ALLIES NORTH AND EA

mans Lost 15,000 Killed

PHAN MAID FACES CHARGE
OF SHOOTING "BERT" MASSEY

**Employer Met Death on the
Steps of His Own Home**

MASSEY OUT OF CITY

**of the Victim Was in the
llar and Heard Nothing—
Newsboy, Who Had Just
Been Paid for His
Papers, the Only
Eyewitness**

t through the heart just out-
his own home at 169 Walmer
Charles Albert Massey, known
siness and society as "Bert"
y, died almost immediately
vening.

short time later Carrie Davies,
nestic employed by Mr. Massey,
rrested by Sergeant Brown of
t police station on Markham st.

Massey is out of town. I then searched the house, and going upstairs I
heard someone in the attic.

"I called out, 'Come on down, you
had better surrender,' and she called
back, 'Come on up.' I went up and
met her on the landing. It was the
maid and she had a revolver in her
hand."

MAN'S OWN REVOLVER.

The weapon with which the shooting was done was a 32 calibre revolver and belonged to Mr. Massey. The
weapon had been used by his son
to shoot at tin cans in the cellar.
This revolver and the woman were
taken to the police station and kept
there till the patrol wagon was sent
up for her.

BROKE DOWN AFTERWARDS.

When the police first entered the
house the girl was up in her own
room dressing, apparently ready to
go out. She had not been crying
and didn't break down till after her
arrest. Then she sobbed bitterly as
she told the police her story. She
claimed that up to this time both

Charles A. Massey and his boy, taken
but a short time ago.

as "Bert" Massey, son of the
late C. A. Massey, and nephew of
Chester D. Massey of the Massey
Harris firm; 34 years of age;
member of the Royal Canadian
Yacht Club and of the Military
tire Association; belongs to
that club connected with the
Chandler Massey Co., the Loco-
mobile Co. of the U.S. States,
and of late York Motors Co.
as salesman.

He was married, his wife having been Miss Rhoda Vanderlift,
of Bridgeport, Conn. She had left
the preceding day on a visit to
Hartford, Conn. He had one son,
Albert, aged 14.

THE ALLEGED MURDERER.

Carrie Davies, an English girl
employed by the Masseys as a domestic for the past two years; 18
years of age; her father was a
soldier in the British army and
is dead; her mother and three
sisters live in England, and a
fourth sister is married and lives
in Toronto. She had saved up
$30 to send home to her mother,
and the police found this in an
envelope.

TIME, PLACE AND WEAPON.

The shooting occurred on the
steps of Mr. Massey's own home,
169 Walmer road, as he returned
from business. A 32 calibre revolver, used by Massey's son for
target practice, was the weapon.

THE MOTIVE.

As alleged by the prisoner, self
protection or vindication.

THE EYE WITNESS.

A newsboy who had been paid
by the victim just before the
shots were fired.

RAGEDY AND SOME OF THOSE CONCERNED

ERNEST PELLETIER
NEWSBOY.

WHERE MR. MASSEY
WAS SHOT

C. A. MASSEY

aid, and the newsboy who witnessed the shooting on the steps of Mr. Massey's home, 169 Walmer road.

up to interview some of the city fathers on the momentous subject of
moving the location of the Women's
Court. She was on her way to be
photographed and have the Bertilion
measurements taken.

The girl's sister was not in court
this morning. Neither were any of
the relatives of the man who was
shot. More like a mild and gentle
Sunday school pupil did she look, and
very subdued and sorrowful this morning.

CAN MAN AND WIFE CONSPIRE

LAW SAYS TWO ARE ONE.

**What the Authorities Say on Ques-
tion Bearing on the Nerlich Charge
of Conspiracy.**

The new charge that Emil Nerlich
did conspire with his wife to commit certain treasonable acts has
aroused an interested discussion
among lawyers as to whether in law
a husband and wife can be guilty of
conspiracy.

"That was the thought that
crossed my mind," remarked a well-
known King's counsel, in discussing
the question this morning. "I think
that they can. A husband and wife
can be charged with theft; they can
be charged with murder, and I think
they can be charged with conspiracy.
Conspiracy is a combining together
to commit an unlawful act, and the

harged with murder. She was
taken to the detective office,

Mr. and Mrs. Massey had been ex-
ceedingly kind to her and that she

street with her, and then he left the
and walked across to go to his own

THE MASSEY MURDER

ALSO BY CHARLOTTE GRAY

Gold Diggers: Striking It Rich in the Klondike (2010)

Nellie McClung (2008)

Reluctant Genius: The Passionate Life and Inventive Mind of Alexander Graham Bell (2006)

The Museum Called Canada (2004)

Canada: A Portrait in Letters (2003)

Flint & Feather: The Life and Times of E. Pauline Johnson, Tekahionwake (2002)

Sisters in the Wilderness: The Lives of Susanna Moodie and Catharine Parr Traill (1999)

Mrs. King: The Life and Times of Isabel MacKenzie King (1997)

The
MASSEY
MURDER

A Maid, Her Master, and the Trial
That Shocked a Country

CHARLOTTE GRAY

HarperCollins*PublishersLtd*

For George

Contents

PART ONE: THE STORY

Chapter 1: Bang!

Chapter 2: The Beak in the Women's Court

Chapter 3: The Corpse in the Morgue

Chapter 4: The Muscle of the Masseys

Chapter 5: A Peculiar Look

Chapter 6: The White-Slave Trade

Chapter 7: Newspaper Wars

PART TWO: THE LAW

PART THREE: THE TRIAL

PART FOUR: AFTERMATH

The Massey Murder

Preface

In Europe, a bloodbath had begun six months earlier. Across Canada, men volunteered to fight, and women prepared to cope alone as they watched husbands and sons march awkwardly away. Politicians talked endlessly of "the War Effort"; generals calculated how many battalions they could raise. A nerve-racking suspicion that the world would never be the same again was seeping into the public consciousness.

And then, on a gloomy February evening in 1915, a gunshot rang out on a quiet Toronto street. A city caught up in the midst of the greatest conflict ever known was suddenly gripped by the strange story of the maid who shot a Massey. The incident itself was unusual and shocking, but it began as a private drama. Yet it quickly mutated into a public scandal on the home front, its flames fanned by passions beyond the control of those most intimately involved.

Ostensibly, at the centre of this story is Carrie Davies, a lowly domestic servant who worked in the household of a member of one of Canada's most famous families. Yet she is the object rather than the subject of events because her fate was taken in hand by so many other actors and forces. This book is a story about Toronto in the early twentieth century, a fast-changing and divided community in the process of reinvention, and about Canada as it embarked on a century of dramatic evolution. A single bullet fired on Walmer Road had an extraordinary significance.

Most of my previous books have been about people or events that made a difference. I looked through the telescope of history and brought into focus lives that created change. Writers who helped shape Canada's literary heritage; an inventor who transformed the world by creating instant communication; a gold rush in the subarctic north that hinted at vast mineral wealth below the snow. In these books, individuals contributed to larger national and international stories, and each book covered several years (in the case of *Gold Diggers: Striking It Rich on the Klondike*), if not decades (in my full-length biographies of Susanna Moodie, Pauline Johnson, and Alexander Graham Bell). For each book, I was able to understand my subject from the inside, because he or she had left personal papers in which I could read what they thought and hear their voice. Yet after finishing each one of these books, I found myself wondering about forgotten lives, the long-dead individuals who left no record behind them. What happens to anonymous, powerless individuals who are swept up by events and currents completely beyond their control?

Then I discovered the case of Carrie Davies. Nobody would ever have heard of the timid eighteen-year-old if she had not run afoul of the law. She herself left none of the traces bequeathed to biographers like me, who want to hear our subjects' voices. There were no letters, journals, notes, or diaries, although I know she was literate. However, I realized I could explore Carrie's circumstances through the record of her imprisonment and trial. I could enter not only the enthralling world of a true crime, but also the story of someone in the shadows of a past era. Carrie Davies herself remains something of an enigma, and she had no immediate impact on history. But the turmoil of her times, on both the home front and the battlefields of France, decided her fate.

So this time I have used the literary equivalent of a microscope rather than a telescope as I gazed backwards across the years. It allowed me to bring into sharp focus day-to-day events that convulsed a city during three crucial weeks. Then I lifted my head from the eyepiece and set the various characters I discovered onto the larger landscape of history that drove the conclusion. No one appreciated it at the time, but the Carrie Davies case gave spectators a glimpse of the Canada to come.

My sources for the legal case that is at the core of the story were limited. I had to rely on the official report of the coroner's inquest, plus newspaper articles. But I was lucky. For reasons that I describe, the day-to-day coverage of this shooting was detailed and vivid. Different newspapers gave radically different accounts. The passions aroused were as strong as any triggered by more recent violent events that have involved difficult ethical questions.

The background to Carrie's case was extensive: my challenge was to prevent the layers of circumstantial detail from overshadowing the story. In 1915, Canada was abuzz with "-isms": militarism, imperialism, feminism, and nascent nationalism. Each of these movements affected Carrie's case, although she herself probably knew nothing about them. But she was a cork floating on powerful cross-currents of assumptions about class, race, and gender: her canny lawyer, Hartley Dewart, used those currents to her advantage.

Nonetheless, Carrie Davies is the central figure of this book, and I have had to use all the conventions of narrative non-fiction to bring this silent witness to life. I imagine, but I do not invent. I do not fabricate characters, events, or dialogue—anything in quotation marks comes from a written source. Physical descriptions, of people and buildings, come from photographic evidence. However, I speculate and I interpret, based on empirical evidence and knowledge of common practice and human behaviour. I do so cautiously, and only when I am confident that I am more likely to be right than wrong. In the words of the historian Modris Eksteins, "For facts to become memorable, an element of fiction [is] essential."

And sometimes, that element is the only way to understand what it was like to actually *be* there, as the ordered world crumbled and war broke the old vision.

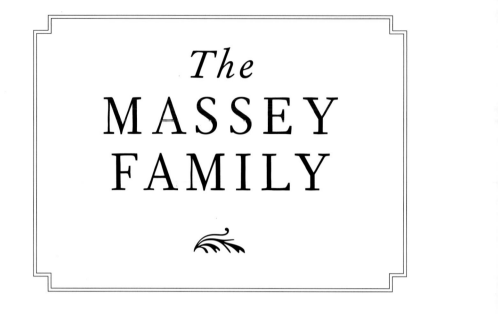

The MASSEY FAMILY

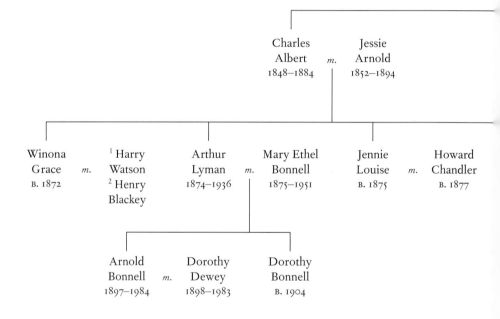

Charles Albert *m.* Jessie Arnold
1848–1884   1852–1894

Winona Grace *m.* ¹ Harry Watson ² Henry Blackey   Arthur Lyman *m.* Mary Ethel Bonnell   Jennie Louise *m.* Howard Chandler
B. 1872   1874–1936   1875–1951   B. 1875   B. 1877

Arnold Bonnell *m.* Dorothy Dewey   Dorothy Bonnell
1897–1984   1898–1983   B. 1904

List of Characters

AT 169 WALMER ROAD, TORONTO

Charles Albert "Bert" Massey, 34, Studebaker car salesman, house owner, and
grandson of the late Hart Massey

Rhoda Vandergrift Massey, 34, Bert's wife

Charles Massey, 14, Bert's son

Carrie Davies, 18, English-born housemaid

AT 326 MORLEY AVENUE, TORONTO

Ed Fairchild, Carrie's brother-in-law, foreman with Jas. R. Wickett, Ltd., a building firm

Maud Davies Fairchild, 22, Carrie's older sister and Ed's wife

Two small children, Bobby and Joyce

MASSEY FAMILY MEMBERS

Arthur Lyman Massey, 41, Bert Massey's brother, resident of 165 Admiral Road

Mary Ethel Massey, 38, wife of Arthur and sister-in-law of Bert Massey

Vincent Massey, 27, cousin, resident of 515 Jarvis Street

Fred Massey, cousin

THE POLICE

Patrol Sergeant Lawrence Brown, from Police Station 11 on London Street

Constable Follis, Police Station 11

Constable Martin, Police Station 11

Inspector George Kennedy, senior detective, City Hall

Constable Mary Minty, Toronto's first female police constable

Colonel Henry James Grasett, 67, chief constable of Toronto

OFFICERS OF THE COURT AND JUSTICE SYSTEM

Colonel George Taylor Denison, 75, chief magistrate, resident of Heydon Villa, Toronto

Mr. Chapman, police court clerk

Rev. Dr. Andrew B. Chambers, governor of Don Jail

Mrs. Sinclair, superintendent of Women's Department, Don Jail

Miss Carmichael, matron of hospital wing, Don Jail

Dr. Arthur Jukes Johnson, 67, chief coroner of Toronto

Sir William Mulock, 72, chief justice of the Exchequer Division of the Supreme Court of Ontario (later simply chief justice of the Supreme Court)

WITNESSES

Ernest Pelletier, 16, newsboy

Dr. John Mitchell, resident of Walmer Road

Beatrice Dinnis, resident of Walmer Road

Joseph Pearson, guest of Walmer Road resident

Mrs. Edna Nesbitt, passerby

Dr. J.E. Elliott, physician who performed post-mortem

John L. Hynes, friend of deceased and resident of 106 Walmer Road

LAWYERS

Dewart, Maw & Hodgson, of Home Life Building, Adelaide Street, Toronto:
Carrie's defence team

> Herbert Hartley Dewart, KC, 54
>
> Henry Wilberforce Maw
>
> T.C. Robinette, clerk
>
> Arthur Roebuck, clerk

Richard Greer, 37, Crown attorney for York County

Edward Du Vernet, 49, Crown counsel

Arthur John Thomson, 37, Massey family lawyer

NEWSPAPERS

John Ross Robertson, 74, proprietor of the *Evening Telegram* (the "*Tely*")

"Black Jack" Robinson, editor of the *Evening Telegram*

Archie Fisher, "The Crow," reporter at the *Evening Telegram*

Joseph Atkinson, 49, owner and editor of the *Toronto Daily Star*

Helen Ball, reporter at the *Toronto Daily News*

TORONTO'S LOCAL COUNCIL OF WOMEN

Florence Gooderham Hamilton Huestis, 42, president

Toronto, 1915

Dundas Street

Arthur Street

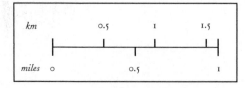

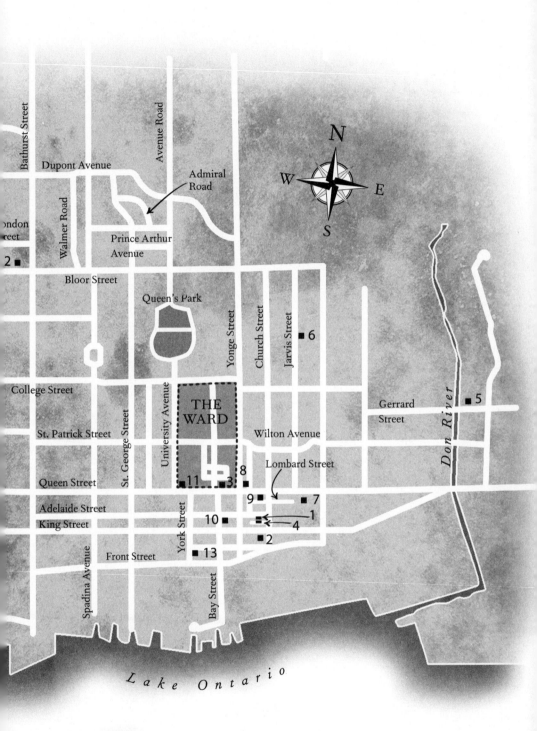

N
W · E
S

Bathurst Street

Dupont Avenue

Avenue Road

Admiral Road

Walmer Road

ondon
eet

2 ■

Prince Arthur Avenue

Bloor Street

Queen's Park

Yonge Street

Church Street

Jarvis Street

■ 6

College Street

University Avenue

THE WARD

Gerrard Street

5 ■

Don River

St. George Street

St. Patrick Street

Wilton Avenue

Queen Street

■ 11   ■ 3

■ 8

Lombard Street

9 ■

■ 7

Adelaide Street

King Street

York Street

10 ■

■ ■◄ 1
■◄ 4

■ 2

Spadina Avenue

Front Street

■ 13

Bay Street

Lake Ontario

{PART ONE}

The Story

{CHAPTER 1}

Bang!

MONDAY, FEBRUARY 8, 1915

Charles Albert Massey sauntered away from the new Dupont streetcar station, heading west into the chilly dusk. Most of a recent snowfall had been shovelled off the sidewalk by Toronto's Public Works department, which meant that heaped banks of dirty snow protected pedestrians from cars, horse-drawn carriages, and delivery trucks. Dupont was a teeming downtown thoroughfare, lined with grocery stores and bakeries. Massey, a slender man of medium height, carefully picked his way around dog excrement and slushy puddles, thankful that, despite a hangover, he had remembered to pull galoshes over his leather shoes that morning.

Bert, as his friends called him, was a member of one of Canada's most prominent families, a dynasty that had built its fortune by producing the wagons, tractors, threshers, reapers, and binders on which Canada's newfound prosperity, and reputation as the "bread basket of the Empire," was based. The thirty-four-year-old cut a stylish figure, with a diamond stick pin in his silk tie and his dark hair slicked back from his wide forehead. Right now, he was probably too eager to get home to let his thoughts linger on either agricultural implements or the fact that his American wife, Rhoda, had not yet returned from a visit to her family, the Vandergrifts, in Bridgeport, Connecticut—a visit that she had kept extending. When she left a week earlier, they had not parted on good terms. Rhoda didn't share her husband's sense of *fun*. A rather shy New Englander, she certainly didn't have his appetite for fast cars and late nights: she preferred to stay out of the limelight.

After a block, Bert Massey turned south past the dairy at the corner of Dupont and Walmer Road. Within minutes, he could no longer hear the Dupont traffic or smell the sour milk from the empty churns in the dairy's backyard. Bert lived in the Annex, the area between Bloor and Dupont, west of Avenue Road, that had been developed over the previous three decades as Toronto's population exploded and streetcars allowed middle-class residents to live farther away from their workplaces. The Bloor Street end of Walmer Road was the fashionable part, with circular towers, portes cochères, and tall chimneys ornamenting spacious stone mansions. Most of the houses near Dupont, where Bert Massey lived, had been hastily constructed and lacked the imposing bulk, wraparound porches, and extensive grounds enjoyed by Toronto's wealthier families—the kind of homes that Bert's rich relatives lived in. Nevertheless, a few of the flourishes of grander mansions had migrated north to Walmer Road's pokier residences. There were pillared porches, stained-glass windows in some front doors, and dormer windows for attic bedrooms in which servants slept.

Number 169, where Albert and Rhoda Massey lived, was particularly shabby. Squeezed between its neighbours, it lacked their balconies and decorated bargeboards. It was not even well maintained. If Massey had raised his eyes to his roof, he would see that a recent warm spell had melted much of the snow from his tiles, blocking the gutters and creating dangerous icicles overhanging the front porch. Did he make this typical homeowner's check? Probably not. It was after six o'clock, so visibility was poor despite newly installed street lamps. And he was tired. After socializing until 1:45 a.m. the previous night at a neighbour's, he had risen early to reach York Motors Ltd. on Yonge Street. Bert Massey did not work in the family firm; instead, he had a job at a

Studebaker dealership, selling cars that were built with American-made parts and assembled in Walkerville, Ontario.

In theory, Bert Massey had a great job in a booming industry. In the past few years, automobiles had gone from exotic rarities to status symbols. Back in 1908, traffic monitors at one Toronto intersection noted only six automobiles in ten hours. Cars were expensive (around $1,400 each—twice the annual salary of a schoolteacher, and four times as much as an ordinary labourer earned), so ownership was slow to gather momentum. But within four years, the motoring craze had taken off, and the same intersection was seeing 382 cars each day. Now, in 1915, there were close to 100,000 vehicles on Canadian roads, the majority of them in the increasingly urban central provinces. It was all quite chaotic: there were no stop signs or traffic lights, and drivers in some provinces stuck to the British custom of driving on the left-hand side of the road, while in others they followed the American custom of driving on the right. Prince Edward Island had banned automobiles altogether until 1913. But what man could resist progress, or the excitement of having a McLaughlin-Buick, or a Ford, or a Cadillac, or a Reo, or a Hupmobile parked outside his home? Even Laura Borden, the irreproachably respectable wife of Prime Minister Robert Borden, cheerfully drove herself through Ottawa's muddy streets in an electric car.

Bert's job as a Studebaker salesman gave him a certain social flash, since his friends could glimpse him cruising down Yonge Street, one hand on the steering wheel as he showed a potential buyer how to signal for turns, or double-declutch during a gear change. It certainly suited his employer to have a Massey as a salesman. This week, Bert had been busy helping hang banners and bunting in York Motors' state-of-the-art showroom for a display of four splendid new Studebaker models in mid-February.

But in practice, Bert's income didn't match the flash: he sold on commission, and with a war on, sales had slumped. The job required him to be smartly dressed, on his feet, and professionally charming all day, no matter how rude or stupid the customers. Today had been particularly exhausting, so icicles hanging off his porch were the least of his concerns. Anyway, Bert Massey didn't bother much with routine chores—in his wife's absence, he had barely bothered to sweep the snow off the sidewalk.

Before Bert Massey reached home, he met Ernest Pelletier, the sixteen-year-old paper boy who had just delivered a copy of the *Toronto Daily Star* to the Massey house. Massey flashed his most charming smile as he pulled out a quarter to pay for delivery of the *Star* for the previous month. Ever since Christmas, the war in Europe had dominated the *Star*'s front page: today, the news was that Britain's Russian allies had attacked German troops in the Carpathians on the eastern front, and its French allies had dynamited a German trench on the western front. As usual, the *Star* had found a poignant local human-interest story for the middle of the page. A short article described how, the day after a local woman had received an official telegram informing her that her husband was dead, a letter had arrived from him containing the message, "Cheer Up Girlie, I'll Be Home by May."

Bert Massey turned off the sidewalk towards his front door. He had no idea what awaited him.

Behind the front door stood the Massey family's English domestic servant, Carrie Davies. Carrie was a mere slip of a girl, a mousy eighteen-year-old who rarely spoke unless spoken to. She was one of hundreds of thousands of demure little housemaids in cities all over the English-speaking world, from Sheffield to Chicago, Manchester to Melbourne, Tunbridge Wells to Toronto. In her black dress, white cap, and starched apron, Carrie blended into the background decor that, similarly, scarcely varied across continents—heavy velvet curtains, dark wood panelling, framed sepia photographs. In the bourgeois world of 1915, the Carrie Davieses barely merited a glance, let alone a footnote in history. Women like her formed the silent army that kept households humming, and yet remained almost invisible to many of its employers. Carrie's life was particularly exhausting because she was Bert and Rhoda Massey's only servant. They couldn't afford the army of cooks, butlers, parlour maids, and lady's maids that kept up the houses of richer Masseys. Carrie had to do everything, during days that began at six in the morning and might not finish until well after 9 p.m.

But tonight, this particular young woman carried a gun—Bert Massey's own .32-calibre Savage automatic pistol. Such guns ("The most powerful, accurate and rapid fire pistol invented") were available in the Eaton's catalogue for $18. And she was standing close to the door because she had just told the paper boy that her employer was not yet home. When she heard Bert Massey mount the steps to the verandah, she raised her right arm. At first, Bert did not see her in the shadows. Then Carrie pulled the door open and stepped forward. A shot rang out. A sharp pain erupted in Bert's left side. He gaped at the young woman before backing quickly down the steps. A second shot rang out. Bert had barely reached the street before he fell and the life began to drain out of him. Carrie Davies lowered the gun, turned round, and disappeared into the house, shutting the door behind her.

Ernest Pelletier was halfway down the block when he heard the shots. For a second, he assumed that the sharp crack was the sound of one of the new electric street-lamp bulbs exploding. Then he swung round—and watched in disbelief as the man to whom he had spoken only seconds earlier staggered down his front steps and collapsed on the sidewalk. Ernest sprinted back to him. Beatrice Dinnis, who lived at 126 Walmer Road, had seen the flash of a gun and heard Bert exclaim, "Oh," as he buckled to the ground. She was one of the first passersby to cluster around the fallen man, who was groaning in distress. One stranger hammered on the doorway of 169 Walmer, but there was no answer. So he went next door and asked for a glass of water, explaining that a man had been taken ill on the sidewalk.

Nobody knew what to do. A woman screamed. There was no observable wound, no gush of blood. Yet Bert Massey was obviously in desperate straits. Curtains twitched in Walmer Road windows as neighbours peered through the gathering darkness at the huddle of shocked witnesses. A youth who lived at number 133 ran to telephone the police. Dr. John Mitchell, who lived a few doors north and was familiar to his neighbours, shouldered through the crowd, loosened Massey's collar, and had him carried into the house next door, number 171. By the time Charles Albert Massey had been laid on a chesterfield there, he was dead. He had not uttered a word since the first shot was fired.

⤜

The police wagon arrived minutes later.

Patrol Sergeant Lawrence Brown and two constables marched up to the front door of number 169 and knocked. Again, no one came to the door. Sending Constable Follis to the back door and instructing Constable Martin to stand guard at the front door, Brown entered the unlocked house. Most of the lights were on in the evening gloom.

The front hall was a cramped space: ahead of him, the sergeant saw a staircase leading upwards, and to his right, through an open door, an empty sitting room. The stocky policeman walked carefully towards the back of the house. In the kitchen, someone had just finished making supper, and there was an unbaked loaf of bread on the table. Brown heard a noise from below, and was startled to see Bert Massey's fourteen-year-old son, Charlie, emerge from the basement in his shirt sleeves. What had he been doing? Perhaps he was smoking one of his father's cigarettes, or even taking a quiet swig from a bottle "borrowed" from the liquor cabinet. Sergeant Brown didn't care. He was more concerned by the boy's expression of shock at seeing a policeman in the house. The noise of the gunshot had not reached the basement, and Brown realized that Charles Albert had no idea of what had occurred. The policeman took Charles to the front door and instructed Constable Martin to look after the boy. White-faced and frightened, Charles kept asking what had happened. Nobody told him.

Sergeant Brown continued his search of the house. The ground-floor rooms were empty, so he cautiously started up the staircase. When he reached the landing, he heard a tremulous call from the third floor: "Who is there?" He replied, "The police." The girlish voice said, "Come on up," but Brown drew his revolver and said, "Come on down."

It was barely half an hour since the two shots were fired. In a bare attic bedroom, Carrie Davies had risen from the table where, in a state of eerie calm, she had just finished writing two short notes. One was to Maud Fairchild, her married sister who also lived in Toronto. The second was to her friend Mary Rooney, another domestic servant who worked for Bert Massey's older brother and his wife, Mr. and Mrs. Arthur Massey, a few blocks away on Admiral Road. Carrie behaved as if in a stupor, oblivious to the furor outside in the street. When she heard the policeman's voice, she had thrust her hands into the arms of a shabby brown cloth coat and picked up the gun again. This time, she held it by the muzzle. Then she started downstairs.

On the second-floor landing, Sergeant Brown stared up in astonishment at the slight figure proffering a pistol as she came towards him. Without taking his eyes off Carrie's expressionless face, the burly policeman grasped the weapon by its handle, and then followed her back to her room.

"I shot him," the young woman announced. Sergeant Brown stared at her, and then gave her the standard caution: "You needn't make any statement unless you like, but any statement you make may be used as evidence either for or against you. [Do] you understand that?" Wide-eyed,

Carrie intoned, "Yes." Almost as an afterthought, she added, "He ruined my character . . . They have been good to me and I have been good to them, but he disgraced my character." The policeman looked at the gun, and then back at her. Carrie began to cry, and repeated, "He has ruined my life . . . Take me out of here."

Brown didn't ask her to explain her remark. He took her firmly by the arm and escorted her out the front door of number 169, through a crowd of shocked onlookers. Carrie kept her head down. She appeared to be clinging to Sergeant Brown rather than being unwillingly frog-marched away from the scene of the crime. After the sergeant had bundled her into the paddy wagon, Constables Martin and Follis, solemn and silent, climbed in after her.

A few minutes later, the paddy wagon drew up outside Police Station 11, on London Street close to Bathurst, so that Sergeant Brown could make a note in the duty register of her name, age, and birthplace. Until now, Carrie Davies had behaved as though nothing had happened: she was her meek little self, doing what she was told. But at the police station, she overheard horrified whispers that Mr. Massey was dead. She gasped, then broke down in tears.

Sergeant Brown knew that this case was more than the London Street station could handle. So Carrie was bundled back in the wagon and driven downtown, to police headquarters at City Hall, at the intersection of Queen and Bay Streets, where Inspector George Kennedy, Toronto's most senior detective, had his office. The police sergeant ushered the now-terrified young woman into the inspector's presence. When the detective began to question her, she admitted in her pronounced English accent that she had pointed a gun at her employer and pulled the trigger. Her motive for the killing, she sobbed, was that "he tried to ruin me."

Brown and Kennedy exchanged shocked looks. Sergeant Brown had already told Inspector Kennedy that this was more than a routine crime, because the dead man was a Massey. Kennedy's eyebrows had nearly lifted off his face when he realized he would be dealing with a family that was already a Canadian legend: the Masseys were respected for their fierce Methodism, appreciated for their public benefactions (Toronto's Massey Music Hall and Fred Victor Mission were only two of the numerous Massey good works), and resented for their power. By the start of the twentieth century, Methodists like the Masseys—along with the Eatons and the Flavelles—were on their way to becoming Toronto's new capitalist class, an elite that challenged the city's Victorian aristocracy in both wealth and snobbery. Bert Massey's relatives lived in one of the grandest houses in Toronto, "Euclid Hall" on Jarvis Street, and Bert himself, as a child, had been dressed like a prince, in velvet coats and *broderie anglaise* collars. The family was not used to seeing its members enmeshed in gossip.

Now this frightened young woman had uttered the sensational accusation "He tried to ruin me," and the two Toronto policemen realized that they had a major scandal on their hands. "Ruin," in this context, meant only one thing: that Bert Massey had tried to have sexual intercourse with his maid. Reporters on the crime beat would swarm City Hall as soon as they got wind of the shooting—Kennedy could already hear a buzz of excitement in the front office. Moreover, at the time of the crime, Bert Massey had been unarmed and several feet from Carrie—an apparently law-abiding breadwinner returning from a long day at work. Carrie had taken him completely by surprise. Was she speaking the truth? And anyway, how many eighteen-year-old domestics knew how to fire a revolver? Under questioning, Carrie stammered that she had worked for Mr. and Mrs. Charles Albert Massey for two years, and she repeated that they had always been kind to her.

The two policemen stared at the wretched girl in dismay. Still, all they could do was follow procedure. Inspector Kennedy began the routine questioning—name, age, height—and then took Carrie through the events of the evening, noting her answers in longhand. Within half an hour, Carrie had answered all the questions put to her, and Kennedy, in a rush to get the paperwork finished so she could appear in the police court the following morning, had instructed his assistant to take Carrie away. In his haste, he forgot to ask her to sign the statement.

Carrie was taken to the Court Street station, the hub of the police department, which was three blocks south of City Hall at the busy corner of Church and Adelaide Streets, behind the elegant Georgian facade of the Adelaide Street courthouse. The police station had cells in the basement for transient prisoners—cells that were cramped, dirty, and stank of human sweat and excrement. There she spent the night in custody, listening to indignant shouts and clanging bolts as drunks, hookers, and other petty criminals were locked up alongside her. In her short life, Carrie had often been uncomfortable—in her overcrowded English home, or the drafty attic bedrooms of employers' houses, or the shared steerage berth when she crossed the Atlantic. But a night in the cells, surrounded by harsh sounds and human misery, with no idea what the next day would bring, must have been the most traumatic night of her life. A shabby cloth coat could not protect her from jailhouse chill, let alone the terror and humiliation of her predicament.

❧

For three weeks, the sensational tale of the Massey killing gripped Toronto. On several days, the case received more coverage than a much more important story—the war in Europe. Thousands of young Canadian men had donned uniforms, crossed the Atlantic, and, in the same month that Carrie faced the court, were preparing to risk their lives in the defence of the British Empire.

This was an extraordinary period in Canadian history. Although the former British colony had entered the twentieth century relatively poor and largely rural, its resources underdeveloped and only a third of its arable land settled, it now had the world's fastest-growing economy. Until war broke out in Europe in 1914, immigrants by the hundreds of thousands had poured into the West, factories had sprung up in the east and railways had criss-crossed the landscape. The Dominion of Canada, still less than half a century old, was riddled with anachronisms and paradoxes—the first gasoline-driven tractors had appeared on Saskatchewan and Manitoba prairies where teams of sturdy Doukhobor women were still harnessed to single-furrow plows. Small general stores served rural housewives, but in the cities huge department stores like Mr. Eaton's on Yonge Street were becoming palaces of consumption. City dwellers were snapping up gadgets like electric toasters, irons, and vacuum cleaners, and filling store cupboards with bottled tomato ketchup, Shredded Wheat, and Palmolive soap, while out west, farm hands still lived in sod huts, ate salt pork and cabbage, and lined their boots with newspapers. A giddy optimism had spread across the country, but though Canada now exercised almost complete control over its internal affairs, it continued to deal with the external world as a ward of Great Britain, the historic "motherland."

Nevertheless, the Dominion was starting to see itself as an autonomous nation. In 1904, Sir Wilfrid Laurier, the country's seventh post-Confederation leader and first French-Canadian prime minister, had made a startling prediction: "Canada has been modest in its history, although its history is heroic in many ways. But its history, in my estimation, is only commencing . . . The nineteenth century was the century of the United States. I think we can claim that it is Canada that shall fill the twentieth century."

The slow evolution of a Canadian identity rubbed up against Canada's passionate attachment to "the Old Country," and in 1915 no province was more profoundly British in its sentiments than Ontario. On the flyleaf of the Ontario *Fourth Reader* of 1910, beneath the Union

Jack, appeared the motto "One Flag, One Fleet, One Throne." On the first page appeared a quotation from Rudyard Kipling: "Oh Motherland, we pledge to thee, Head, heart and hand through years to be." The first picture in the *Reader* was a portrait of the late King Edward VII. Loyalty to Britain suffused Canada's most populous province, even as its residents watched their own country develop economic muscles and political sinews unthinkable at Confederation.

At the same time, no Canadian city was undergoing more wrenching changes than the province's largest city. Toronto was almost unrecognizable from the muddy town it had been when the Dominion of the North was established in 1867. Back then, with only about fifty thousand residents, it was smaller than Halifax, Nova Scotia, in population and area. But in the 1880s it absorbed adjoining Riverdale, Yorkville, the Annex, Seaton Village, and Parkdale, and within a few years it was linked by electric trolleys and steam railways to outlying communities like Scarborough, Richmond Hill, and Newmarket. In the first decade of the new century, the city's population had grown by a staggering 81 percent, from 208,040 to 376,500, and by 1915 it had over half a million residents—with at least one-third born outside the country. Montreal was still the Dominion's largest city and financial centre, but Toronto had emerged as Canada's industrial leader.

Now, within a city and country under stress, Carrie Davies's actions played into contemporary disquiet about the dissolution of Old World standards of behaviour. Whatever did Carrie Davies think she was doing? Was this the kind of thing that would happen if people didn't know their place, and women were given the vote? Did Charles Albert Massey's death presage more fundamental shifts, perhaps—at best, Canada's evolution towards its own unique national identity; at worst, a slide into social chaos within Toronto thanks to growing numbers of immigrants?

CHAPTER 2

The Beak in the Women's Court

TUESDAY, FEBRUARY 9

THIS IS THE 189TH DAY OF THE WAR.
Today's report notes a heavy German bombardment of Ypres.
—*Evening Telegram*, Tuesday, February 9, 1915

Mrs. Edward Fairchild, sister of Carrie Davies, stated this morning that the only reason that she could advance for her sister's act was that she was in a state of nervous depression caused by the fact that all the money she earned had to be sent home.
—*Toronto Daily Star*, Tuesday, February 9, 1915

The day after Bert Massey's abrupt death dawned chilly and damp: a thick, grey layer of cloud hung low in the sky, blotting out the winter sun. Despite the biting wind that whistled down Queen Street and the slush on the sidewalk, people had been scurrying towards City Hall since dawn. This massive municipal palace, opened only sixteen years earlier, epitomized Toronto's growing commercial muscle and expansive self-belief. Replacing a more modest building on the dirty waterfront, it had been built around a courtyard and covered a whole city block: it housed both Toronto's City Council and the police courts, and it was close to Osgoode Hall, home of the Law Society of Upper Canada and the province's first law school. Like a judge's dais in a courtroom, City Hall's imperious bulk was elevated above the street by twenty wide granite steps so that it dwarfed surrounding buildings.

But the eager court watchers were indifferent to the building's Romanesque gargoyles, rusticated stone arches, and gigantic clock tower; they clustered on the steps and waited impatiently for one of the three large oak doorways to be unlocked. Once inside, the crowd milled around the base of the Grand Staircase, below the monumental stained-glass window that depicted (with typical Toronto braggadocio) "the Union of Commerce and Industry." At the rear police entrance on Albert Street, eager rubberneckers stamped their feet and waited for the police wagons to arrive from the Court Street station with the previous night's crop of arrests.

Detective Inspector Kennedy's gloomy fears had been realized: the editors of Toronto's six newspapers rushed to cover the bloody death of the grandson of pioneering industrialist Hart Massey. For the past few days, the front page of the *Globe,* the paper that served the city's business and political elite ("Canada's National Newspaper," boasted its masthead), had featured exclusively war news. Today, it had a startling change of topic in column five: "C.A. Massey Killed By House Servant. Carrie Davies, Aged 18, Under Arrest. Shot At His Own Door." The story began with a breathlessness unusual for the establishment's favourite paper: "A murder of sensationally dramatic and personal interest took place in Walmer Road last evening . . ."

The more down-market *Toronto Daily Star* had placed the story in the third column of its front page, under the headline "C.A. Massey Shot By Domestic As He Returned Home. Prominent Toronto Society Man Drops Dead on Own Doorstep. No Motive Known For Awful Deed." Reports of German spies in the Port of Halifax, and of German bombs falling on the little French town of Soissons, had been typographically elbowed aside.

News of the sensational event had rapidly spread beyond the city. New York reporters had called to ask about the story, which was covered in the *New York Times.* Montreal's *Gazette,* the most important English-language paper in Canada's largest city, devoted a column to it on page four: "C.A. Massey Shot and Killed by an 18-year Girl: Domestic in His Home Met Him at Door and Shot Him Through the Heart." In its eagerness to highlight the prominence of the Masseys, the paper exaggerated Bert's significance in the mercantile dynasty. "Dead Man Was the Eldest Member of the Famous Massey Family Known Throughout Canada."

The first stage of Carrie Davies's journey through the legal system was her appearance in a police court, which would decide whether she should be allowed out on bail or remain in custody. Carrie's remand hearing would take place in an unusual judicial institution: a police court that dealt exclusively with women. South of the border, such courts had been established in Chicago, Los Angeles, and New York City, but this was the only one of its kind in Canada.

Toronto's Women's Court was the result of efforts by the local branch of a powerful organization called the National Council of Women (NCW). Toronto's Local Council of Women (LCW) had fought for a separate court for women because the LCW's leaders insisted that judicial decks were stacked against women who fell afoul of the law. Women had no way to participate in the development or the administration of the law: they could not be voters, legislators, coroners, magistrates, judges, or jurors. At City Hall's law courts, all court officials and almost all the police were men, and for every woman detained, nineteen men were arrested. Male spectators leered and jeered at women prisoners. Underage girls arrested for "vagrancy" (a euphemism for soliciting) were often followed home and dragged down, in the words of an LCW member, "to Heaven knows what infamy."

In the early twentieth century, most women and men believed that, while men committed *crime*, women committed *sins*. The LCW argued that, since women could be "saved," they should be treated differently from hardened male criminals. Most important, they should be shielded from the idle throng of male hangers-on, loafers, and lawyers hanging around City Hall, on the hunt for scandal and gossip.

The reasoning of LCW activists seems well intentioned but naive today: they wanted to protect women because, as the "weaker sex," they needed to be shielded from the full force of the law. This was the heyday of "maternal feminism"—the belief that women and men had different roles in society, thanks to women's "motherly" perspective. Proponents of this view did not argue for gender equality: instead, they suggested that women should have a role in the public realm because their maternal values and influence would improve debate. Some LCW leaders were ambivalent about the Votes for Women campaign because they felt that women could exert their influence indirectly. Others were ardent suffragettes because they believed that the values and behaviour of mothers would elevate the public realm. Out west, Canada's leading suffragette, Nellie McClung, argued early in the war that "women are naturally the guardians of the race," and that if there had been women in the German Reichstag ("deep-bosomed, motherly, blue-eyed German women") they would have stopped the Kaiser going to war.

Despite their differences on the suffrage issue, Toronto activists were united in their abhorrence for the way that women were treated in the rough-and-tumble atmosphere of City Hall's police courts. LCW lobbying had paid off: in February 1913, the Women's Court was established. Women arrested by Toronto police could now be remanded in a court to which no men were admitted, unless they were witnesses or officers of the court. All spectators, including reporters, had to be female. The courtroom was located on the second floor of City Hall, in No. 1 Committee Room, and unlike the stark courtrooms on the floor below, it featured walls painted a soft brick colour, pictures hanging on them, and an ordinary chair rather than a railed dock for prisoners. Most important, women who were discharged from the court could slip away without being harassed by onlookers. The *Globe* remarked, "To the onlooker it seemed all as simple as being called to the teacher's table at school."

The muckraking journal *Jack Canuck* enthused over this new institution, suggesting that "the new and humane order of things will work wonders in the reclamation of the unfortunate daughters of Eve." Mrs. Florence Huestis, the formidable president of the Toronto branch of the NCW, reported that her members attended the court regularly and "did their best to help fallen girls and women." This was where Carrie Davies, already en route from Court Street police station cell, would appear.

By 9.30 a.m., when court sessions were scheduled to begin, the tiled corridors of City Hall were thronged with idlers eager for a glimpse of the trigger-happy domestic. The sensational tale of the murdered Massey had swelled the throng, but Carrie Davies wasn't the only draw. Toronto's police courts, where 90 percent of the city's criminal cases began and ended, always pulled a crowd. Local newspapers covered these courts as if they were covering circus acts and music hall turns, reducing a day's slate of individuals charged with crimes to a cast of ridiculous stereotypes—drunken Irishmen, comic African Americans, naive hayseeds, tarts with hearts. Rubberneckers cheered for decisions they supported and booed those they disagreed with.

The *Evening Telegram* ran a regular column, "Police Court To-day," with brief and often tongue-in-cheek entries. A typical report, under the heading "Judicious Mixture," described how "John Keyler showed some discrimination in his thefts from the Robert Simpson Company Limited. When he took some jam and candies he also annexed a quantity of cascara and headache wafers. Sent down for fifteen days."

Why did the city's residents find justice so entertaining? Largely because of one man: Colonel George Taylor Denison, a tall, silver-haired character with a bony face and walrus moustache who was the police court magistrate—an office that did not require a law degree or any special training, but did imbue its holder with immense authority. Magistrates in England and Canada were often referred to as "beaks," but in Toronto there was only one court official who was invariably called "The Beak," and he was a favourite of the Press Gallery. Denison was the unchallenged monarch of City Hall's police courts. One journalist had recently written that a trip to Toronto without visiting a Denison courtroom "would be like going to Rome and not seeing the Pope."

Police Magistrate Denison stood for everything that was most British about Canada in 1915. Denisons had fought for Canada from the earliest days, and the name was synonymous with loyalty to the

British Empire, the Anglican Church, and conservative political principles. There were well over a hundred Denisons in Toronto by 1915, and there had been scarcely a single event in Toronto's development in which a Denison hadn't played a starring role. The Beak's grandfather, the first Colonel George Taylor Denison, emigrated to British North America from Yorkshire in 1792 and fought under General Brock in the War of 1812. The second Colonel George Taylor Denison helped suppress the 1837–38 uprisings and founded a family cavalry regiment, Denison's Horse, which eventually became the Governor General's Horse Guard. Before becoming the police court magistrate, City Hall's Colonel Denison saw service in the militia against the Fenians at Ridgeway in 1866 and the Metis and Indians during the Northwest Rebellion in 1885. He had also made himself an authority on military tactics, especially the élan of the cavalry charge: in 1877, he had travelled to Moscow to receive an award from the Russian tsar for his book *History of Cavalry*. This Colonel Denison's most passionate commitment was to Canada's destiny as an integral part of the British Empire: chief organizer of the United Empire Loyalists and president of the British Empire League in Canada, he crossed the Atlantic frequently to remind British politicians of the importance of Empire to Canada, and Canada to Empire.

Heydon Villa, George Denison III's red-brick mansion on the western outskirts of Toronto, was a temple to high Victorianism. Far grander than Bert Massey's house on Walmer Road, where Carrie Davies had worked, it was a cross between a shrine to imperialism and a stuffy gentleman's club. The first sights to meet a visitor's eye were the looming stuffed head of a gigantic bison and an elaborate Denison family tree that hung in the hall. The adjacent library featured a Zulu spear, a quiver of Sioux arrows from the massacre of Custer's men at Little Bighorn, and a vast collection of military books. In the drawing room, where the Colonel entertained like-minded men, a sword he had found at the Battle of Ridgeway did duty as a poker in the grate. In the 1880s, the house had been a gathering place for those who, like Denison, simmered with outrage about Canada's lack of national spirit. Members of the Canada First movement (the most prominent was poet Charles Mair) railed against threats to the new nation from Riel and his followers ("traitors") or the "wrong" kind of immigrants. Imperial crusaders from Britain, including writer Rudyard Kipling and politician Joseph Chamberlain, were regular visitors, and over port and cigars their after-dinner conversations invariably touched on the need for closer ties between Britain and its colonies—and with Canada in particular. Colonel Denison was single-minded about Canada, and most particularly, his version of Canada.

The Beak was distrustful of French Canadians and Roman Catholics and was horrified by socialist or suffragette ideas. He dismissed the notion of closer commercial ties with the United States as a dangerous slide towards continentalism, and had nothing but contempt for Americans—in his eyes, American cities like Chicago were "filled with disease, bad water and ruffians." He belligerently defended the social order that he saw being undermined by industrialization, urbanization, and immigration. His lip curled at the thought of Toronto's new mercantile barons, like the Masseys, and his nose wrinkled at the smell of exotic substances like garlic.

All in all, Colonel George Denison was a nineteenth-century figure increasingly at odds with the twentieth century. But he was not alone in a Toronto that, despite the city's rapid growth, was still run by a Protestant elite of families who flaunted their British origins. Some proudly traced their arrival in Canada to the late eighteenth century, when they had fled democracy, in the shape of the American Revolution, as self-proclaimed "United Empire Loyalists." Many (like Denison) were descendants of the Family Compact, the tight little Tory clique that ran Upper Canada in the first decades of the nineteenth century. Their names—Strachan,

Beverley Robinson, Boulton, Jarvis, Simcoe—guaranteed their social prominence from one generation to the next.

By 1915 Toronto was a metropolis that had spread far beyond its original boundaries. Ornate brownstone office buildings had replaced the brick townhouses that the old elite had built along King Street and Queen Street. But Union Jacks still fluttered off buildings, and the WASP grip on Toronto was powerful. The names of streets like Jarvis, Beverley, or Strachan were permanent reminders of old-guard influence. Social divisions were not rigid: the class system was more porous in the New World than the Old, and successful businessmen like department-store mogul Timothy Eaton or meat-packing entrepreneur Joseph Flavelle were welcomed into the top strata once they had made their fortunes. But ties between old-money families were quietly strengthened during regular encounters at St. James' Anglican Cathedral, or at Rosedale "At Homes," or in Toronto's three clubs: the National Club, the Albany Club, and the Toronto Club. Almost all the men in Toronto's overlapping business, social, and military elites belonged to at least one of these social institutions. The National Club, founded by members of the Canada First movement, was now considered the unofficial Liberal Party headquarters in the city, and despite his dinosaur views and insistence that he was not a party man, Colonel George Denison was its longtime president.

How would this martinet and roaring snob treat Carrie Davies? By the time she appeared before him, Denison had completed nearly four decades on the bench to which he had been appointed in 1877, twenty years before her birth. Carrie could expect speedy treatment, because Denison ran his court like a well-oiled machine. Boasting that he presided over "a court of justice, not a court of law," he cantered through cases at a breathtaking pace, relying more on intuition than evidence, and flaunting his impatience with legal technicalities and procedural niceties. Denison handled an average of twenty-eight thousand cases a year, which, according to Harry Wodson, police court reporter for the *Evening Telegram*, constituted an astonishing caseload of over five hundred a week. To the exasperation of the magistrate's seven clerks, Denison routinely cleared his docket in a couple of hours before lunch, ordered the court adjourned, and then, stick in hand and homburg hat on head, strolled off to the handsome dining room of the National Club, at 303 Bay Street.

Perhaps Carrie, a British-born woman in the most traditional of employments, might have expected a touch of compassion. In Denison's court, people who "knew their place" (retired soldiers, hard-working British immigrants, and the penitent) could expect leniency. In contrast, striking workers, people of Irish or African-American descent, and the *nouveaux riches* found little mercy. Admirers like Harry Wodson, who shared Denison's outlook, thought he was a terrific fellow: "A swift thinker, a keen student of human nature, the possessor of an incisive tongue, he extinguishes academic lawyers, parries thrusts with the skill of a practiced swordsman, confounds the deadly-in-earnest barrister with a witticism, [and] scatters legal intricacies to the winds . . . His mind is more or less remote from the affairs of the rank and file of humanity . . . Just what mental process is used to make the punishment fit the crime, only the magistrate himself knows." But Denison infuriated those who regarded him as a whip-cracking fossil, mired in the assumptions of a borrowed class system. Phillips Thompson, a journalist and labour sympathizer who worked on the publication the *Western Clarion*, excoriated the magistrate in print: "He is true as hell to the ideals of his Tory U.E. Loyalist ancestors, and holds like them that all popular notions of liberty are rank delusions and that the masses were bound to be exploited for the benefit of the ruling class."

Denison had no interest in what drove individuals to break the law. One woman whom he regularly fined for drunkenness amused Harry Wodson by reproaching the magistrate: "The only diff'rence between me and Lady O'Flaherty up in Rosedale is that I have no powdered flunkeys to carry me up to bed whin I'm drunk." Denison paid no attention and sent her to the slammer.

Only a sense of humour softened Denison's paternal Toryism and patrician bias. He filled scrapbooks with cartoons of himself (he was easy to caricature), and Harry Wodson enjoyed watching the Beak suppress a chuckle at the cheeky remarks from court regulars. Dodson suggested that his genial manner endeared him to most defendants who appeared before him. A 1913 cartoon pictured a tattered husband and wife jostling each other in front of Denison's seat, and the woman saying to her husband, "Ain't I got as much right to enjoy the pleasure of bein' tried by Colonel Denison as you have?"

Carrie knew none of this when Miss Mary Minty, the beefy, square-jawed Scotswoman who had become Toronto's first female police constable in 1913, escorted her into the Women's Court on the second floor of City Hall. Exhausted and traumatized after a night in the police cells, she barely understood that the stern, snappy man presiding over the court would decide whether she should be kept in custody or allowed out on bail.

The women on the public benches craned forward to see the eighteen-year-old, as she sat on the prisoners' bench alongside gaudily dressed prostitutes ("petticoated birds of paradise and prey," in Wodson's phrase), petty thieves, and haggard drunks. In her worn brown cloth coat and black hat, Carrie seemed out of place in such company. Her face was swollen with tears, and her hands played nervously with her knitted gloves as she looked around the large square room.

Colonel Denison launched proceedings like a Gatling gun at full throttle. The morning's case list began with a handful of cases involving drunkenness, vagrancy, and petty theft, which were dispatched before most people had drawn breath. The prisoners' bench rapidly emptied, until only Carrie's slight figure was left. Finally, Carrie's name was called above the subdued whispering that filled the courtroom. She rose, and stumbled forward to stand in front of the magistrate. This case was too serious to give the Beak any cause to slow down. He fixed his eyes on her and, in his parade-ground bark, addressed her: "Carrie Davies, you are here accused of murder."

There was a collective gasp. The most serious accusation possible had been brought against Carrie—an accusation that, if upheld by trial, could take her to the gallows. In early-twentieth-century Canada, the death penalty was regularly invoked and frequently imposed. Only the previous year, thirty-one people had been sentenced to death: sixteen of them would see their petitions for clemency dismissed and would feel the noose around their necks.

Had the court clerk, Mr. Chapman, not wedged a chair behind Carrie, she would have collapsed on the floor. She sat, hunched forward, without saying a word as Colonel Denison consulted the Crown attorney about the court calendar. He announced that Carrie should return to the Women's Court in a week's time, on February 16, after evidence had been gathered and the coroner's inquest completed, so that the date for her criminal trial might be set. Meanwhile, she should be remanded in custody.

Miss Minty stepped forward, took Carrie's arm, and led her back to the bench. Denison made a few general remarks to his clerks, slammed his casebook shut, and strode out of the court. Miss Minty escorted Carrie back into the corridor. None of Carrie's friends or family, nor any members of the Massey family, was present this morning, nor did Carrie have a lawyer. Accused of murder, she was not eligible for bail— but even if she had been, there was nobody to stand bail for her. At this point, she was completely alone in the justice system's grip.

Newspapers that catered to the city's elite reported simply that Carrie had been remanded for a week. They devoted more ink to portraying the dead man as an agreeable *bon vivant*. The *Globe* described "the late Mr. Massey" as "well known about town. He was fond of motoring and took much enjoyment out of life . . . A diamond ring and stick pin worth several hundred dollars and some money were found on him." The *Toronto Daily News* mentioned that he was educated at Albert College, Belleville, later attending an American preparatory school, and was a "prominent figure among the young social set."

But reporters from papers with a blue-collar readership put the spotlight on Carrie. Was her impassivity the result of dazed terror or hard-boiled criminality? The *Evening Telegram* portrayed her as young and guileless: "a rather short, fair-haired girl, of eighteen, whose blue-grey eyes looked as though they had wept most of the night . . . More like a mild and gentle Sunday School pupil did she look, and very subdued and sorrowful this morning." The *Toronto Daily Star* took a very different line: "The heaviness over her eyebrows resembles the Slavic type more than the English, and her mouth is strong, showing capacity for resentment out of all keeping with a round, childish chin."

As spectators streamed out of the courtroom, each made her own judgment as to whether Carrie Davies was subdued Sunday school pupil or resentful, aggressive immigrant. That evening, readers of the *Evening Telegram* were able to glean more about the young girl now accused of murder. A day earlier, soon after Bert Massey had been killed, a *Tely* reporter named Archie Fisher who had been at City Hall when she was brought in had discovered that Carrie Davies had a sister living in the distant east end of Toronto. Fisher had hurried along Gerrard Street for six kilometres until he reached Morley Avenue, where a jumble of wooden telegraph poles and tiny brick houses, many single-storey and all squatting on small lots, lined a soggy gravel thoroughfare just south of the train tracks. Cursing the darkness, he stumbled north, up an incline, until he found number 326. A woman came to the door after he knocked, and looked at this stranger with surprise.

The reporter realized he had got there before the police. "Are you Maud Fairchild, Carrie Davies's sister?" he demanded in a voice sombre with authority. Maud Fairchild said she was, and immediately asked, "What has happened to Carrie?" The reporter continued to grill her as Maud's husband, Ed Fairchild, emerged from the kitchen with a baby in his arms. "Does your sister work for Mr. Massey?" Maud looked anxious. "Yes. Tell us what is the matter." The reporter stepped importantly through the door into an ill-lit, narrow hall and announced that Carrie had shot her employer.

The Fairchilds were devastated. As Ed asked, "Was Mr. Massey badly hurt?" his wife gasped, "Poor Carrie." By now the reporter had manoeuvred them into the tiny parlour: Maud sank into a chair and a toddler immediately ran to her and clung to her skirts. Neither Ed nor Maud could believe that Carrie would do such a thing: she was such a shy little thing, she could barely kill a fly. She had worked for the Masseys for two years, and always said the Masseys were good to her. She had been taken poorly the previous summer, Maud stuttered, while she was with the Masseys at their summer cottage, and they had looked after her so well. She had been her normal, quiet self when she spent Sunday afternoon with the Fairchilds.

Then Ed remembered something. When Carrie was with them on Sunday, the Fairchilds had friends visiting, so she hadn't been able to talk much to her sister. However, she had taken her brother-in-law aside in the kitchen and whispered to him that Mr. Massey had tried to kiss her the previous day, when she was cleaning up after a dinner party. Ed insisted that Carrie hadn't seemed particularly upset. "I told her not to think about it too much about that," said Ed. "Probably he was feeling a little good and he would forget about it. She said that she guessed he would be ashamed of himself." As Carrie was leaving at the end of the evening, Ed had mentioned Mr. Massey's behaviour to his wife. Maud was concerned, but she didn't stop her sister returning to Walmer Road.

Now, a day later, she recalled telling her sister that if anything should happen, to run right out of the house and rush into a neighbour's house, "no matter whether she was fully dressed or not."

But now Carrie was in real trouble. Ed Fairchild grabbed his coat and insisted he must leave immediately and get downtown: he planned to stand bail for his sister-in-law and get her out of police custody. The reporter had not yet divulged that Bert Massey was dead. He immediately offered to accompany the distraught man downtown. The two men disappeared into the February dark—but not before the man from the *Tely* had asked Maud to lend him a photograph of Carrie which he knew his editor would publish in the next edition. On the following day, after Carrie's appearance in the Women's Court, it appeared next to the *Tely*'s scoop—the most informative account of the murder so far, under the headline "News of What Had Happened a Cruel Blow to a Little East End Household."

Carrie, an uneducated eighteen-year-old who had taken a man's life, had barely uttered a word on the day of her first court appearance. Over the course of the next three weeks, her own words would be recorded on only three occasions. A century later, those remarks are all we have in her voice on which to base speculation on her state of mind: she left no diary or letters that reveal what she was thinking or feeling. We know her reactions to events only if they were noted in others' accounts or newspaper articles. However, observers have always been happy to project their own assumptions onto her. In 1915, she was on her way to becoming a lightning rod for the fears and prejudices swirling around Canada's largest English-speaking city.

CHAPTER 3

The Corpse in the Morgue

TUESDAY, FEBRUARY 9

PARADE OF 4,000 SOLDIERS THROUGH CITY
Mounted rifles swing into Queen Street at the foot of University Avenue.
BRITISH LOSSES TOTAL 104,000
*Premier Asquith speaking in the [British] House of Commons to-day
said that British casualties in all ranks in the western arena of the war, from the
beginning of hostilities to February 4, amounted to approximately 104,000 men.
This includes killed, wounded and missing.*
—*Globe*, Tuesday, February 9, 1915

*Mr. Frederick Massey . . . said that he had viewed the body in the morgue,
and recognized it as that of Charles A. Massey, whom he knew intimately.*
—*Toronto Daily Star*, Wednesday, February 10, 1915

Once Colonel Denison had closed the Women's Court proceedings, Miss Minty marched her prisoner through the spectators gathered at the courtroom door, round to the other side of City Hall's second floor, and waited for the elevator to rattle up in its metal cage from the ground floor. When its doors opened, a group of self-assured women in smart hats and fur coats bustled out. Carrie shrank back, but nobody took any notice of the shabby domestic: these women had other concerns. The members of Toronto's Local Council of Women were on a mission to persuade Mayor Thomas Langton Church and the Board of Control that the Women's Court must not fall prey to government cuts. Once these women had stomped off, Carrie and Miss Minty stepped into the elevator for the creaky ascent to the third floor. There, the policewoman escorted her charge to the police office, where Carrie would begin the ordeal of being admitted, on remand, to the notorious Toronto Jail, better known as "the Don."

Carrie was told to remove her hat and coat. First, she was photographed from the front and both sides. Next, a police clerk bustled up to her, wielding a pair of steel calipers. Carrie's eyes widened with alarm, but Miss Minty reassured her. There followed a lengthy procedure in which twenty-five dimensions of Carrie's body were measured, including her height, head length, left foot, left little finger, right ear, nose size and shape, ear lobe, chin, teeth, and the width and tilt of her forehead. All these measurements, plus her birthplace, occupation, and hair colour, were noted down in a big, brown leather-bound volume: the Toronto police force's "Bertillon" register.

The Bertillon system of identification had been invented forty years earlier by Alphonse Bertillon, a pale-faced, misanthropic records clerk in the Paris Police Department. As police forces in Europe and North America expanded and became more professional in the nineteenth century, they found themselves hampered by their inability to track offenders. Hardened criminals were often sentenced as first offenders because there was no accurate way to identify recidivists or escapees. Bertillon, a self-important, obsessive little man with a thrusting beard and deep voice, was exasperated by this haphazard approach to identification. His father, an anthropologist and statistician, had spent his career researching the unique variations in physical characteristics in every human being, and Bertillon built on this research to develop a criminal identification scheme. He used his father's measuring techniques on arrestees and convicts, carefully recording physical features (eye colour, shape and angles of the ear, brow, and nose) that no disguise could hide. He accumulated a vast amount of data on cards, which were then categorized and cross-indexed.

In the late nineteenth century, when innovations like photography, the telephone, and the gramophone were taking off like wildfire, Bertillon's system won instant popularity. No wonder—as the first use in history of scientific detection to catch a criminal, it combined two obsessions of the time: science and crime. Adopted in 1882 by the Paris police, "Bertillonage" became all the rage in France after it successfully identified 241 multiple offenders. In 1887, the warden of the Illinois State Penitentiary introduced it into the United States, and its use quickly spread across the continent. By the mid-1890s, Alphonse Bertillon was an international celebrity. Sherlock Holmes, Arthur Conan Doyle's fictional detective, showed "enthusiastic admiration of the French *savant*," and in Conan Doyle's 1901 novel *The Hound of the Baskervilles*, another character described Holmes and Bertillon as being the two best detectives in Europe.

However, there were flaws in both the system and its author. Pumped by success, Bertillon also claimed to be a handwriting expert. In the 1890s he had testified for the prosecution in the explosive Dreyfus affair, when a Jewish officer in the French army was wrongly accused of being a German spy. Bertillon's rambling evidence helped condemn the innocent Captain Alfred Dreyfus to life imprisonment on Devil's Island. Moreover, Bertillonage was fallible: different officers could make their measurement in different ways, while two individuals with the same measurements could be confused. In 1903, two men—one named Will West and the second William West—were convicted in Kansas for different crimes, yet were found to possess the same Bertillon measurements.

The decline in Bertillon's credibility was as rapid as his rise, after another set of unchanging human characteristics, fingerprints, was shown to be more reliable. By the early 1900s, police departments in Britain and the United States were switching over to a fingerprint classification system developed by Commissioner Edward Henry of Scotland Yard. Fingerprinting offered odds of 67 billion to one of any two individuals having identical prints. Alphonse Bertillon died in 1914, a year before Carrie faced the calipers. By then, the Toronto Police Department was one of the few forces still laboriously measuring lobes, noses, and feet. Judging by the skimpy records in its leather-bound Bertillon Register, it did so with dwindling conviction of its usefulness.

Toronto's police department was old-fashioned and struggled to keep up with its British equivalent, the Metropolitan Police Force in London's Scotland Yard. The man in charge of Toronto's police, Colonel Henry Grasett, was a contemporary of Colonel Denison's who shared the Beak's militaristic pretensions and patrician attitudes. The two men saw each other regularly at the Toronto Club. A militia officer born into a prominent Toronto family (his father was rector of St. James' Cathedral, bastion of elite Anglicanism), Colonel Grasett had fought alongside Denison against Fenian invaders in 1866 and had led operations against Chief Big Bear in the Northwest Rebellion in 1885. The chief constable believed in spit-and-polish discipline and parade ground drills, but he was not a dinosaur. Interested in progressive policing, he tried to keep abreast of modern policing trends.

When Grasett had become chief constable in 1886, there were only 172 police officers in the city and the force's toughest challenges were vagrancy, burglary, and fistfights. Now there were over six hundred police officers, the majority of them British (particularly Protestant Irish) immigrants, with a far greater range of rules to enforce. Not only were they dealing with street traffic, insurance frauds, and violent crimes, they were also responsible for regulating parades, processions, dance halls, gambling, liquor laws, censorship, Sabbath-breaking, the ages of newsboys, and any new forms of "immorality" that came to police attention. As reporter Harry M. Wodson observed, Toronto had become a city of "shall nots," where it was more important for citizens to memorize six thousand bylaws than the Ten Commandments. In 1902, Chief Constable Grasett was elected vice-president of the Police Chiefs Association of the United States and Canada, in recognition of the growing muscle of the Toronto boys in blue. But police resources were stretched—by the city's dramatic growth, by the loss of many constables to the army in 1914, and by the city fathers' determination to impose their morality on the working classes.

Grasett had replaced an informal "rogues' gallery" of photographs of criminals with the Bertillon system after a visit to the state-of-the-art Chicago Police Department in 1897. But technological innovations like the telegraph and telephone cost money, and Toronto was slow to adopt them because City Council was not always sympathetic. Grasett finally managed to establish a motorcycle squad in 1911 to enforce the new fifteen-mile-per-hour speed limit on city streets. (Riders often wore business suits so that speeders would not realize they were being monitored.) Nonetheless, in 1914 the Toronto force was still using horse-drawn police wagons: it was another three years before the department acquired motor cars. Although the Dominion Police, with its headquarters in Ottawa, abandoned Bertillonage soon after the turn of the century (partly because many of its technicians had dropped their calipers and joined the stampede to the Klondike goldfields in 1898–99), the Toronto Police Force continued to take Bertillon measurements until 1915, although they also began finger-printing suspects in 1906.

Carrie Davies's Bertillon measurements would never be used, but the process was part of the intimidating ordeal of arrest. After she had been Bertillonaged, Carrie was escorted downstairs by Miss Minty, and then driven off in a police wagon to Toronto Jail, three and a half kilometres away on the other side of the Don River. There, she stepped out of the paddy wagon at the intersection of Gerrard Street and Broadview Avenue and looked up at the monstrous building in which she was to be incarcerated. Constructed of cold grey stone and black iron, with small barred windows set high in its walls, it was one of the largest jails in North America and often described as the "Riverdale Bastille." Built half a century earlier to hold about three hundred prisoners, it had recently been condemned by the provincial inspector of prisons as "over-crowded, ill-ventilated and unsanitary, a fire-trap, and the worst jail on the continent of America." Conditions for women were especially disgusting. The *Toronto Star* had recently revealed that a woman confined to the punishment cell there had killed seventy-three rats and thirteen mice. A group of women visitors had discovered that women inmates were not supplied with underwear or socks (male prisoners got both) and had no access to books. A particular disgrace was that "the night toilet pails [do] day duty for scrubbing. [This is] neither sanitary or modern. As many of these women are victims of social diseases, it stands to reason in the light of modern bacteriology that this state of affairs should desist."

There was little chance that the current governor of the jail would take any action on these complaints: he was as ineffective as he was well meaning, and he had no idea how to run a large, complex institution. The Reverend Dr. Andrew B. Chambers, vice-president of the Upper Canada Bible Society, had got the governor's job solely on the grounds of his Conservative Party links, and in the words of a contemporary, he "simply wanted to be a friend to everybody, especially those in trouble." Most people, including the chief turnkey and the guards, took advantage of him.

But Dr. Chambers's soft heart did save Carrie from exposure to the Don's toughest elements. He decided that this woebegone young woman was far too feeble to be locked up with the other women prisoners, many of whom were delusional, violent, or worse. Since Carrie's days on this earth seemed likely to be numbered, they should be as comfortable as possible. He sent her up to the prison hospital and put her in the charge of Mrs. Sinclair, superintendent of the Women's Department. For the rest of the day, Carrie refused to eat or speak: she just stared around her in fear.

❧

Oblivious to Carrie's lonely journey, the Local Council of Women delegation was still busy on the second floor, protesting to Mayor Church and the Board of Control against a proposal to move the Women's Court out of City Hall.

The number and range of Toronto's women's organizations in 1915 were truly startling. A middle-class Toronto woman could spend every afternoon or evening attending the Women's Conservative Club's knitting circle, the sale of homemade dainties by the Women's Christian Temperance Union, a knitting tea sponsored by the Political Equality League, or the Toronto Women's Patriotic League's collection drive for mufflers, socks, and wristlets for soldiers. The Heliconian Club ran regular sessions on literature, travel, and music for its members. In addition, there were church-sponsored groups, arts-focused clubs, and other get-togethers that allowed the wives of Toronto's swelling professional classes to meet each other.

All this activity stood in dramatic contrast to the way that the wives of Toronto's elite, or those who aspired to join it, had conducted themselves until recently. The cornerstone of sociability in the late Victorian era was the "At Home," an elaborate and suffocating ritual that might include a few intimates or a cast of hundreds, and took place in private houses during the afternoon. The rules were set by the wives and daughters of Toronto's most patrician families, who shared their husbands' stout belief that moral superiority sprang from good breeding and lots of money.

An At Home event was rigidly formal. It began with a stiff white card, engraved with the holder's name and address, and with a handwritten note of a weekday on the lower left-hand corner. The card was an invitation to join the holder for a tea on the day prescribed: it would be left with a maidservant at a door—but only *after* the hostess and her prospective guest had been formally introduced. Each society hostess had her At Home on a particular day, and over the years the occasions had grown increasingly competitive. Should the hostess offer a rose tea, a strawberry tea, a tea-and-talk, or a five o'clock tea?

The city's *grandes dames* slowly patrolled the drawing rooms of their social equals, sipping from bone china cups and making small talk. Their daughters dutifully handed around dainty sandwiches and *petits fours* and displayed their fathers' or husbands' wealth in the form of sable collars and diamond brooches. Grace Denison, niece by marriage of the police magistrate, wrote a society column about them in *Saturday Night* magazine, under the sobriquet Lady Gay. Over time, these afternoon receptions had become increasingly crowded, arduous, and competitive, as hostesses scheduled their teas on the same day so that guests had to rush between them. Lady Gay regularly complained about "the crush," in which she risked being "trodden upon, prodded in the ribs, squeezed, smeared and rent." For women whose waists and ribcages were already uncomfortably squeezed into unnatural shapes by whalebone corsets, At Homes could be purgatory. A *Saturday Night* article in 1906 had bemoaned the monotony of "the same decorative mums and roses, the same orchestral accompaniment, the same women, in the same frocks, the same suffocation in the tea-room."

Such events were still going strong in 1915, but with the new century, fashions and rituals began to change. Even the corsets loosened up—the new Tango model, made by the Dominion Corset Company of Toronto, claimed to "mould the figure, enhancing nature's charms without strain or compression." Most of the wives and daughters of Toronto's middle and upper classes did not expect to go to university or to look for paid employment. Only a few years earlier, the widely circulated medical journal *Canada Lancet* had belittled educated women as "withered, shrunken-shanked girls" with "stooping gait and . . . spectacles on nose." Who wanted to look like that? But many younger women did want to do something more useful than pass around Royal Doulton teacups.

As the city expanded, so did the options for women to escape from crowded parlours and the accumulation of social debts. Public tearooms, like McConkey's on King Street or the Savoy on Yonge Street, became fashionable meeting places where women could gather without having to disrupt their own households. Sometimes it was the same small talk in these commercial establishments as it had been in Rosedale drawing rooms, but frequently women gathered to talk about larger national issues and shared projects. Concern for public welfare, the campaign to eliminate alcohol from public life, women's right to vote—in tearooms, churches, and Women's Institutes, women in unprecedented numbers at different social levels were discussing these topics. Clubs, committees, groups, and associations were formed at a rapid rate to exchange information and opinions. The daughters of Yonge Street, Forest Hill, and Annex families showed the same enthusiasm for taking initiatives as Manitoba farm wives. The activities of the McConkey's set inspired some pejorative comment about "clubwomen" who had nothing better to do. While they sat discussing the vote, women like Carrie Davies were scrubbing their floors, cooking their dinners, and polishing their silver. But even if these women did not question some aspects of the status quo, they were genuinely concerned with improving conditions for the poor and exploited. And with the outbreak of war, a whole new range of challenges—from fundraising and knitting to encouraging enlistment—had opened up for them.

Seventy-two of these women's groups belonged to Toronto's Local Council of Women, the federation of early feminists that had successfully lobbied for the Women's Court. LCW membership was almost entirely Anglo-Saxon, Protestant, and middle or upper class; nevertheless, it represented a wide range of opinions and priorities. Some groups operated exclusively in their own neighbourhoods; others monitored provincial and federal politics. Some focused on philanthropy, others on educating their members. Some groups passionately supported female suffrage, particularly now that women out west were close to winning the right to vote in provincial elections; others felt that women didn't "need" the vote and shouldn't be demanding it while the nation was at war. The LCW maintained cohesion by focusing on maternal feminist goals: fresh from its success getting the Women's Court off the ground, it was now lobbying for safe milk, clean water, mothers' pensions, and children's playgrounds. The organization's philosophy was that "women and particularly mothers had the capacity to infuse social institutions and political life with superior moral virtue and maternal qualities."

No one worked harder to infuse Toronto with superior moral virtue than the LCW's president, Florence Gooderham Hamilton Huestis, who led today's delegation to see Mayor Church. Mrs. Huestis had social status. She was married to Archibald Morrison Huestis, a sweet-natured but retiring man from a Nova Scotia United Empire Loyalist family who worked at Toronto's Methodist Book Room—but Florence's status didn't derive from Archie (relatives referred to him as the "Prince Consort," because he was overshadowed in every way). Florence Huestis cut a swath through Toronto because of her two middle names. Florence's grandfather was William Hamilton, a wealthy Toronto industrialist whose fortune came from ironworks and toolmaking: his foundry produced the ornate iron fence that encircled Osgoode Hall. She was also part of the Gooderham dynasty, founded by William Gooderham, who with his nephew and partner James Worts had built a massive whisky distillery in the city's east end that by 1861 was the world's largest, producing 7,500 gallons of spirits a day. Flush with whisky profits, Gooderham had gone on to amass a fortune from railways, livestock, and banking. Mrs. Huestis had a gold-plated Toronto pedigree and sufficient family wealth that Mayor Church, for one, would be foolish to ignore.

An attractive, self-assured woman, Huestis was a fearless champion for those less fortunate than herself, and she was widely admired for her efforts. Always elegantly dressed, in the latest long-jacketed suit and brimmed hat, Mrs. Huestis smiled sweetly at male adversaries as she crisply dismissed their arguments. However, there was more to Florence Huestis's commitment to the underdog than benevolence. Unknown to many of her admirers, Mrs. Huestis had a secret. Her pedigree was not as gilded as it seemed, because her parentage was (and remains) shrouded in mystery. Born in 1873, little Flora Hamilton had been raised first by her grandfather Hamilton, and after his death by William's daughter Mary and Mary's husband, Henry Gooderham. Who were Florence's own parents? Was she the orphaned child of a distant relative? Had one of William Hamilton's several children given birth to her—presumably an illegitimate birth, since she wasn't even christened until age seven, when her grandfather died and she was shunted into the Gooderham household? Did a female member of the extensive Gooderham clan get herself into trouble, so that baby Florence mysteriously appeared after her mother had vanished from society for a few months? Or was she the offspring of one of Mary Hamilton Gooderham's brothers and a family maid?

Growing up, Florence herself was haunted by the mystery; she never forgot the taunts about her origins that she endured at the hands of toffee-nosed fellow students at Bishop Strachan School, where the daughters of Toronto's wealthy families were educated. She had emerged from the humiliation determined that she, and other women, should not be condemned to powerlessness. The stigma of her origins had been channelled into a powerful commitment to social welfare and women in peril.

By 1915, Mrs. Huestis was the mother of four daughters (whom the Huestises sent to Havergal Hall, Bishop Strachan School's rival). Firmly entrenched within Toronto's elite, she was "poised, capable and enthusiastic, a gay hat lending charm to her animated face." She was personally responsible for establishing the Big Sisters movement in Toronto, and she worked hard to expand the Women's College Hospital, where she presided over the board of governors. When the Toronto Council of Women held their monthly meetings, she stuck to the issues the members were comfortable championing: the Women's Court, pensions, playgrounds. But she never hid her personal conviction that women should be reaching for more radical change and demanding the vote. When the British suffragette Sylvia Pankhurst visited Toronto in 1911, Florence Huestis invited her to tea at her mansion at 10 Homewood Place, a block east of Jarvis Street. As the two women sat in the Huestis drawing room, surrounded by Florence's collection of fine English china, it must have been a stimulating meeting of minds. These two individuals came from completely different backgrounds, but shared a belief that the fastest solution to the world's problems was for women to win political rights.

The case of Carrie Davies touched Mrs. Huestis with particular intensity, and she followed the case avidly in the newspapers. But on February 9, while Carrie was being Bertillonaged on the third floor of City Hall, Mrs. Huestis was fighting another battle. The mayor was trying to brush off the LCW delegation with the specious argument that the city could not afford a dedicated court space for women until the war was over. *Tely* reporter Harry Wodson couldn't agree more strongly: he had no time for the "petticoated fiends" who "luxuriated in a court of their own" and who were often, in his view, arch hypocrites and menaces to society. But the LCW delegation was determined not to lose the court it had fought so hard for, in which "fallen girls and women" could be helped to see the error of their ways. They were also determined to improve the grim conditions for women at Don Jail, where Carrie was now incarcerated. One of Florence Huestis's colleagues, a Madame Ratti, spoke about her visits of inspection to the women's sections of prisons and reformatories throughout Canada. Madame Ratti expressed perfectly the tension that she and some others felt between appropriately "feminine" behaviour and reformer tactics when she explained that prison wardens had been effusively helpful because "I did not use suffragette methods. I am a French woman and I get what I want."

❧

However, as a strange scene the same evening revealed, Carrie Davies had not been completely abandoned to the court system. A couple of blocks east of City Hall, on Lombard Street, stood the bleak two-storey city morgue. Bert Massey's corpse had been bought here from Walmer Road, because the law required a coroner's inquest in cases of violent death. The inquest was held on the second floor, but the whole building stank with the stomach-wrenching odours of decaying flesh and disinfectant that leaked up from the room downstairs. Bert now lay on a marble mortuary slab alongside unclaimed bodies found in the streets after the previous week's cold snap.

In 1915, a coroner's inquest into the death of a crime victim required a jury of twelve. At 8 p.m., Chief Coroner Arthur Jukes Johnson was eager to start, and he waited impatiently as a coroner's jury was sworn in. The foreman was a contractor named James Burford, and his eleven fellow jurors were all men; not until the 1950s would women be admitted to jury service in most Canadian jurisdictions. Like Burford, most of the jurors were skilled workers with British names: they included an electrician, a butcher, and four merchants. Only a John McMahon, of Albany Avenue, described himself as a "gentleman." The point of an inquest, as spelled out in law, was to decide who the deceased was, and how, when, where, and by what means he had died. The jurors would hear witnesses so they could answer these questions, but it wasn't their job to make any decisions about who was responsible for the death. Their focus was Charles Albert Massey, not the individual who had held the gun. But their verdict would decide Carrie's journey through the legal system. Since Carrie Davies had already been remanded in custody on a charge of murder, most of those present expected that she would be there to give her side of the story.

Coroner Arthur Jukes Johnson and his jury soon found themselves stuck in the middle of a legal dogfight. Carrie was not present, but representatives from two different law firms had appeared, each claiming that his firm had been retained to represent her. Neither had actually spoken to Carrie.

Outside the morgue's filthy windows, feeble street lamps carved tiny circles in the dark February night. Inside, bright electric lights hung from the ceiling, casting inky shadows on faces and making the coroner's brows look even more ferocious than usual. Dr. Johnson, the city's first chief coroner, was not amused. A former surgeon who owed his appointment to a fascination with crimes and poisons, Johnson was in his late sixties and known for being snappy and churlish. He was an expert at his job: he had written a book on a coroner's duties, and he had written it in excruciating detail. "Before going to an inquest," he instructed his disciples, "the Coroner should see that he has with him convenient writing materials—a good pen and ink, a box of adhesive seals, some double sheets of foolscap, together with certain forms." Now Johnson gave a sigh of exasperation as he looked from one lawyer to the other, and then at the jury, which was patiently waiting to hear from witnesses what had happened the previous night. Should he proceed without Carrie, or should he adjourn? He was inclined to adjourn: "Where a person is accused of a serious crime like this, they have the right to give evidence on their own behalf," he told the jury. "I think it would be better to adjourn until she can be here."

At this point, the older and more confident of the two legal representatives spoke up. Mr. Henry Wilberforce Maw, a partner in the law firm Dewart, Maw & Hodgson, insisted he had been officially retained by Ed Fairchild, Carrie's brother-in-law. The other law firm's emissary turned out to be a law student sent on spec, looking for business, so he was quickly dismissed. Maw spoke with great authority about his client, although he had been unaware of her existence until Fairchild had managed to secure an interview with him that day. "I don't wish her to be here tonight," he announced. "She is very much agitated and upset. . . . The thing is so sudden that we have not had time to form conclusions as to the best form of procedure to take. Most of her relations and friends are in the Old Country. She is very excited and it would be very unwise to bring her here tonight."

Relieved to have an experienced lawyer on the case, Coroner

Johnson would have been happy to adjourn for the night until Carrie could be present. But that is not what Henry Maw wanted. He had not yet spoken to his client; he only knew what he had heard from Carrie's brother-in-law and read in sensationalist newspaper stories. He didn't know the exact details of Bert Massey's death, let alone what Carrie had told the police. It was rumoured that the girl was so distressed he'd never get a decent account of events from her. He needed to know the official story before he could decide how to proceed. But he was not an experienced courtroom lawyer, so he was on uncertain ground. He was unsure about the need to enter a plea of guilty or not guilty on behalf of his client in the coroner's court (it was unnecessary), so he prevaricated. Turning to the coroner, he said, "I am prepared to hear what evidence you have here, but I think it most unfair to ask us to decide what our election will be before a tithe of evidence has been given . . . I have not seen the statement she is alleged to have made to the police. The girl is not in a fit state of mind to talk matters over quietly. I think you should take the evidence so far as you can and then adjourn for a week. Then we will be in a position to decide whether we will bring her here or not."

Chief Coroner Johnson was not impressed by Maw's obfuscation, and blatant play for information before he developed a defence strategy. If the coroner wanted Carrie at the inquest, he would order her brought from jail. But Richard Greer, Ontario's attorney general, was sitting at the back of the room, drawn to observe what was going on in this shocking case. He could see that Maw would need more information if he was going to represent his client adequately. He rose to give his views. "It seems to me a breach of the fundamental ideas of British Fair Play when a girl is not given an opportunity to instruct counsel . . . The woman is young. She has not many friends in this country. Counsel has not been properly instructed by her."

Johnson harrumphed, but conceded that Carrie's lawyers might at least hear the outline of events from the witnesses present before the inquest adjourned. He raced through the rest of the formalities. Who would identify the deceased? Two well-dressed young men at the back of the room came forward: Mr. Frederick Massey, a distant cousin of the deceased, accompanied by his lawyer. Bert's brother, Arthur Massey, had not stinted in defence of his family's interests: he had hired Arthur John Thomson. A Harvard graduate and son of a distinguished lawyer, Thomson had been the Osgoode Hall Law School Gold Medallist in 1900. Thomson stuck close to his client, alert for any procedural errors.

Fred had already been downstairs to identify the body: he reappeared, white-faced and gagging, and ready to confirm that yes, the dead man was Bert Massey. Next, the coroner and the jury heard evidence from two Walmer Road residents: Dr. John Mitchell, who had watched Bert Massey take his last breath, and Beatrice Dinnis, who had seen the gun flash. Neither witness had any doubt that the Masseys' maidservant had aimed and fired a gun at her unsuspecting boss. But nothing like this had ever happened on Walmer Road before, and Miss Dinnis had been dizzy with excitement ever since. She had replayed the whole macabre drama several times in her head, and now told the jury that she saw a dark figure come out onto the verandah, adding in a whisper, "but that may have been my imagination."

The inquest was then adjourned for five days. The body of what the newspapers continued to refer to as "the murdered man" was loaded into a hearse and transported to the Hopkins Burial Company's undertaking parlour on Yonge Street.

As Henry Maw walked away from the solid, squat morgue building, he must have wondered if there was any chance at all of getting the charge against Carrie Davies reduced from murder to manslaughter. The eyewitness accounts were damning. The Massey family was so powerful. No wonder the woman was hysterical.

Yet the beginnings of a defence for Carrie Davies were starting to emerge—if she could find the right courtroom lawyer.

The first possible element in the defence story came the following day, when the *Globe* ended an account of the inquest with the paragraph: "Miss Davies . . . had a sweetheart who is with the Canadian contingent at Salisbury Plain. She had known the young man for eight months."

Carrie's boyfriend (who was never named) must have been among the thirty-one thousand Canadians who had volunteered to fight for King and country as soon as war was declared. He would have left Canada for England the previous October and, along with the rest of the Canadian Division, been sent to Salisbury Camp, the army training ground 145 kilometres southwest of London, for additional training. The Canadians endured a wretched winter on Salisbury Plain. Violent windstorms blew down the men's tents; torrential downpours transformed the chalky ground into a sea of mud; an epidemic of spinal meningitis killed at least twenty-eight men. Morale sank. Government censorship had prevented details of the sodden conditions reaching soldiers' families, but hints appeared in the papers, including stories about the "plague" of meningitis deaths.

The hardships endured by these men en route to the battlefields had not yet undermined the enthusiastic support from Toronto residents for the war and the brave young men who had volunteered. *Globe* readers who glanced at the coroner's decision to adjourn the Massey inquest could see, in the same edition, a stirring editorial entitled "King and Country Need You—Always." The editorial writer appealed to every young man to enlist, and "to give himself, body, mind, and spirit, to the dull drudgeries of drill and to the deliberate risks of death for the unseen ideal called 'King and Country.'"

Carrie's anonymous sweetheart on Salisbury Plain, drilling in a downpour in defence of Empire, was as good as a character witness for her.

{CHAPTER 4}

The Muscle of the Masseys

THURSDAY, FEBRUARY 11

———

RUSSIANS FORGE AHEAD IN EAST PRUSSIA
"BABY-KILLERS" STILL BUSY IN TOWNS ALONG AISNE
BRITON WINS THRILLING AIR DUEL
. . . Thousands of Belgians watched the terrific battle in the air.
When the [German] Taube pitched earthwards, signalling the victory of the British flyer,
the crowd broke out in a great chorus, singing "God Save the King" . . .
—*Globe*, Wednesday, February 10, 1915

The relatives express extreme indignation that any suggestion of indiscretion
should be made against the murdered man.
—*Toronto Daily News*, Wednesday, February 10, 1915

Charles Albert Massey's funeral took place three days after his death. Rhoda, Bert's widow, had returned the previous day from Bridgeport, Connecticut, after what must have been a shocking telephone call from her brother-in-law Arthur Lyman Massey. The trip home, which had involved at least two changes of train (likely in Boston and Montreal), had taken twenty-four hours, and probably felt much longer. A front-page story in the *Toronto Daily News* said she was "Prostrated with Grief." Arthur Massey met her at Front Street Station and escorted her to his house at 165 Admiral Road. Admiral Road was only five blocks from Walmer Road, but with its leafy elm trees, spacious lots, and turreted homes it was several degrees smarter. There Rhoda was greeted by her son, fourteen-year-old Charlie, who was traumatized by the death of his father and the arrest of Carrie, the shy young woman only four years older than him with whom he had often been left alone in the house. He used to chat to her while she cooked and cleaned in the kitchen, and in the basement he had enjoyed demonstrating to her his skill with his father's firearm. Arthur Massey and his forceful wife, Mary Ethel, had swept Charlie off to Admiral Road immediately after the dreadful events of the previous Monday. Now they were busy burying the whole business, including Rhoda's husband, as fast as possible. They had already made arrangements for the funeral.

Rhoda Massey wanted her husband to receive a Masonic burial. Like father and grandfather before him, Bert had been an active Freemason, belonging to the Ashlar Lodge on Yonge Street, one of more than a dozen Masonic lodges in Toronto. His wife relished this connection with the secret brotherhood that was deeply rooted in Toronto's WASP establishment. "It was my husband's wish that he be buried under Masonic auspices," she told the *Toronto Daily Star,* adding querulously, "but although I returned home just as soon as possible, I was not in time to give his lodge . . . the three days' notice required." Either the Ashlar Lodge, or her brother-in-law, had decided that an elaborate ceremony for Brother Massey would be inappropriate. Arthur briskly informed her that there would be a short service, for family only, at 165 Admiral Road, and then the Hopkins Burial Company would convey the coffin and family party to Mount Pleasant Cemetery.

Mount Pleasant was the final resting place for *haute* Toronto: among those buried in its two hundred and five carefully groomed acres of graves and memorials were Sir Oliver Mowat, the former premier of the province, and both of the men who had revolutionized the Dominion's retail business: department store kings Timothy Eaton and Robert Simpson. One of the cemetery's most lavish memorials was the massive Massey mausoleum, designed by architect Edward J. Lennox. Lennox had also designed City Hall, where Colonel Denison held sway in the Police Courts, and the architect had used the same heavy Gothic hand to memorialize the Massey family's illustrious forebear, Hart Almerrin Massey. The monument, a shrine to Massey muscle, was a solid lump of rusticated masonry encrusted with every excrescence imaginable—steps, windows, gables, pillars, and a turret. It was topped by a life-size statue of a hefty woman standing on a small Greek temple, gazing westward and radiating a grim power.

When the Hopkins hearse drew up outside the Arthur Massey residence, there were a couple of reporters loitering outside, hands thrust into the pockets of their wool coats as the February wind whipped the bare branches of the trees along Admiral Road. They watched the coffin carried through the front door, followed by an Anglican minister, the Reverend Mr. James of Bloor Street's Church of the Redeemer, who arrived to conduct the service. Mary Ethel Massey had imported Anglicanism into this branch of the family. The reporters were still there when, less than an hour later, the black-clad mourners straggled out for the drive to the cemetery. "Many beautiful floral tributes testified to the popularity and esteem in which the late Mr. Massey was held by a host of friends and acquaintances," the reporter from the *Star* noted respectfully. The paper listed Bert's friends who acted as pallbearers by name: "Messrs. James McFadden, H. H. McNamara, Kenneth Zimmerman, John L. Hynes, Howard Frederick Massey, Arthur A. Allan." It was left to readers to wonder why Frederick Massey, a distant cousin, was the only pallbearer related to the dead man. Bert's twenty-seven-year-old first cousin Vincent Massey, then a member of the University of Toronto's History Department, attended the service. (He noted in his diary, "Went to Bert Massey's funeral from Arthur Massey's house.") But he had darted out early because he had more pressing priorities. He had already been obliged to miss a lecture on musketry at the university. That evening, former U.S. president William Taft was scheduled to speak at the University of Toronto's Convocation Hall, and the ambitious Vincent had wangled for himself the honour of being an usher.

From Admiral Road, the funeral cortege drove slowly up Yonge Street into Mount Pleasant Cemetery. By now, the press had lost interest. Had a reporter from the *Star* or *Evening Telegram* followed the cortege, he would have watched the sad little straggle of mourners skirt the Massey mausoleum and head towards a snow-covered, treeless southern corner of the cemetery. The procession finally stopped in an area of modest memorials and unmarked graves close to the cemetery wall. The undertakers swiftly lowered Bert's coffin into a hole in the ground;

equally swiftly, the handful of mourners dispersed. There would be no grave marker for half a century.

The physical distance between Hart Massey's mausoleum and Bert Massey's grave reflected a bigger gulf—the distance between a hard-nosed entrepreneur and his less-favoured descendants.

Of all the industrialists who helped lay the foundations for the Dominion's wealth, Bert Massey's grandfather was the best known inside and outside Canada. By 1915, he had been dead almost two decades, but the Massey name was stamped on Toronto's largest factory, on millions of pieces of agricultural machinery, and on buildings dotted around Toronto. His fame and philanthropy guaranteed that his grandson's untimely death would become a sensational news story.

But there was another side to Hart Almerrin Massey, and one that Charles Albert Massey knew well. Bert was sixteen years old when his grandfather died, aged seventy-three, and he had clear memories of the tall, gaunt, frock-coated figure with the white beard, gimlet eyes, and forbidding demeanour of an Old Testament prophet. For the first few years of his life, Bert and his siblings had been the darlings of their grandparents' eyes. Abruptly, when Bert was about ten, Hart had pushed them all to the margins of the Massey empire. The Massey name was an ambiguous inheritance.

❧

Massey family history has all the characteristics that Canadians once relished—log cabin beginnings, devotion to duty, efforts rewarded.

However, the first Masseys to set foot in British North America arrived for commercial reasons rather than through loyalty to the Crown or imperial ambition. The Masseys were Yankee Methodists who came up from Vermont in 1802. Hart Massey, Bert's grandfather, had archetypal pioneer beginnings: he started life in 1823 on a hardscrabble family farm north of Lake Ontario, close to the little port of Cobourg. These were years when Canadian agriculture consisted of an annual cycle of backbreaking drudgery: land-clearing, rock removal, plowing, seeding, scything, and threshing—all done by hand. Land was cheap, but the work was brutal and monotonous. The hardships prompted the English immigrant Susanna Moodie to write, in *Roughing It in the Bush*, "My love for Canada was a feeling very nearly allied to that which the condemned criminal entertains for his cell." Subsistence farmers like the Moodies and Masseys scratched a living from primitive farms on the harsh Canadian Shield and struggled to feed their families. They seized on any primitive labour-saving device, such as patented stump-pullers and improved harrows, that local blacksmiths hammered into existence. By the time he was six, Hart Massey knew all about rising at dawn to fetch water, feed chickens, collect eggs, harness horses, and gather kindling.

But Massey men shared a valuable talent: an aptitude for fiddling around with bits of metal. Hart's father, Daniel, was fascinated by mechanical inventions and acquired a workshop in nearby Newcastle. From an early age, Hart too had demonstrated primitive engineering skills, and in 1851 he took over the Newcastle works, which was now a solid local foundry. Hart had vision, and an intuitive understanding of market forces, and the family foundry's reputation rapidly spread beyond the rock-strewn farms around Newcastle. Hart geared the "Newcastle Foundry and Machine Manufactory" to the production of mechanical mowers and reapers. His machines made farmers' lives incomparably easier, and Massey products were soon winning prizes at agricultural shows. In 1867, the year of Canada's Confederation, Hart Massey's combined reaper and mower won a gold medal at an international exposition in France. The foundry expanded, profusely illustrated Massey catalogues were widely distributed, and Hart Massey was on the road to becoming one of Canada's first self-made millionaires.

Some of the Massey success was due to Massey mechanical and marketing skills, but much was due to the larger national context. Massey machines appeared when there was a scarcity of farm labour, increasing demand for wheat production, and (thanks to the U.S. Civil War) little competition from the States. Massey machines continued to win international prizes as Canada expanded westwards and the population grew. By the end of the nineteenth century, there were over six million Canadians, and the most popular image of Canada for decades to come was of acres of golden wheat, waving in the prairie breeze, awaiting the Massey thresher. Massey reapers had helped transform Canada from a handful of sparsely populated colonies (with a population of less than a million when Hart was born) into the breadbasket of the Empire.

Hart Massey and his wife, American-born Eliza Phelps, would have four sons (a fifth died as an infant) and a daughter. Their eldest child, Charles Albert (Bert's father), was born in 1848. The Masseys had retained close links with family and business interests in the United States, and when Charles was a lanky, lantern-jawed twenty-three-year-old, his father left him in charge of the family's Newcastle factory and moved to Cleveland, Ohio, for health reasons.

Charles Massey had inherited from his grandfather and father their entrepreneurial flair and appetite for work. However, he was also a gentler character, with a sweet smile and a passion for music: he began playing the organ at services in Newcastle's Methodist Church when he was only thirteen. He and his pretty American wife, Jessie, lived next door to the Newcastle works in a white clapboard house. Their first surviving child, Winona Grace, was born in 1872; four more babies would follow. Jessie reported to her own mother that her husband would frequently come home during the day to visit his growing family: "Charley plays with [the baby] so much, she cries for him now when he goes out and wants to stay with him all the time he is in the house." But Charles did not neglect the foundry. Under his shrewd management, business increased 50 percent in the eight years after his father's departure.

In 1878, the Massey Manufacturing Company introduced its first machine of wholly Canadian design, the Massey Harvester. Plans called for two hundred of these reapers to be made the first year: more than five hundred orders flowed in. Business boomed. By 1879, the company had outgrown the Newcastle premises and Charles took the bold decision to move it to Toronto. He commissioned "the largest and best equipped factory ever built in Canada" on a six-acre site on King Street West, sandwiched between railway tracks (it had its own spur line) on the outskirts of the city. The main plant consisted of a huge four-storey building of solid red brick, lit by gas and safeguarded from fire by an automatic sprinkler system. A couple of years later, the company opened a branch plant in Winnipeg just as immigrants began to pour into Manitoba. By 1883, the Massey Manufacturing Company's aggregate business was a million dollars, more than ten times the amount done in 1870, the year of its incorporation. With seven hundred employees, it was Toronto's largest factory.

Charles, Bert's father, worked like a dog through these years, keeping the Newcastle plant running while building the new Toronto works, then switching production to Toronto and ramping up to meet increased demand. As general manager, he ran the works and was responsible for all the advertising, wages, hiring, stock purchases, banking, and correspondence—he wrote as many as a hundred and fifty letters a day. He and Jessie left their modest Newcastle home and moved to a town house in Clarence Square, at the southern end of Toronto's Spadina Avenue, that was a ten-minute drive, in a horse-drawn carriage down tree-lined dirt roads, to the new Massey factory. Their fourth child, and second son, Charles Albert ("Bert"), was born here in August 1880. A year later, Bessie Irene completed the family.

Charles was popular with Massey employees because he remembered names and promoted social activities. His love of music prompted the formation of the Massey Band, String Orchestra, and Glee Club, as well as the Massey Cornet Band, which was in constant demand at provincial fall fairs and at skating rinks throughout the winter. But he was seriously overworked, and by 1882 his father, Hart, now in robust health, had returned to Canada and resumed control of the company. His management style was a great deal harsher than his son's, but Charles was too incapacitated to dilute his father's iron rule.

Massey fortunes surged and Hart purchased a twenty-five-room mansion—an architectural frenzy of turrets and balconies—on fashionable Jarvis Street that he named Euclid Hall (433, subsequently renumbered 515). Charles and his family built a house close by and began to raise their children alongside those of Toronto's expanding plutocracy. Toronto's industrial boom was phenomenal in these years: furniture and clothing manufacture, piano-making, meat-packing, engineering, and breweries had all taken off. Furnaces, rubber and paper goods, carriages, chemicals, corsets, brass fittings, railway bolts—the catalogue of products churned out in hastily built factories was endless. The Bell Electric Light Company moved from London to Toronto in 1883 and was soon selling equipment across the continent. In 1884, the Toronto Electric Light Company began lighting central streets with steam-generated electricity. Several of Hart Massey's counterparts were fellow Methodists, including Joseph Flavelle, a prominent financier who had begun in the meat-packing trade, and the department store dynasty the Eatons. Nevertheless, in this heaving mass of entrepreneurial vigour, the Masseys stood out. The Massey Manufacturing Company was the city's biggest employer and single largest contributor to the city's wealth.

But the city's social elite was an exclusive club. Toronto's Fine Old Ontario Families ("FOOFs," as they had come to be called) resented the new mercantile class. "I do not care for Toronto as I used to do," Colonel George Denison, who typified the old guard, told a friend in 1911. "Parvenus are as plentiful as blackberries, and the vulgar ostentation of the common rich is not a pleasant sight."

As Methodists and tradesmen, the Masseys were regarded as *nouveaux riches* by Toronto's self-designated gentry, even though they certainly didn't flaunt their success. On Sundays, the Masseys attended the dour Metropolitan Methodist Church at the corner of Church and Queen Streets, where they droned gloomy psalms about lost sheep. Not for Hart the displays of finery and feather-trimmed hats sported by the parishioners of St. James' Anglican Cathedral, farther down Church Street, where cheerful hymns such as "Jerusalem the Golden" reflected the sense of entitlement shared by FOOFs. Hart Massey and his relatives rarely appeared in *Saturday Night* magazine's social columns, and no Massey matron would be included alongside the opera singers, society leaders, and wives of governors general in turn-of-the-century Canada's equivalent of *Hello! Canada:* Henry J. Morgan's volume of gushing prose about 358 women, *Types of Canadian Women,* published in 1903. Hart Massey barely noticed: he had no interest in joining any Toronto club, and he regarded drinking, dancing, and theatre-going as sins.

Various producers of agricultural machinery had sprung up in the young Dominion, but there were only two of real size: the Masseys, who dubbed their binder "The Mighty Monarch of the Fields," and A. Harris, Son and Company of Brantford, whose binder was known as "The Little Brantford Beauty." Rivalry between the two companies was intense. Reaping tournaments were held in hundreds of sweltering, dusty harvest fields scattered from Nova Scotia's Bay of Fundy to Alberta's Bow Valley. Given the ups and downs of agricultural life (poor harvests, weather disasters), farmers found themselves both grateful for every improvement in the machines they relied on and beholden to distributors to whom they were often in debt. It was said that the Dominion's farmers were divided into three camps—those who swore by Massey, those who swore by Harris, and those who swore *at* both of them.

By the end of the nineteenth century, Hart Massey had won the Great Harvester War. The Massey and Harris firms merged in 1891, but Hart was the boss. He presided over the Massey-Harris Company and the Massey family controlled the largest block of shares and all the patents, production methods, and facilities. The Masseys were brilliant at promotion, churning out colour catalogues, house organs, leaflets, agricultural pronouncements, and the ambitious, general-interest *Massey's Magazine*. (Canadian writers such as Charles G.D. Roberts, Bliss Carman, and Duncan Campbell Scott, along with artists Charles W. Jefferys and George Reid, were regular contributors.) In 1892, Massey-Harris advertised that it was the largest maker of farm implements and machinery under the British flag. Massey-Harris equipment was used on the Royal farms at Windsor. Orders from around the globe now kept fifteen hundred men in Toronto employed flat out in a fifty-nine-hour workweek.

Thanks to influence in Ottawa, Hart's monopoly in the domestic agricultural implement market was reinforced by tariff policies that kept his American competitors out of Canada while protecting his own exports to Imperial markets like Australia and South Africa. "How can he contend that he can compete with the American manufacturers in their country but not in his own?" asked a *Globe* editorial in 1893. Like his American contemporaries Andrew Carnegie and Nelson D. Rockefeller, Hart Massey insisted that what was good for his company was good for his country. Massey Manufacturing was shipping tractors, threshers, reapers and cutters, and binders, some steam-driven and others gas-fuelled, to markets from South America to the Middle East. Surely he deserved to be made a senator? "My long experience has enabled me to systematize and put into successful operation one of the largest manufacturing industries in the world," he told Conservative Prime Minister Sir John Thompson in 1893.

The aging millionaire had additional reasons to believe that he was entitled to a seat in the Upper Chamber. In accordance with his Methodist principles, in his later years he devoted increasing amounts of time and money to philanthropic enterprises. Best known of his projects were two institutions familiar to everybody in Toronto: the Fred Victor Mission for homeless men, named after his youngest son, who died aged only twenty-three in 1890, and the Massey Music Hall, a major concert auditorium from the moment it opened in 1894 with a performance of Handel's *Messiah*. Dozens of other institutions benefitted from Massey benevolence: Methodist colleges all over the country, a Methodist camp in Muskoka, the Methodist Social Union of Toronto, industrial training initiatives in Toronto's schools, organs for various Methodist chapels, the Salvation Army's Rescue Home in Parkdale, the Chautauqua summer festival in upstate New York, and Victoria College at the University of Toronto, which received an endowment for a chair in religious education. Toronto boasted many wealthy businessmen as the Victorian age drew to a close, but none gave more generously—or more carefully—than Hart Massey.

Nevertheless, entrepreneurial success and good works were not enough to win the elderly industrialist a seat in the Senate. Politicians were aware of a western backlash against the monopolist who had managed to exclude from the Canadian market his American competitors and their agricultural machines that were more suitable for heavy prairie soils. The nascent labour movement sniped at the enormous wealth of an authoritarian businessman who kept wages low and who fought the reduction of the working day from ten to eight hours because, argued Hart Massey, such a short working day would mean that his employees would not be able to make ends meet. Daniel John

O'Donoghue, leader of the Knights of Labour, described Hart Massey as a "brute . . . devoid of soul."

Hart Massey died, aged seventy-two, on February 20, 1896. He had built an insignificant colonial village smithy into the mightiest manufactory of its kind in the British Empire. But he was a stern moralist and strict disciplinarian—the kind of rigid, self-righteous Methodist who insisted that Toronto should remain a repressed, closed-on-Sunday, God-fearing, and fun-shunning city. It was the influence of prominent citizens like Hart Massey that prompted a British visitor to the city to comment that "Sunday is as melancholy and suicidal a sort of day as Puritan principles can make it." Alongside the fulsome eulogies to an outstanding businessman was a layer of hostile comments. "His was not the impulsive charity that springs from an exuberant disposition," read the obituary in the *Toronto Daily Star*. "He gave because he thought it was his duty, not because he loved much." The man who could be a devoted husband and father could also be mean, as his family had already discovered.

Bert Massey, Carrie Davies's employer, knew firsthand what a tyrant his grandfather could be.

In 1884, Hart Massey had suffered a tragic loss. Only weeks after moving his family into the new house on Jarvis Street, his eldest son and heir apparent, thirty-five-year-old Charles Albert Massey, had caught typhoid fever. Doctors had tried all the newest therapies, including direct blood donation and a desperate, experimental injection of milk directly into the patient's veins. But Charles's health was already impaired by stress and exhaustion. In his final hours, the sick man admonished his three older children to study their Bibles, and gave each of his two babies, Bertie and Bessie, a last kiss. Then his eyes closed for the last time. The Massey who had done more than any other member of the family to develop and consolidate the company's success was gone.

Hart Massey commissioned a stained-glass memorial window for the factory's offices that portrayed a seraphic Charles above a field of ripened grain, in which one of the company's Perfect Binders was parked. But the old man did not let grief dilute tight-fisted business instincts. Jessie Massey, now a thirty-one-year-old widow with five children, found herself with no right to any share of the family company's revenue, and a drastically reduced income. Less than a year after settling on Jarvis Street, she was obliged to move to a narrow brick house at 288 Ontario Street, in far less fashionable Cabbagetown. Jessie continued to be welcome in Euclid Hall's drawing room, with its thick carpet and thicker drapes, and Hart and Eliza made a fuss over their five grandchildren. But Hart's love and ambitions were now focused elsewhere. He turned to his sons Chester and Walter to fill their brother's shoes. It was soon evident that Chester had little interest in business; he focused on his art collection and the family's philanthropy, while Walter, aged only twenty, became secretary-treasurer of the company. (At this stage, Fred Victor was still a schoolboy.)

In 1887, Jessie Massey remarried. Her new husband was a clerk in the Dominion Bank named John Haydn Horsey. By now, only Hart Massey's thirty-three-year-old daughter Lillian still lived at home, and he missed the energy of a household of children. Jessie's three elder children were in boarding school, and Hart Massey suggested that the two youngest, Bertie and Bessie, should come and stay with their grandparents for a while to allow Mr. and Mrs. John Haydn Horsey a little privacy.

Jessie gratefully accepted this invitation, and on Saturday, April 14, 1888, Hart triumphantly noted in his daily journal: "Charley's children came to live at Euclid Hall." Eight-year-old Bert Massey and his seven-year-old sister left Cabbagetown for the opulence of 515 Jarvis Street, where an elegant fountain played in the marble-floored front hall and a coachman called Dick groomed horses in the carriage house. In a photograph from this period, Bessie and Bertie are dressed in the elaborate children's outfits with which prosperous families displayed their own success. Bert looks like Little Lord Fauntleroy in a tiny velvet frock coat with silver buttons and a lace collar, and well-polished black ankle boots. But after a year, Jessie told her father-in-law that she wanted her children back. The old man prevaricated, and then began insisting that Jessie could visit her children only at set times. On a couple of occasions, Bessie and Bertie were allowed to visit their mother, but their grandfather's carriage stayed on the curb, waiting to take them back to Jarvis Street. Jessie became more insistent that the children should rejoin her. Hart wouldn't let them go.

It must have been painful for the two youngsters, torn between two households. One day, as Bessie would tell the Massey biographer Mollie Gillen, Jessie had had enough. She hired a cab, drove to the school that the children attended, and asked the principal if she could see them. When they appeared, she led them out to the cab and asked them solemnly whether they wanted to come and live with her and her new husband, John Haydn Horsey. Bertie and Bessie didn't hesitate: they wanted to rejoin her. Jessie quickly told the cab driver to take them all to her own house. She then sent the driver to Euclid Hall with a note for Hart in which she assured her former father-in-law that the children were safe in her hands, and could he please send their possessions?

Hart Massey was furious. Few people had challenged him so directly and got away with it. He refused to send a single one of their belongings. Jessie remained fearful that the family autocrat might try to reclaim the children, but she needn't have worried. To all intents and purposes, Hart Massey slammed the door on Charlie's children. Soon he had two more small grandchildren to dress in velvet and photograph on his knee: Vincent, born in 1887 and the elder of Chester's two sons, and Ruth, the first of Walter's four children, who arrived in 1889. Most of the Massey clan now lived in grand mansions on Jarvis Street. Only Jessie's five children lived elsewhere, in a far more modest home, with their mother, stepfather, and half-brother, Clifton Manbank Horsey, who was born in 1890. Jessie herself died in 1894, when she was only forty-two. By now, her older children were about to leave home, and Haydn Horsey appears to have taken responsibility for the younger Massey stepchildren as well as his own four-year-old son. Hart Massey grudgingly advanced funds for fourteen-year-old Bert's education.

Two years after Jessie's death, her father-in-law died. Hart Massey left a huge estate of almost $2 million (worth close to half a billion dollars today in purchasing power). The larger part of his money went to charitable and educational causes, and almost all the rest (after taking account of his widow's needs) was divided among his surviving children, Chester, Lillian, and Walter. Bequests to the "poor" Masseys, now orphaned and struggling, were grudging, given the size of the estate: Bert Massey and his four siblings each received only $15,000 (about $402,000 today)—from which money advanced by their grandfather for their education was deducted. Belleville's Albert Business College, the school Bert had attended, received $10,000 in Hart's will—not much less than Bert himself. For several years, there had been ugly rumours that Hart Massey had quietly wrested a large portion of stock back from Charles Massey's estate, to ensure that it would never be sold outside the family. This suspicion, and the stingy bequest, triggered a family lawsuit, finally settled out of court, that caused a bitter rift in family relations. The details were always hushed up.

From then on, Jessie's children never cropped up in the family photograph albums or in news reports of Massey triumphs. Hart's widow, Eliza, was equally stingy: when she died in 1908, almost all her estate went to Chester, Walter, and Lillian. She left nothing to her five grandchildren by her eldest son, Charlie, although an elderly brother-in-law and sister in the States each received $1,000.

Both of Charles Albert's two sons appear to have inherited the Massey mechanical aptitude. Arthur, six years older than Bert, had invented and patented a particular design of bed for invalids while still in his early thirties. Bert had opted for a career in the booming automobile industry. Yet there is no suggestion that either Arthur or Bert was offered a job at the Massey works, although there was no Jarvis Street heir in the next generation. (Chester's two sons had little interest in farm machinery. Although Vincent was briefly in charge, he quickly moved into politics, while his younger brother, Raymond, was always determined to be an actor, not a tractor maker. It was unthinkable that one of Walter's three daughters might join the company, while his son Denton—born in 1900—was still too young.) After Walter Massey's death in 1901, the former general manager of the Harris firm, Lyman Melvin-Jones, took over the ever-expanding Massey commercial empire. Ironically, Melvin-Jones won the prizes that Hart felt he himself had deserved—a seat in the Canadian Senate and a British knighthood.

With a name like Massey, Bert was welcomed at smart clubs, and his friends were drawn from the Toronto establishment. Membership in the Masons (he benefited from family tradition) allowed him to troll for useful contacts and present himself as a *bona fide* businessman. He and Rhoda had started their married life in a smart house with elaborate wooden trim and twelve-foot ceilings on Madison Avenue, not far from his mother's house in the newly named Annex district. However, money was tight, and the move to nearby Walmer Road was probably a sign that his grandfather's legacy was gone and his income was dwindling.

But in 1915, few knew about the nasty family politics behind closed Massey doors. Masseys were Masseys—rich, powerful people who lived like kings. Number 169 Walmer Road might be a modest dwelling compared to such baronial piles as George Denison's Heydon Villa or Hart Massey's Euclid Hall, but it was still a comfortable detached house with room for servants and a carriage house in the backyard. And Bert Massey appeared to symbolize the thoughtless presumption of a playboy. He wore a diamond stick pin and sold Studebaker cars to wealthy

Torontonians. As a married man with a young son, perhaps he could be forgiven for not rushing to join the armed forces. Nonetheless, plenty of other thirty-four-year-old family men had already volunteered to fight for King and country.

Newspaper reporters latched onto the name Massey, unaware that the dead man belonged to a spurned branch of the family with no access to Massey millions. In 1952, the critic B.K. Sandwell made the same blithe assumption when Bert's cousin Vincent Massey, a fourth-generation Massey to achieve eminence, was appointed Canada's first Canadian-born governor general. Sandwell made the famous quip:

> *Let the Old World, where rank's yet vital,*
> *Part those who have and have not title.*
> *Toronto has no social classes—*
> *Only the Masseys and the masses.*

But it had never been quite as simple as that.

{CHAPTER 5}

A Peculiar Look

THURSDAY, FEBRUARY 11

———

GREAT RUSSIAN VICTORY IN THE CARPATHIANS

DESPERATE BATTLE, IN WHICH GERMANS GO BRAVELY TO DEATH

THE SLAUGHTER APPALLING

ASSAULTS ON RUSSIAN TRENCHES REPELLED WITH BAYONET

. . . SLOPES DOTTED WITH SLAIN

—*Globe*, Thursday, February 11, 1915

CARRIE DAVIES NOW IN JAIL HOSPITAL

IS NOT CONFINED TO BED BUT HAS HAD SEVERAL FITS

All day Tuesday the girl sobbed and refused to be comforted or take any meals.
She slept little at night and it is stated had several epileptic fits, to which
she is supposed to be subject.

—*Toronto Daily News*, Thursday, February 11, 1915

The unfolding drama of a shocking death within a prominent family provided titillating relief for Toronto's citizens. Gossip was easier to absorb than the welter of confusing stories out of distant countries on the far side of the Atlantic. The only sources of information about the war, now in its seventh month, were newspaper reports and the rumours they triggered: there was no radio, let alone any of the information technology we take for granted today—television, Internet, streamed videos of battles in real time, captured on cell phones by ordinary citizens. In Carrie's world, newspaper readers were accustomed to getting the news when it was at least a day old, and to wondering if it had already been overtaken by events.

The official story in early February 1915 was that the war was going well. This was a contrast to the previous year, when for a ghastly moment Britain and its allies risked defeat in northern France and Belgium. Grey-uniformed German troops had headed for Belgium in 550 trains a day, some with "to Paris" chalked on their sides. By late August, German forces had captured Brussels, massacring civilians and pushing the remnants of the Belgian army out of the way as they moved into northern France. The French army had failed to contain the German surge across the border and were ill-equipped to mount an offensive to the southeast. French troops went into battle in eye-catching blue coats and brilliant red trousers that, in Adam Hochschild's words, "had long made them the most flamboyantly dressed of Europe's foot soldiers." It was a matter of Gallic pride: when a reformer at a parliamentary hearing had suggested toning down the colours two years earlier, the minister of war had bellowed, "*Jamais! Le pantalon rouge c'est la France!*" In case the vivid uniforms were not enough to guide German snipers, there was sound as well. Brass bands often led French infantry units into the attack.

Nevertheless, disaster had been narrowly averted. The French had halted the German advance towards Paris at the First Battle of the Marne in September, and the following month the British had crushed a clumsy German attack in the First Battle of Ypres. Canadians had been shocked by the horrendous casualties during these first three months of the war—the French lost 800,000 men (300,000 dead and the rest wounded or taken prisoner) and the British suffered a total loss of 95,000. Canadian newspapers described in blood-curdling detail how corpses littered the ground where Allied troops spent November and December extending the network of trenches—and getting their first taste of the months of misery ahead. Winter weather meant that the trenches were soon flooded and foul, and guns clogged with mud. Since Christmas, the western front had been relatively quiet.

Yet during this first year of fighting, an air of unreality lingered. *Saturday Night* had published a letter from an English officer in the North Staffordshire Regiment about the events on Christmas Day 1914, when German and British troops mingled freely in no man's land, between the trenches. "This morning, after reveille, the Germans sent out parties to bury their dead. Our men went out to help, and then we all, both sides, met in the middle and in groups began to talk and exchange gifts of tobacco, food, etc. All the morning we have been fraternizing, singing songs. I have been within a yard, in fact onto their trenches, and have spoken to and exchanged greetings with a colonel, staff officers, and various company officers. All were very nice . . . The Germans are Saxons, and a good-looking lot, only wishing for peace, in a manly way, and they seem in no way at their last gasp . . . The whole thing is extraordinary . . . It is weird to think that tomorrow night we shall be at it again hard." A German juggler who had been onstage in London gave an impromptu performance to both sides in no man's land. British soldiers from the Cheshire Regiment barbecued a pig and shared it with their enemies, and Saxon troops rolled a barrel of beer over their parapet and into British trenches.

The Christmas truce seemed to suggest that perhaps there was something noble about these warriors—that hostilities were a test of manhood rather than a brutal bloodbath. Such magical thinking didn't last long. On December 26, snipers on both sides resumed their job of picking off easy targets. Screams, groans, and whimpers of pain replaced the sound of carols.

Immediately after Christmas, most of the fighting had been on Germany's far distant eastern borders. In the lakes and forests of northeastern Poland, Russians and Germans had pounded each other with deadly machine gunfire, rifle shots, shell splinters, and whirling shrapnel. Phrases like "terrific slaughter" and "inferno of shells" were scattered through printed reports of the bloody Battle of the Masurian Lakes, which began in early February in a blizzard. Once again, the carnage was shocking: the Germans killed 56,000 Russians and captured 100,000 more. According to War Office spokesmen, the Masurian Lakes battle was a victory for the Russians, who had checked a German offensive.

Meanwhile, on the western front, the Allies' artillery had captured two little towns on France's border with Flanders, towns with names no one back in Canada could spell—Passchendaele and Langemarck. But these lofty pronouncements could not blot out the tales of bloody mayhem on both fronts that were seeping across the Atlantic. Some of those stories were propaganda, deliberately spread by government warmongers in London and Paris to encourage enlistment. Others were straightforward reporting from the battlefield. Canadians bombarded with such reports had no way of knowing the difference.

"French Government Tells of the Fiendish Atrocities Perpetrated by the Kaiser's Men" read one headline, over a story alleging that German soldiers had used scissors to gouge out the eyes of French soldiers. Army doctors reported that German shells were packed with phosphorus, which poisoned wounds and led to men dying of necrosis. At a medical triage station, a correspondent for the *Toronto Daily News* met men who were "tired, tired, tired . . . their eyes are heavy with gazing over-long in Death's face" as they sat on trolleys and held up their "frost-bitten, bandaged feet." The German navy had been given instructions, according to a Canadian Press dispatch, to drown any innocent women and children travelling on captured vessels. "Fiendish Determination of Germans Marks the Latest Development of Prussian Kultur." A report from Poland asserted that the Germans were using "a new explosive, the fumes of which temporarily blind combatants." The reporter described how the fighting was so intense that "it is no longer possible to distinguish individual gun explosions from the rattle of infantry. All are mingled in one inarticulate battle shriek. At night as if in a thunderstorm the darkness is pierced by intermittent flashes of fire while sickly green rockets shed a ghastly light over the lines."

Gruesome reports like these circulated through Canada endlessly by word of mouth. The war news was increasingly unsettling: German tactics were not just belligerent, they were immoral. What kind of men assaulted women or deliberately blinded their enemies? In the little town of Leaskdale, eighty kilometres north of Toronto, the writer Lucy Maud Montgomery (who had a two-year-old son) confided to her journal, "There have been such hideous stories in the papers lately of [Germans] cutting off the hands of little children in Belgium. Can they be true? They have committed terrible outrages and crimes, that is surely true, but I hope desperately that these stories of the mutilation of children are false. They harrow my soul . . . I cry myself to sleep about them and wake again in the darkness to cringe with the horror of it."

What was happening to the brave lads who had left farms, factories, and families to defend the Empire? Families with menfolk at the front silently whispered prayers. Few people yet questioned the righteousness of the cause, or suggested that their boys' bravery was anything less than heroic. "'Tommy' is majestic in his suffering," the *Toronto Daily News* proclaimed on its front page. The fortitude of the rank and file despite appalling conditions and losses awed reporters. "These, mark you, are earth's common men, the unnoticed men in the street," wrote the *Daily News* correspondent. "Where do they learn it?"

A wave of sympathy for Canadians who found themselves helpless cannon fodder began to build. Somehow, the untoward death of a thirty-four-year-old man on the streets of Toronto didn't seem quite so outrageous . . .

॥

Nevertheless, for the Masseys, Bert's untimely death was a dreadful blot on the family name. Even if Bert Massey did not live on Jarvis Street like his cousin Vincent, or enjoy the perks of wealth, his close relatives were determined to protect his name and reputation.

Two papers had already quoted Carrie Davies's assertion that her employer had "tried to ruin me." Had Bert Massey assaulted the girl while his wife was away? In theory, this was a shocking suggestion; in practice, within Bert's circle for as long as anyone could remember, girls at the bottom of the social ladder had often been regarded as "easy prey" by male employers. Bert wouldn't have been the first man in Toronto to embark on such a dalliance, which might be justified either by blaming the servant for the seduction, or by dismissing it as a "harmless flirtation." His friends probably spent more time discussing Bert's foolishness in getting caught or his bad luck in hiring the wrong maid. If they spent any time on Carrie's role, it would have been to speculate on how an eighteen-year-old girl had got her hands on Bert's pistol and knew how to fire it. What really alarmed them was the idea that a "harmless" backstairs seduction led to Bert's death. Moreover, it looked as though the girl had planned the death: this wasn't a crime committed in the heat of a struggle. But Bert's relatives didn't appreciate the salacious gossip that was starting to spread. The first step towards suppressing the story was burying the corpse. Step two was promoting the Massey version of the facts.

Rhoda Massey, newly widowed and facing an uncertain future, remained out of sight. She did not appear at any of the court hearings in the days to come, and she made no public statements. Most likely, she and her son remained in the guest room at 165 Admiral Road, rather than return to unhappy memories and the lack of domestic help at Walmer Road. Arthur Massey's two children, eighteen-year-old Arnold and eleven-year-old Dorothy, could keep their fourteen-year-old cousin company. Meanwhile, Arthur and his wife, Mary Ethel, were more than up to the task of promoting the Massey side of the story.

Arthur Massey was a more successful professional than his brother. Trained as a bookkeeper, with his friend Walter Chandler he had set up a hospital and physician supplies business called Chandler and Massey. It was a family affair: his sister Jennie was married to Walter Chandler's brother, and the two men had persuaded John Haydn Horsey—Arthur's stepfather, who now managed a Dominion Bank branch office—to be vice-president. Now forty, Bert's brother was the picture of bourgeois respectability (although he maintained his youthful taste for rather flashy bow ties.) When a reporter from the *Toronto Daily Star* appeared at his Admiral Road door before the funeral, Arthur spent several minutes with him on the doorstep.

Sporting a black armband, and speaking in a pained but stoic tone, Arthur explained, "We have only a feeling of sympathy for the unfortunate girl. We feel sure that the crime was committed in a fit of temporary insanity." He mentioned that there had been an episode the previous summer when Carrie had behaved strangely—"she was probably deranged." Perhaps, he suggested, she had worked herself into a frenzy because she had not heard from her young man in France. "There can certainly be no suspicions against Mr. Massey, and there is absolutely no truth in any report that credits him with any indiscretions."

A reporter from the *Toronto Daily News* was given the same spin. The paper featured it on its front page: "'Our family bears absolutely no resentment towards the girl, because we do not believe that she knew what she was doing,' said Mr. A.L. Massey today. 'It was very unfortunate for us that my brother should have been the victim. She might have shot anybody who happened to come along.'" The *Daily News* reported as fact that the doctors who had treated her the previous summer "will testify at the trial as to her mental state," adding, "The relatives express extreme indignation that any suggestion of indiscretion should be made against the murdered man."

In 1915, newspaper reporters automatically treated a man of Arthur's position with deference. With his firm Massey chin and air of authority, his "more in sorrow than in anger" tone struck the right note of patrician forbearance as he gently sketched a compelling picture of an unhappy, unstable, and not very bright girl. He made it clear that the Masseys were not looking for revenge. Protecting the family name took priority over punishing a simpleton.

However, Mary Ethel Massey did not share her husband's subtlety. After the family's return from Mount Pleasant Cemetery, Rhoda Massey had gone upstairs to rest when a reporter from the *Evening Telegram* rang the doorbell and asked to speak to the grieving widow. The reporter was an unprepossessing-looking character in a long black coat and with a battered bowler hat perched on the back of his head. Mary Ethel Massey, an impatient woman used to getting her way, knew that Rhoda would never speak to the press, so she led him into a room where they would be undisturbed. Undaunted by the reporter's scruffy appearance, or the pencil hovering over his notebook, she let rip.

"Motive? Why, there wasn't any motive. We are all perfectly satisfied that the girl was not mentally responsible when she shot Bert. I know that it has been hinted that Mr. Massey may have been indiscreet and acted improperly towards the girl, but the whole story is ridiculous. No person who knew Bert will believe that for a minute. He was not the kind of man to act that way."

The reporter must have realized that a snobbish *grande dame* in full flow would give him a great article—one that would grip and shock his paper's working-class readers, and that might play into the resentment of wealthy shirkers that was starting to bubble through Toronto. All he had to do was ensure that his shorthand was accurate and fast enough to stay abreast of Mrs. Massey's tirade, and then he could slot the interview almost verbatim into the *Telegram*'s columns. He carefully noted how Mrs. Massey always referred to the unfortunate Carrie as "the girl" and never by name, and kept returning to the rumours of an attempted seduction.

"We are satisfied, we are sure," continued Mary Ethel, "that Mr. Massey was innocent of wrongdoing, and that the girl had no cause to kill him. There was no motive, except that the girl was out of her head. Of that I am quite satisfied."

The reporter lifted his head from his pad to ask, "What leads you to believe that there was something wrong with her mentally?"

Mary Ethel settled back to give a long account of the incident from the previous summer to which her husband had referred. "Last summer Mr. and Mrs. C.A. Massey visited us at our summer home on the island. One night while we were over at the National Yacht Club this girl went out in the park with our maid. She suddenly became ill. She was carried from the park to our house, and when we returned from the club she was attempting to tear her hair and bite her fingers. It took six people to hold her." The notion that it took six people to hold a girl who could not have weighed more than fifty kilograms must have seemed a stretch to the reporter, but he didn't challenge Mrs. Massey. She continued her story, describing how the Masseys had summoned two doctors and a nurse, who suggested that Carrie had "suffered a spell."

After Monday night's shooting, Mary Ethel Massey explained, she and her husband had spoken to one of the doctors. "Since talking it over, we are convinced that another spell came on . . . The fact that she shot Mr. Massey on the steps seems to me to prove that she was not mentally responsible. If she had shot him in the house then her story might be substantiated . . . Mr. Massey was not a man who would bother about servant girls or attempt to act indiscreetly."

The reporter then revealed that he had already talked to someone else about the case—that he had, in fact, found out a lot more about Carrie Davies than any member of the Massey family had bothered to learn. Watching his interviewee carefully, he mentioned, "The girl told her sister that Mr. Massey once came into her room in quest of a buttonhook." (In the days before zip fasteners and Velcro, buttonhooks were used to fasten the rows of tiny buttons on women's boots.) Unblinking, Mary Ethel brushed aside the suggested impropriety. "Well, I was just going to explain that. Mrs. Massey was going away one time and she told Bert that she was taking her buttonhook. . . . While Mrs. Massey was away, Bert invited a number of married couples to the house for a party. We were invited but Mr. Massey had the grippe and we could not go. When the guests were ready to go one young woman had to put on her overshoes. Bert was asked for a buttonhook and he ran up into the maid's room and got the one she had. That is all there is to that story."

Had Mrs. Massey ever noticed anything wrong with the Davies girl?

"Well, to my knowledge her character was perfectly good. She was a straight little girl as far as I know. Once or twice I was struck by a peculiar look which she seemed to have but I put it down to her English ways and the fact that she had only been in the country two years. A seamstress who calls at my house to do work told my maid that she shouldn't go out with the girl as there seemed to be something wrong with her mentally."

The reporter noted down Mrs. Massey's dismissive comments. Mary Ethel Massey rose to signal that the interview was over. With the blind self-assurance of a woman who had never had anything to do with the press, she assumed that her story would have more credibility than anything a half-educated child said. She was confident that she had convinced this obsequious newspaperman that Bert Massey, and the Massey family, were blameless.

Mary Ethel could not have made a worse choice of reporter to whom to unburden herself. The newspaperman, whose name was Archie Fisher, was equally satisfied with the interview for very different reasons. His story about Mrs. Arthur Lyman Massey would appear in the *Evening Telegram* under the headline "Family of Dead Man Explain the Tragedy," alongside an article that gave a very different picture of a young Englishwoman with "a peculiar look."

CHAPTER 6

The White-Slave Trade

FRIDAY, FEBRUARY 12 TO SUNDAY, FEBRUARY 14

═══════

NEW WAR TAXES

ALL CLASSES HELP TO CARRY THE BURDEN

*Hon. W.T. White, Finance Minister, is being congratulated on all sides today
for his able budget speech . . . He needed money to carry on our share of the Empire's
struggle. He placed his taxes where wealth is accumulated, and as far as possible
placed the burden on the rich rather than the poor.*
—*Toronto Daily News,* Friday, February 12, 1915

GIRL HAD PERIODIC FITS OF DEPRESSION

CARRIE DAVIES IS STILL IN JAIL BUT IS FEELING BETTER

*. . . The rumors of indiscretions on the part of the murdered man prior to the
shooting are not credited by the majority of the police officials.*
—*Toronto Daily News,* Friday, February 12, 1915

In the Don Jail, Carrie Davies heard little about the war or anything else going on outside the prison's high walls. She remained confined to the hospital ward, under the medical supervision of jail physician T. Owen Parry. Dr. Parry was a no-nonsense, unsmiling man who rarely showed sympathy for his patients: one of his duties was to attend executions so he could sign the death certificate after the hangman had done his job. But he felt sorry for Carrie and allowed her to remain in the hospital ward, where better food was served. After a good night's sleep, on her third morning in jail she tucked into porridge, syrup, coffee, bread, and milk. For her first two days in prison she had sobbed uncontrollably and refused to be comforted, but now she was reported to be "more cheerful" and mingling with fellow prisoners. However, on Friday morning she fainted, and Dr. Parry was quickly summoned. Was this the mental instability that the Masseys had spoken of? A diagnosis of "epilepsy" had been bandied about—devastating if true, in an age when there was no treatment and the condition was often seen as a form of demonic possession. Dr. Parry batted off the suggestion. "She has shown no signs of epilepsy. We have been watching her very closely for this since she came to the jail . . . She has not had any fits, but has been weak and hysterical. There was a marked improvement in her condition today."

By now, Toronto's newspaper readers knew a little more about the young woman who shot Bert Massey, thanks to the indefatigable *Evening Telegram* reporter Archie Fisher. Three days after his first visit to the Fairchilds, on the night of the killing, Archie Fisher again made the long journey east to Morley Avenue for another chat with Carrie's sister Maud and brother-in-law Ed Fairchild. He was under instructions to milk the pathos of Carrie's life for all it was worth in a lengthy *Tely* feature.

In the fuggy warmth of the Fairchilds' parlour, Maud poured out her fears and her family history to the reporter. It was a story of a miserable working-class English family spiralling towards destitution—a story with no redeeming note of virtue rewarded or generosity extended. Maud and Carrie were among the nine children of a British army sergeant and his wife. Carrie was born in Woolwich, an army town on the Thames River, and spent her early childhood in Aldershot, a military town in southern England. Army pay was low, but the family had kept its head above water because Mrs. Davies had run a small store. Carrie, "just a cheerful, normal girl" according to her sister, had attended an army primary school. But life took a downturn when Sergeant Davies was severely injured in an accident while in charge of an army transport wagon during the South African War. Discharged from the army, he came limping home with no pension and no prospects. The Davies family moved to a grimy village called Sandy in Bedfordshire, on the main Great Northern Railway line, seventy-four kilometres north of London. They tried to make ends meet with what Archie Fisher called a "wayside inn," but it was a struggle—especially with the arrival of more babies.

The Davies's poverty was not unusual in the area, which until recently had been a largely agricultural district. Families at the bottom of Sandy's social scale (and there were only three thousand residents) relied on small holdings, where they grew their own vegetables and kept a few chickens and a pig. Children slept head to foot, several in one bed. No one could afford a doctor, so mothers relied on traditional remedies such as applying brown paper coated in goose grease to bronchial chests, or soaking toes swollen with chilblains in urine. A little girl like Carrie could earn extra pennies by collecting acorns for the pigs, picking mushrooms, blackberrying, and catching sparrows for sparrow pie. Mrs. Davies took in sewing, and probably participated in the local cottage industry of lacemaking.

But when Carrie reached her twelfth birthday, there was no money to keep her in school or feed her in the crowded Davies cottage. Moreover, the demands of sewing in an ill-lit cottage had ruined Mrs. Davies's eyes—"the doctor told her to leave off as she was going blind," Carrie would later explain. It was time for the thin, probably undernourished child to leave home: as Charles Dickens wrote, "the poor have no childhood; it must be bought and paid for." Carrie was sent to an aunt in London to learn the skills required for "service," as domestic work was known. As a domestic servant, Carrie might be able to put aside a little money to send home. And "service" was more respectable than the limited other options for young girls such as fieldwork, or (in the north) work in textile mills. Her aunt was apparently very strict: Maud Fairchild said Carrie "went out little, but always to Sunday school."

When she was a skinny thirteen-year-old, Carrie was eligible for her first job. Small for her age and easily intimidated, she bravely packed up her few possessions into a small trunk and set off for Aldershot, on the other side of London from her mother in Sandy, to work as a maid in the home of an army officer who had known her father. In his article, Archie Fisher didn't include details of Carrie's employment history before she left England three years later. Did she stay with the Aldershot family, or switch to another house? Was she treated well or badly? Was she ever allowed a night off, and could she afford the third-class rail ticket she would need to visit her mother? We don't know.

Servants are everywhere and nowhere in history. Carrie and women like her worked too hard to have any energy left for writing diaries or letters, and if any of them did manage to scribble down something, it has probably been lost. When a youngster like Carrie went into service, she walked into the shadows. The underclass of servants in middle- and upper-class homes was expected to be "seen and not heard," exhibiting deference and modesty. In *Mrs. Beeton's Book of Household Management*, published in 1861, the famous guru of Victorian domesticity wrote, "A servant is not to be seated, or wear a hat in the house, in his master's or mistress's presence; nor offer any opinion, unless asked for it; nor even to say 'goodnight' or 'good morning,' except in reply to that salutation." It was a hard, hard life. In novels set in city homes, writers of the period—from George Eliot to Virginia Woolf—rarely mentioned the women who kept their characters' gowns ironed, brass shined, and chamber pots emptied. The only exception to this rule is Charles Dickens—but too often, in novels like *The Pickwick Papers* or *David Copperfield*, the servants provide one-dimensional pathos or comic relief.

Yet at least until the Second World War, middle-class households throughout the British Empire ran on servants, and most women expected either to be servants or to keep them. Without electricity or many labour-saving devices, domestic labour was strenuous and time-consuming. And being "in service" differed dramatically from other forms of employment, because the live-in status of household staff required personal relationships with their employers. Today, if we try and imagine the lives of servants, we are most likely to think about armies of well-treated staff in an aristocratic establishment like TV's *Upstairs, Downstairs* or *Downton Abbey*, where the population below stairs is as comfortable and self-sustaining as the one upstairs. But most female servants were drudges—maids-of-all-work like Carrie, expected to work alone for sixteen-hour days, seven days a week, for paltry wages. Their

FLANDERS BATTLE GROWS VIOLENT--ADVANCES BY ALLIES NORTH AND EAST OF YPRES REPORTED

Enemy Using Fiery Projectiles Against Soissons---Germans Lost 15,000 Killed in Battle of Borjimow

BRITISH-BELGIAN FORCE REGAIN TWO TOWNS?
HEAVY FIGHTING IN THE FORESTS OF ARGONNE

ORPHAN MAID FACES CHARGE OF SHOOTING "BERT" MASSEY

Germans Send Troops from Rheims District to Reinforce Northern Line, Where They Are Meeting With Heavy Losses — Strategic Bridges North of Dixmude Wrecked by French Artillery

GIST OF THE WAR GRIST

WHAT GIRL TOLD HER SISTER

WALMER ROAD TRAGEDY AND SOME OF THOSE CONCERNED

The *Evening Telegram* was on top of the Massey murder case from the start.

The Masseys were one of Toronto's most prominent families: Bert Massey's grandfather lived in a magnificent mansion on Jarvis Street.

Hart Massey with his grandchildren Vincent (Chester's elder son) and Ruth (Walter's eldest daughter).

In June 1915, four months after Bert Massey's death, his cousin Vincent Massey married Alice Parkin in Kingston's St. George's Cathedral. None of Bert Massey's siblings were invited.

The Massey mausoleum in Mount Pleasant Cemetery.

Left: City Hall, completed in 1900, was a landmark building for Toronto.

Below: Yonge Street was lined with imposing multi-storey office buildings and festooned with telephone wires.

CTA FONDS 1244 ITEM 323G

City Hall's marble staircase and stained-glass window reflected Toronto's solid sense of self-worth.

CTA FONDS 1244 ITEM 1008

At the intersection of King Street and Yonge Street, a member of Toronto's police force struggled to keep up with Toronto's explosive growth in population and traffic.

The Denison dynasty in 1877: Colonel George Taylor Denison III (*seated at left*) was proud of the family's military traditions.

The National Club (*right*) was the scene of regular white-tie-and-tails dinners (*above*) for members such as Colonel Denison.

Hartley Dewart, QC (*above*), had his offices in the Home Life Building on the corner of Adelaide and Victoria Streets (*right*).

Florence Huestis, president of Toronto's Local Council of Women, lobbied for mothers' pensions, children's playgrounds, and votes for women.

Sir William Mulock, chief justice
of Ontario and the Grand Old
Man of Anglo-Canada.

All of Ontario's lawyers had to be admitted to the bar at Osgoode Hall.

skin glistened from steam and sweat, and their hands were raw and red from being dipped in cold water and dried on coarse aprons. If any man in the household deigned to notice the "slavey," as such domestics were known, and was tempted into careless sexual exploitation, it was the maid's job that was at risk, not the employer's reputation.

Nevertheless, even girls as young and naive as Carrie knew more about their employers' personal tastes and habits, marital relations, and family conflicts than anyone outside their homes. When there were only one or two servants, the lives of employers and employees were intertwined. As she scoured grease and hair from the bathtub, or laundered soiled underwear, or prepared meals, a servant in a middle-class home, however vulnerable, wielded a precarious power. But a girl like Carrie was unlikely to use it.

While Carrie learned in Aldershot how to scrub floors, dust pelmets, carry loaded trays, polish silver, starch linen, cook a decent leg of lamb, and lay fires, two older sisters had achieved what was still universally regarded as the most desirable destiny for a woman: marriage and children. With their husbands, they had also managed to flee Britain's class-ridden society. One sailed off to Australia, the other to Canada.

Arriving in Toronto in 1908, Carrie's sister Maud Fairchild had quickly found her feet. Her husband, Ed, had a skill much in demand in the rapidly growing city: he was a bricklayer. New stores and offices, working-class cottages and row houses, and whole neighbourhoods of solid-brick middle-class homes were springing up. Ed got a job in the thriving construction industry as a foreman with Jas. R. Wickett, Ltd., a building firm, and the Fairchilds rented a home in the working-class neighbourhood of Leslieville, at the very end of the Toronto Railway Company streetcar line, where there were several brick factories. Soon there were two more Fairchilds: first a son, Bobby, and then a little girl, Joyce. Maud stayed at home on Morley Avenue with the children, and on Sundays (Ed's only day off) the little family crossed Gerrard Street and attended St. Monica's Anglican Church.

As Toronto expanded, Maud could see that its emerging professional class was eager for the same creature comforts as its British counterpart. The papers were filled with articles about "the servant girl problem," as the chronic shortage of domestic servants was called. The Canadian government paid agents to recruit young women in the British Isles for domestic service on the other side of the Atlantic. An agent who brought a servant girl to Canada could earn more than $15 (around $1,400 in today's terms, given the rise in the value of wages since then): a $5 bonus from both the federal and the provincial governments, a $2 commission from Ottawa for finding her a job, and a finder's fee from the girl's employer. Youngsters who arrived by themselves, with no relatives or friends in the New World, often faced loneliness and exploitation. But Carrie would have a sister here. And Maud decided that Carrie, who was four years younger than her, could find a much better job in Canada than in England, where the supply of trained household servants outstripped demand. So Maud sent her younger sister $45 for her passage.

As soon as sixteen-year-old Carrie arrived in Ontario, she went to work for Mr. and Mrs. Charles Albert Massey on Walmer Road. The wide-eyed young immigrant, with her stick-thin limbs and hunched shoulders, was their only live-in servant, on call twenty-four hours a day, with Thursday and Sunday afternoons off to visit her sister. Carrie carried her suitcase up to the stuffy attic bedroom, where she found her new uniform laid out on the thin straw mattress—a black cotton ankle-length skirt, plain dark blouse with long sleeves and detachable white collar, white cotton apron, and white cap. Eaton's sold such self-effacing uniforms on the third floor of their Yonge Street store for about $2.50. Employers insisted on uniforms because they reflected their own genteel status. Moreover, it meant that their maids were not dressed in their mistresses' cast-offs, leading to the embarrassment of the employee being mistaken at the door for her employer. Carrie was paid $14 a month plus room and board for her first four months, $15 a month for the next four months, and $16 a month after that. But Mrs. Massey took the cost of Carrie's uniform out of her first few weeks' meagre wages, and when that was paid off, Carrie started to pay her sister back for her transatlantic ticket. Once that debt was settled, her thoughts turned to her widowed mother in England, and her needs.

"Only last week," Maud Fairchild told the *Evening Telegram*'s Archie Fisher, "she had $30 ready to send home." At Christmas for the past two years, Carrie had sent presents to each of the siblings who remained in Sandy with her mother, "down to little three-year-old Marjie, the youngest, of whom she was very fond."

⇜

Carrie Davies was one of thousands of young women drawn to Toronto to work "below stairs" for Toronto society. Canada's largest English-speaking city attracted youngsters with little schooling from farms and villages throughout Ontario and the Maritime provinces, as well as those like Carrie from England. New arrivals scanned the "Help Wanted, female" advertisements in the newspapers for cooks, kitchen maids, parlour maids, ladies' maids, and maids-of-all-work. According to the 1911 census, there were nearly twelve thousand women in domestic service in Toronto—about one-quarter of the total number of single "working girls" in the city. Their hours were unregulated and their wages pathetic.

At Walmer Road, Carrie was plunged into the demanding but inflexible routine followed in middle-class homes across Canada. Lily Reid, a young Ontario woman who went to work in a small-town rectory in 1912, would later recall the monotonous weekly schedule of "washing on Monday, ironing on Tuesday, Wednesday for baking and extras, Thursday for upstairs cleaning, Friday for downstairs, and Saturday to make all preparations for Sunday." With coal or wood fires as a main source of heating, soot and cinders coated furniture, floors, and drapes. Washing was done manually, wet clothes were dried on an outside line no matter how cold the weather, and women like Lily and Carrie ironed the garments with heavy steam irons on a kitchen table padded with blankets.

In addition, Carrie was expected to prepare the family meals, using ingredients with unfamiliar brand names (Five Roses Flour instead of Spillers, Redpath sugar instead of Tate and Lyle), strange new vegetables (corn, squash), and even confusing new names for products she had used in Aldershot (lard was called shortening in Canada; biscuits were cookies; scones were biscuits). On Thursday afternoons she might go to the local YWCA to meet her friend Mary Rooney. On Sunday afternoons she tried to reach the Fairchilds' house in time to attend the evening service at St. Monica's Anglican Church nearby. But it was always a scramble to get there on time: as the Masseys' only live-in servant, she had to prepare supper for the family before she hung up her apron for her afternoon "off."

However, by the time Carrie arrived in Toronto in 1913, the growing commercial and industrial metropolis was spawning a wider range of jobs for women. While middle- and upper-class women like Florence Huestis were joining clubs, committees, and associations and agitating for social change and the right to vote, working-class women were voting with their feet. They walked away from domestic service in favour of jobs as sales ladies, stenographers, waitresses, switchboard operators, and production-line workers. Toronto's new sweatshops in the garment district required dressmakers, sewing-machine operators, hat makers, knitting-machine operators, box makers. The workforces in commercial bakeries, paper-bag factories, and book binderies were overwhelmingly female. And these jobs offered both set hours (ten to twelve hours per weekday, plus a half day on Saturdays) and better wages than domestic service—up to $10 a week (the equivalent to an unskilled wage of $950 a week today). This was still just over half the average male wage in similar jobs, but it was far better than Carrie's $3 a week ($285 today) from the Masseys, even though office and factory workers had to cover the costs of room and board themselves.

Toronto authorities were profoundly unsettled by the speed with which unmarried women turned their backs on jobs as round-the-clock "slaveys" in dingy basements. These were the days of "Toronto the Good," where a Morality Department had been established within the police force in 1886. A man employed in a factory or sales job was regarded as a family's essential breadwinner and an indispensable cog in the wheels of industry. However, a woman employed outside a home was regarded as a potential moral problem. City fathers didn't like the idea that young single women working in offices and factories were no longer safely lodged in family homes where middle-class matrons would keep a close eye on how they spent their off-hours and whether they went to church.

The city fathers were howling in the wind, completely out of step with what young women wanted: freedom. The women themselves flocked to live in boarding houses or shared apartments and enjoy unsupervised fun. Photographs taken in pre-war Toronto show gangs of "good-time girls" cavorting in the waves on Scarboro Beach during the summer, while in winter they piled into sleighs in High Park (both these activities were forbidden by law on Sundays). Vaudeville houses, nickelodeons, and dance halls actively courted their custom. Their high spirits and easy ways challenged conventions.

Who wouldn't prefer the camaraderie and chatter of a garment factory, however cramped and noisy, to the grim loneliness of a damp basement? But the women who took jobs in factories, offices, and shops "lingered in the murky light of sexual suspicion," as historian Carolyn Strange has put it. In 1898, Toronto journalist C.S. Clark had published a book called *Of Toronto the Good*. A lurid look at the underside of the "Queen City," it was a deliciously shocking read. Clark painted a picture of rampant sin and corruption, and insisted (with little evidence to support his claim) that the city was "an immense house of ill-fame." He argued that most girls were lured into prostitution through moral weakness and cupidity, and described how a woman signalled her availability with "a flash from her eyes." If a woman exchanged glances with a man, she was obviously fair game. How was a decent man supposed to know the difference between flirting and soliciting?

Not all reformers shared Clark's assumption that working girls drifted voluntarily into prostitution through the casual bartering of sexuality. Toronto's Local Council of Women had a different, although equally prurient, fear: the so-called white-slave trade. One organization reported in 1912 that Canada was losing 1,500 girls per annum to the international traffic in girls for brothels, and that many of the girls disappeared into the dens of American red-light districts. Pamphlets inveighing against this sex trade whipped up a moral panic. The Reverend Dr. John Shearer, a Presbyterian watchdog, talked of respectable girls being lured across the border like "innocent lambs go[ing] blindly to slaughter." According to George J. Kneeland of New York's American Social Hygiene Association, an unnamed "king" of the slave trade controlled three hundred men who procured thousands of young women who had been drawn to the bright lights of the city. (Kneeland made the preposterous assertion that schoolteachers were particularly inclined to accept the "yoke of slavery" because they resented the restraints put upon them as public servants.)

White-slave trade propaganda was as full of fantasies as Clark's sensational claims about Toronto's sex-ridden streets. The salacious appeal of such scenarios had made encounters between working-class heroines and evil slave traders a staple of early silent films. The irony was that young women were often the main audience for such movies: if they could scrape together the ticket price, domestics like Carrie Davies and Mary Rooney spent their weekday afternoons off in movie houses, watching films like *Traffic in Souls,* thrilled by the flickering images of themselves transformed into vivacious and brave urban survivors. The popularity of these films with the so-called victims reinforced dark suspicions of working girls' moral laxity.

The truth was that it was neither liberation from Victorian roles nor organized gangs that propelled women into prostitution. It was poverty, and the complete absence of a social safety net. Women's wages were so low that they barely covered the cost of housing, food, and clothing. If a single woman lost her job, there was often nowhere to turn. Her downward fall could be rapid. If she "ruined" her reputation, she was transformed into a despised "fallen woman" rather than a pitiable figure more sinned against than sinning. A woman who bore a child out of wedlock, or wandered about the streets at night the worse for alcohol, was described in police or court records as "hardened" or vicious. Both contraception and abortion were against the law, so infanticide was a cruel but common occurrence, with as many as thirty dead infants a year turning up in the city's privies, rubbish heaps, and vacant lots.

Carrie had lined up alongside several "fallen women" when she appeared in the Women's Court, in front of Colonel Denison, the previous Tuesday. Her only shock would have been to find herself among them. Reports of women accused of infanticide, men acquitted of the rape of their servants, or girls lured into prostitution appeared regularly in Toronto's evening papers. While Carrie was in jail, the *Star* featured a photograph of Lena Nisnevitz, aged nineteen, who had committed suicide by drinking carbolic acid. No reason was given for her painful suicide—readers like Carrie could fill in the missing details for themselves.

For two years, Carrie had also seen evidence of urban poverty on her afternoons off, when she left Walmer Road to catch an eastbound street-car for a visit to Morley Avenue. With the rapid expansion of Toronto in the previous decade, and the arrival of thousands of immigrants, levels of destitution and street crime had shot up. Since the late nineteenth century, Toronto mayors had tried to control the public drunkenness, disorderly conduct, begging, and prostitution that characterized North American cities during these years. Carrie likely avoided the red-light district around Adelaide Street, but she couldn't avoid crossing Yonge Street, where men brawled, barefoot children begged, and girls her own age openly solicited.

The most notorious area in Toronto was the Ward, which British-born girls like Carrie rarely entered. This was a warren of lanes and streets bounded by Queen Street to the south, College Street to the north, University Avenue to the west, and Yonge Street to the east. From the 1890s onwards, this area had gradually been taken over by waves of Jews from Eastern Europe. Living side by side with them, but in smaller numbers, were groups of Chinese, Poles, Finns, Italians, Slavs, and West Indians. Over twelve thousand foreigners were cooped up in the Ward's mean streets in 1915. Unlike Montreal or New York, where poverty-stricken immigrants crowded vertically into multi-storey tenements, the Toronto immigrant quarter was a horizontal sprawl of roughly built single-storey homes that often housed several families. Window sashes sagged; roofs leaked; drinking water came from back-street wells; Jewish and Italian ragpickers blocked the laneways with their merchandise; filthy backyard outhouses stank. Grocery shops dis-played fly-ridden sides of beef, unfamiliar sweetmeats, and big dishes of melting fat in their windows. Rats scurried along the edges of build-ings and clods of horse dung fuelled smoky fires. In spring, when the snow melted, a vile slop of dog shit, sodden newsprint, and discarded bones filled the potholes and puddles.

Few residents of the Ward had the time or inclination to notice the wretched conditions and pungent smells. They were too busy scraping together the money to bring to Canada the relatives they had left facing poverty or pogroms in the Old Country. Yet the Ward was not a relentlessly dark place. Its unpaved streets were lively with entertainers, local preachers, and small stores selling fresh vegetables. Women wearing brightly coloured shawls over their heads haggled in unfamiliar languages over prices. Today, we would describe the neighbourhood as "exotic." But in the Toronto of 1915, it was "foreign." Eighty-five percent of the city's population still came from British backgrounds, and the terms "multiculturalism" or "melting pot" had yet to be introduced. The Ward, literally in the shadow of City Hall, was perceived as a both a physical and a moral scar on the city's landscape.

Four years earlier, Dr. Charles Hastings, the city's energetic medical health officer, published a report in which he described its overcrowding, unsanitary water closets, contaminated water, windowless rooms, filthy lanes and alleys, and cesspools rising up through the back lots. In one building, he had discovered seven men sleeping in a single room measuring seven feet by twelve, and in another house he found nineteen men crammed together in three equally small rooms. An insidious assumption underlay Dr. Hasting's report—an assumption that the Ward bred not only dirt and disease but also sin. "A child born and reared amid such surroundings has about the same chance of escaping a life of shame or crime as an un-vaccinated baby confined in a pest-house would have of escaping small-pox," he wrote. Moreover, the report suggested that it was the foreigners' fault that conditions were appalling: Dr. Hastings did not even consider the possibility that the fault might lie with landlords' refusal to upgrade their properties, or the city's failure to provide services. He urged the obliteration of the Ward for health reasons.

The gulf between old and new Torontonians was already wide, and Dr. Hastings' report widened it. A fearful, uneducated eighteen-year-old like Carrie might be defenceless and invisible, but on this divide, she was on the "right" side. Why? Because she was British. Nevertheless, she must have felt so vulnerable, and scared of ending up in some rat-infested hovel in the Ward. The appalling double standard of the day dictated that if she were branded as "ruined," it would be seen as her fault, not her employer's—even if he had forced himself on her. With her character besmirched and no reference letter from Mrs. Massey, she had little chance of finding another job. As a result of this Victorian hypocrisy, the prurient fantasies of filmmakers, journalists, and preachers were the stuff of nightmares for Carrie. She could be swept up by the white-slave trade. She could be forced to earn her living on the streets and find herself pregnant. Granted, Carrie Davies had a sister and brother-in-law to whom she might turn—but hadn't they encouraged her to return to Walmer Road despite her employer's fumbling attempts to kiss her? Maud Fairchild herself told Archie Fisher that Carrie "used to say she didn't want to be a burden on anyone." Carrie could see that the Fairchild household already had enough financial pressures without an extra mouth to feed. And her family back in England could not help: her mother counted on Carrie to send some of her earnings home.

Almost a century later, it is easy to brush away such fears. With women already shedding the cap-and-apron life of domestics and enjoying the regular wages and hours of office work, why didn't Carrie learn how to become a "hello girl" (as telephone operators were then known) or an assembly-line worker in a factory? When the boys marched off to war in 1914, employment opportunities for women expanded still further. Jobs previously restricted to men were now opened to women: new jobs in military uniform factories were available. Within a few months, the Munitions Department in Ottawa would announce that women would now be permitted to work in munitions factories, as long as they had a doctor's certificate attesting they could bear the burden. Four thousand women across Canada, 2,500 in Toronto alone, immediately signed up. With her customary self-assurance and commitment to progress, Florence Huestis, from the Local Council of Women, rallied opinion behind the campaign to get women to come forward and temporarily take over men's jobs, to allow the latter to fight for King and Empire. If Mrs. Huestis endorsed the cause, many felt that it must be the right thing to do. Women were elbowing their way into public life.

But not Carrie. She was not the kind of girl to grab the future in both hands; she was too timid, too conventional. Nevertheless, she had been swept up in the patriotic fervour that the war had sparked—recruitment drives, military parades, route marches through city streets, public drill sessions. The previous August, huge crowds had gathered in driving rain to see Toronto's soldiers off to war. Military bands had played martial music on August 20 at Cherry Street Station as the first contingent left; by the end of the month, over four thousand men had gone. In her brief off-duty hours, Carrie had even managed to acquire the anonymous male admirer—a young man about to depart to the battlefront. Perhaps he was a friend of her brother-in-law. Or perhaps she had met him the previous summer, when she had accompanied the Masseys to their "cottage" on Toronto Island. While wealthy cottagers took tea on the verandah of the Royal Canadian Yacht Club clubhouse, their servants could spend their off-duty hours at Dotty's Hippodrome, riding the switchback railway or taking a spin on the carousel. Or they could hang around the shooting gallery, hoping that one of the newest recruits to the Queen's Own Rifles or the 48th Highlanders might hit a bull's eye, win a kewpie doll or ice-cream cone, and look around for a pretty girl to give it to.

Carrie's anonymous beau in Europe may not have realized that there was a shy eighteen-year-old in Toronto treasuring the memory of a casual encounter the previous summer. There were many stolen kisses and impetuous promises in the summer of 1914, as young men, irresistibly macho in their new khaki uniforms, flirted with female admirers. Carrie always refused to disclose her boyfriend's name, suggesting perhaps she knew she exaggerated the romance. Maud Fairchild was aware of her little sister's soldier. But she was sure that Carrie was a good girl who would never do anything to bring shame to her family. As she sat in her kitchen in February 1915, with two small children clinging to her, she wondered what on earth her sister had been thinking. Archie Fisher exuded sympathy as Maud answered his questions and confided her fears to him. Carrie Davies's sister gave the reporter all the ammunition he needed for his tear-jerking article about the vulnerable youngster from an impoverished British family.

Close to the article headlined "Family of Dead Man Explain the Tragedy" in the *Evening Telegram* ran Archie Fisher's piece entitled "Mother Waits Carrie's Letter, Sister Will Miss Her Letters." It began with a poignant image. "In a hamlet in Bedfordshire, England—'Sandy Beds' the villagers call it—a widowed mother and five young children look every week for a letter from a missing daughter and sister—Carrie Davies, the eighteen-year-old girl held for the death of C.A. Massey." No matter that Sandy was never known as "Sandy Beds," or that it was and is a grubby railway town in Bedfordshire rather than a picturesque "hamlet," or that Carrie was charged with murder rather than passively "held for the death" of Bert Massey.

An equally poignant image ended Archie's account of his interview with Maud Fairchild: "The tears that had been kept back so bravely came in a bitter flood of weeping—weeping that was not for herself."

What a contrast with hoity-toity Mary Ethel Massey.

{CHAPTER 7}

Newspaper Wars

SATURDAY, FEBRUARY 13 TO SUNDAY, FEBRUARY 14

There was quite a stir at the [Halifax] steamship terminals today when the C.P.R. liner Missanabie docked from Liverpool, and fourteen "alien suspects" from the first Canadian contingent at Salisbury Plain disembarked under a strong guard, with each man handcuffed to a guard, and taken to Citadel.
—Globe, Monday, February 15, 1915

Mrs. C.A. Massey is bearing up bravely under the sudden blow. She was well enough to go out for a while today . . . The family still express the belief that the unfortunate girl will be adjudged insane.
—Toronto Daily Star, Saturday, February 13, 1915

The enforced passivity of the women's hospital ward felt strange to Carrie Davies, whose days in service began before 6 a.m. with fire-laying and breakfast preparations. A handful of visitors relieved the prison tedium. News of Carrie's whereabouts spread rapidly within the Fairchilds' East Toronto neighbourhood, which led to a prison visit from the Reverend Robert Gay, minister at St. Monica's Church. Next, Mr. Maw appeared; he introduced himself as her lawyer and explained the legal process she faced. He told her that both the initial hearing in the Women's Court and the coroner's inquest had been held over until she was in a fit state to attend and the police court magistrate and the chief coroner had established the facts of the case. She was a lucky young woman, he informed her. His partner Hartley Dewart had agreed to represent her in court. Dewart was one of Toronto's most eminent courtroom lawyers—a King's Counsel, an honorary title that denoted seniority and merit (and, frequently, good political connections) within the legal profession.

Lawyers and KCs, as King's Counsels were known, had almost certainly never intruded on Carrie's narrow little world up to now. The circles in which Bert Massey moved included more salesmen than solicitors. If she had ever opened the door of 169 Walmer Road to a lawyer, he would likely have handed her his hat and coat without even glancing at her. Carrie knew nothing about the difference between a suit-and-tie lawyer like Mr. Maw, who handled civil issues like marital, property, and commercial law, and a courtroom specialist like Mr. Dewart, who wore a silk-lapelled gown when he defended clients in court on criminal charges. But Carrie had been catapulted into an alien world, filled with expensive professionals, Latin phrases, and impenetrable legal process. She was the centre of the action, but she must have been totally bewildered.

The visitors whom Carrie most longed to see, Maud and Ed Fairchild, appeared in the jail's cold, dank visitors' room the day after Mr. Maw. When Carrie, clad in a regulation grey wool gown, was brought in by Mrs. Sinclair, the women's superintendent, the sisters stared at each other, white-faced and mute with helplessness. Ed Fairchild reassured Carrie that he was doing everything he could. But it was a terrible time for the three working-class British immigrants. Even ignorant young Carrie recognized that she was in a predicament, facing the most serious charge in the Criminal Code. How could the trio possibly find the funds to pay Mr. Maw's fees, let alone those of the famous Hartley Dewart, KC?

As it turned out, Carrie needn't have worried. A wave of populist sympathy was about to wash over the eighteen-year-old, for reasons that had little to do with her. Toronto was in the middle of a brutal newspaper war. Newspaper wars always involve not only a battle for subscribers and advertisers, but also competing editorial visions for the society they serve. In the pre-television, pre-Internet era of the early 1900s, the stakes were much higher than today because newspapers were the *only* public sources of news. As British ties loosened and an autonomous Canada began to emerge, newspaper proprietors and editors were as important as politicians in shaping the national self-image.

The two newspapers involved in the battle for eyeballs in 1915 were the *Evening Telegram* and the *Toronto Daily Star*. Carrie's case furnished each side with ammunition to attract readers and to promote their proprietors' views of where the Dominion's loyalties should lie. The editors of each paper already differed on a crucial issue in the Walmer Road shooting: Who was the real victim?

❧

In 1915, at major downtown intersections in Toronto, the shrill shouts of newsboys (some as young as nine years old) rose above the din of automobile engines and horses' hooves throughout the day. Toronto boasted no fewer than six daily newspapers, and "special editions" and "extras" kept the newsboys' lungs busy, filling any empty hours between regular print runs.

There were three morning papers, each costing two or three cents an issue, that were filled with lengthy political articles tailored to the interests of the professional classes who read them over leisurely breakfasts. The oldest, most serious, and self-important of these papers was the *Globe*, founded by George Brown in 1844 to promote his Reform politics, which now generally (but not always) leaned towards the Liberal Party. Its two morning rivals were the *Mail and Empire* and the *World*. In the evening, three one-cent papers hit the streets, with short, punchy articles designed to be read by blue-collar workers at the kitchen table after a day of manual labour. The three evening "rags" were the *Toronto Daily News*, the *Toronto Daily Star*, and the *Evening Telegram*.

Toronto could not yet claim to have Canada's most important paper. That distinction belonged to Montreal, the largest city in the Dominion. The *Montreal Star* had the biggest circulation and the closest relationship to the Conservative government in Ottawa of any newspaper. But the Toronto newspaper market was booming alongside the city: most households took two papers a day. And one particular Toronto paper, the *Evening Telegram* (established in 1876 and usually known as the *Tely*), had already transformed both the city's administration and Canadian journalism with its innovative and brash approach to the news.

The 1915 newspaper war was nothing new in Canada. Throughout the nineteenth century, newspapers had proliferated as fast and frequently as the small towns they served. If a man (and it was always a man) wanted to broadcast his views in his community, all he needed was a few dollars to invest in a hand press, some boxes of movable type, and a nimble-fingered typesetter. The next day, the local *Examiner, Expositor,* or *Intelligencer* would be on sale, its smudgy columns filled with advertisements for local stores, verbatim reports of political debates, news items copied from larger papers elsewhere, and (the backbone of the paper) inflammatory editorials. One of the noisiest newspapermen in Canadian history was the politician William Lyon Mackenzie, the fiery leader of the 1837 rebellion who founded the *Colonial Advocate* as a vehicle for his outrage at the way Upper Canada was governed. But even the great polemicist himself was shocked by the invective in rival publications. He complained that the hundreds of newspapers circulating in Upper Canada had become "the denier resort of the venal, the profligate and the unprincipled in society."

Local papers thrived, pulling isolated market towns and scattered farm families together into communities with their own heroes, habits, opinions, and rituals. By the 1880s, for example, the town of Port Hope, on the shore of Lake Ontario, had a population of about six thousand and no fewer than three papers, each a mouthpiece for its proprietor's political views. These community papers were regularly put out of business by deaths, debts, or libel suits. But new ones always sprang up in their place, with owners eager to air their views.

As the twentieth century approached, and the Toronto newspaper market expanded, new technology changed the look and the economics of newspapers. They could now feature photos, thanks to photogravure. Keyboard-operated Rogers Typograph machines allowed one man to work as fast as three manual typesetters. The enormous, clanking new presses churned out papers for mass circulation, but they required proprietors with deep pockets. So big-city papers like the *Globe* or the *Tely* had wealthier owners, as well as more pages and readers, than the scruffy small-town rags. Yet they were equally partisan, with editorial pages skewed to Conservative or Liberal opinion.

The *Tely*'s success was due to the knuckle-dusting commitment of its founder, John Ross Robertson, to produce a Conservative newspaper that appealed to "the masses not the classes." He regarded "quality" papers like the *Globe* and the *Mail and Empire* as hopelessly stuffy, feeding their readers lengthy reports of parliamentary debates and indigestible, partisan editorials on national politics. The *Tely* was enthralling: it gave its readers punchy stories from city council, police courts, sports events, hospitals, high-life soirees, and low-life streets. Reporters combed downtown hotel registers for scandals; drunks hauled up before Colonel Denison's court were named in the *Tely*'s columns. And the paper shone a light on municipal corruption by printing details of city contracts, so readers could decide whether their local taxes were being wasted. The paper's appeal went far beyond Toronto's rapidly expanding working class: it was soon the second paper in professional households. In the words of a contemporary writer, the paper was an "institution . . . read by every one from the fashionable belle in her boudoir to Biddy in the basement!"

The size of the *Evening Telegram*'s circulation attracted the most classified ads of any paper, and these money-spinners occupied the front pages of the paper, spilling into a further two pages in a sixteen-page issue, and a whopping five or six pages in the fat, twenty-eight-page Saturday *Tely*. "Business and Residential Properties" (for sale or rent) were plastered over the eight columns of page one, followed by columns of "Properties Wanted," "Lost Items," "Found Items," "Unfurnished Rooms," "Furnished Rooms," "Business Chances,"

"Wanted—Male Help," "Wanted—Female Help," "Domestic Help," "Employment Wanted," "Situations Wanted, " "Articles for Sale," "For Sale or Exchange," "Motor Cars," "Articles Wanted," and "Personals." The front page often included an eye-catching display advertisement for a fashionable new product like Shredded Wheat ("A Canadian Food for Canadians") or Royal Vinolia Vanishing Cream ("for those who dislike the sticky, grimy feeling of the usual cream.") Above the fold on the right-hand side of the page there was a cartoon, featuring Colonel Denison, Prime Minister Borden, John Bull, or some other instantly recognizable target of satire. The paper also grabbed the lion's share of splashy display ads from the new department stores of Timothy Eaton and Robert Simpson. The *Montreal Standard* reported that when Robertson's five o'clock edition of the *Tely* appeared, it was "One of the sights of Toronto . . . literally hundreds of men on the streets seizing copies as they came out to read the Want Ads." The paper made its proprietor money—a lot of it— almost from the first day.

The *Telegram* promulgated views that were bigoted even by the standards of the time. Like Colonel Denison, John Ross Robertson was convinced that Canada's role within the British Empire was the Dominion's most important feature, and the only defence against annexation by Uncle Sam. A stocky man with a goatee beard who was perpetually in a hurry, Robertson had been born in 1841 in a Toronto that was an unpretentious town of brick rowhouses, where the cobbled streets rang with English, Scottish, or Irish accents. The Robertsons themselves claimed impeccable Scottish heritage—direct descent from Duncan, born in 1347, chief (according to John Ross Robertson) of the Struan Robertson clan. Now Robertson found himself in a thrusting metropolis of company headquarters housed in steel-framed and marble-pillared skyscrapers, where you could hear Polish, Yiddish, and Italian alongside English on the paved roads around City Hall. Like

Colonel Denison, Robertson didn't hide his antipathy to people from backgrounds different from his own, and he directed particular venom towards French Canadians and Roman Catholics. In September 1885, when Quebecers rioted in Montreal at the prospect of Louis Riel being hanged for leading the Northwest Rebellion, the *Telegram*'s proprietor had editorialized that Prime Minister Sir John A. Macdonald should "throw the French overboard." A ferociously proud member of both the Orange Order (the fraternal Protestant organization) and the Masons, Robertson announced that it was time French Canadians understood that Canada was "a British colony, and that British laws, British customs and British language must prevail."

For over thirty years, Robertson's verbal fusillades appeared in the columns of the paper he owned. He had also spent some years as a member of Parliament in Ottawa: ornery as ever, he had run as Independent Conservative. By 1915, he was a seventy-four-year-old millionaire press baron in a three-piece suit, watch chain, and spats who didn't hesitate to express fervent affection for the British monarchy and implacable hostility towards women's suffrage.

These days, his devotion to the Masonic Order, patronage of Toronto's Hospital for Sick Children, and collections of historical memorabilia took most of his time, and others wrote his editorials. But he continued to keep tight control over the *Evening Telegram*, although his alter ego, editor Jack Robinson, ran the paper day to day. Robinson didn't share his boss's dapper style and was never part of Toronto's privileged elite: he was a large, ungainly man, and his rumpled suits, quipped an associate, looked as though they were made in a tent factory. But "Black Jack," as he was known on account of his thick thatch of dark hair, was as noisy and forceful as the boss he had served for twenty-seven years, and equally committed to temperance, the Orange Order, and the *Tely*. One of his *Tely* reporters described Black Jack as "A splendid bigot. And he believed in being a bigot."

The newspaper locked in competition with the *Tely* for readers among the new British blue-collar immigrants was the *Toronto Daily Star*. This younger publication had a very different history. Originally established in 1892 by a group of printers who had been locked out in a labour dispute at another paper, the *Star*'s early years had been rocky. In 1899, it was bought by a group of influential Toronto businessmen who had decided that the city needed a staunchly Liberal evening newspaper to counter the influence of Robertson's Tory *Tely*. The group included some of Toronto's commercial heavy hitters: department store owner Timothy Eaton, Peter Larkin (founder of the Salada Tea Company), William Christie (head of the Christie, Brown biscuit company), George Cox (former president of Canada's biggest bank, the Bank of Commerce, and now a Liberal senator). There were three more members of this elite little band of financiers whose influence would reverberate, explicitly or implicitly, through the Carrie Davies case sixteen years later. One was William Mulock, at the time a Liberal cabinet minister. The other two were the most important men in the Massey-Harris farm implement company: managing director Lyman Melvin-Jones and company president Walter E.H. Massey, Hart Massey's son—and Bert Massey's uncle.

This small, wealthy (and largely Methodist) clique of Liberals offered the job of editor and manager to an ambitious young newspaperman called Joseph Atkinson. Like Walter Massey, Atkinson was a Methodist who had started life in the little lakeside town of Newcastle. The similarities ended there: unlike the Masseys, the Atkinson family lived hand to mouth, and Joe's widowed mother had run a boarding house for workers in Massey's iron foundry.

A keen-eyed, clean-shaven thirty-four-year-old with a penchant for checkered suits, Joe Atkinson insisted that he should have total editorial freedom. At first, Senator Cox and Minister William Mulock were apoplectic at the idea: why would any smart politician invest in a news outlet over which they had no control? But their fellow investors, and Prime Minister Sir Wilfrid Laurier himself, persuaded the two men to accept Atkinson's terms since they were all confident that their new employee's loyalties lay firmly with the Liberal Party. Despite the paper's big-business ownership, Joe Atkinson fought off political interference and insisted that the *Toronto Daily Star* was, as he repeatedly said, the champion of the "little people." The co-owner who backed Atkinson through thick and thin, with both financial and moral support, was Walter Massey. "I know the other shareholders haven't much interest in the paper any more," he told his editor soon after Atkinson was appointed. "But you and I will see it through its troubles."

Over at the *Tely,* John Ross Robertson regarded with skepticism Atkinson's much-vaunted "editorial independence." The *Star*'s slogan was "A Newspaper Not an Organ," but Robertson told everybody in earshot that it should read "An Organ Not a Newspaper" because, he said, it was just a mouthpiece for plutocratic owners like the Masseys.

The only thing the two papers had in common was their determination to recruit working-class readers. Otherwise, they were poles apart. The *Tely* stuck to classified ads at the front of the paper: the *Star* followed modern practice and put news on page one. While John Ross Robertson's *Telegram* took swipes at rail barons and the provincial government, Joe Atkinson's *Star* portrayed the world as a place of progress, where business was enlightened, workers had rights, and government worked in everybody's interests. While the *Tely* continued its anti-Laurier, anti-American, pro-Empire campaigns, the *Star* endorsed Laurier's Liberal platform, which included free trade with the United States, Canadian nationalism, an aggressive immigration policy (limited, however, to Europeans), and support for labour unions. The *Star* did not share the *Tely*'s casual anti-Semitism: in 1906, the *Star* noted that in the past five years Jewish newsboys had almost totally displaced boys of British origin. "They are a better class and easier to handle than newsboys used to be. They are also more trustworthy . . . The street sales of *The Star* fall off 1,500 to 2,000 on Jewish holidays." By contrast, the *Tely* would no more have praised Jewish work habits than it would have recommended Irish home rule or endorsed the campaign to give women the vote.

From 1899 onwards, the battle lines were drawn. The *Tely* spoke with the voice of Old Canadians and for Crown, Union Jack, and British immigration. The *Star* did not question the pervasive pride of Empire, but it added to the mix a note of vigorous Canadian nationalism: its reporters rode on immigrant trains to the west and ate with railway construction crews in their camps. The clash of visions resonated far beyond Toronto's King Street, where both papers were printed. In 1909, when Britain requested support from Canada for the expansion of the British navy, the *Telegram* led the chorus of approval for granting the request while the *Star* backed the Laurier government's proposal to build a Canadian navy. For the next half century, as Canada struggled to define itself as a nation, there would be skirmishes between Conservative loyalty to British traditions and Liberal support for a more inclusive, autonomous country. The two Toronto newspapers embodied this tension.

The most dramatic clashes usually erupted over Toronto issues. The *Star* championed the widening of Yonge Street; the *Tely* opposed it. The *Star* lobbied the city to acquire the frontage on Lake Ontario; the *Tely* accused its rival of representing the business interests that would benefit. In 1909, the *Star* led the campaign to have Toronto's water supply chlorinated and filtered. The *Telegram* refused to join the crusade until typhoid fever spread the following year. Behind the rhetoric, both the *Telegram* and the *Star* spoke for powerful capitalist interests. They would take opposite sides, for instance, in 1910, when two different consortia vied for control of Toronto's streetcar and street-lighting systems. It was no coincidence that, in each case, the newspapers' proprietors were personal friends with the men who ran the consortia.

❧

The early years of rivalry between the *Star* and the *Tely* were amicable: John Ross Robertson regarded Atkinson and the upstart paper with benign amusement. The proprietor of the *Tely* was a generation older than the editor of the *Star,* and although he still considered himself an outsider in Toronto social circles, he belonged to clubs to which this self-educated son of a small-town miller would never be admitted. Besides, the *Star*'s circulation in 1900 was less than 7,000, compared to the *Telegram*'s 25,144. When Robertson met Atkinson on King Street, he would ask, "Well, Joe, is it paying yet?" When the *Star*'s editor replied, "No, it is not," the old man would guffaw and tell Atkinson to give up the struggle and join the staff of a paper with a real readership.

But one day, Atkinson answered, "Yes, it paid last month." In 1906, the *Star*'s circulation topped 37,000 copies a day, overtaking the *Telegram*'s, and John Ross Robertson and Black Jack Robinson were no longer laughing. Only the *Globe,* with a circulation of 50,000, outsold the *Star* within the city. By 1913, the *Star* had the city's largest readership, and Joe Atkinson, who had been steadily buying up the stock owned by the original investors, was the controlling shareholder. Walter Massey had sold his stock to Atkinson several years earlier, cementing the editor's independence.

In the next few years, the papers indulged in a price war as competition for readers and advertisers grew vicious. Toronto's paper wars followed the pattern established in New York, where Joseph Pulitzer's *World* and William Randolph Hearst's *Journal* went flat out to steal readers from each other with screaming headlines, breathless stories, gaudy comic strips, the latest fiction, sports news, and women's pages. Joe Atkinson was particularly good at dreaming up schemes that encouraged *Star* readers to enjoy a sense of shared goals. In 1906, the paper founded its Santa Claus Fund (still a feature today), with the goal of ensuring that no child under thirteen was overlooked at Christmas. In 1912, during another typhoid outbreak, the *Star* sponsored a "Swat the Fly" contest in an attempt to reduce the spread of disease from garbage to food. A girl called Beatrice Webb collected the prize after killing 543,360 flies.

In this fevered battle to entertain, the Carrie Davies case was irresistible to penny-press editors looking for sensational headlines. Stories of assaults on young women always increased circulation, and how many Toronto citizens could walk past a newsboy who yelled, "Massey Murder"? Only a decade earlier, Montreal newspapers had made such a meal of the murder of a young girl that one publisher remarked that the papers "were hardly fit to be picked up with a pair of tongs." No Toronto newspaper would ignore Carrie's case, but the *Evening Telegram* and the *Toronto Daily Star* were the papers that devoted the most column inches to the murder of a Massey by his maid.

At the *Telegram*, John Ross Robertson and Black Jack knew that Bert Massey's death put their main rival in an uncomfortable situation—a dilemma that revealed the social and class divisions within the Anglo-Canadian population of Toronto. Even though Walter Massey no longer held shares in the *Star*, the paper owed its success in part to Massey money, and Joe Atkinson must have felt some vestigial loyalty. Could Atkinson walk away from the corpse on the sidewalk, even if the slick car salesman Bert Massey had little appeal to a working-class readership?

Black Jack Robinson had no time for the *Star*'s editor: he called Atkinson "Whispering Joe" because he considered him so devious. The *Tely* could use the Carrie Davies case to paint the *Star* as a Massey mouthpiece. Meanwhile, the *Tely* could pursue a much more enticing storyline: the predicament of a helpless young English woman who had been assaulted by a member of one of Toronto's leading families. Even though there was no doubt Carrie had fired the gun, or that Bert Massey had met a brutal and untimely death, Robertson and his editor decided the *Telegram* would go to bat for the shooter. Helpless little Carrie Davies, the soldier's daughter from the Motherland, would be treated as a working-class heroine. The *Tely*'s printing presses, housed in a massive four-storey building with plate-glass windows at the corner of King and Bay Streets, would clank into action on her behalf.

One of the *Tely* editor's first steps had been to put Archibald McIntosh Fisher, one of his sharpest and most persistent reporters, on Carrie's case. With black eyes flickering under dark brows and a cigarette hanging from his lip, Archie was known in the *Tely* newsroom as "The Crow," because of his hooked nose and the long black overcoat he wore winter and summer. Archie was extremely good at ferreting out information (as he had proved by finding the Fairchilds the night of the shooting), then returning to the *Tely*'s offices and whispering it into Black Jack's ear. Once on a story, he kept it moving faster than any other reporter in the city. The interview with Mary Ethel Massey, in which she came across as snobbish and sly, was a triumph of Archie's style.

Next, Robertson and Robinson watched how the rest of the Toronto press was handling the Walmer Road shooting. After a week, the upmarket morning papers had decided that a crime committed by an underage servant girl was not a major event. War news took up all the front pages.

The *Globe* even had a major scoop on Monday, February 15: "Several aeroplanes make a raid into the dominion of Canada," read its big, black headline. "Entire City of Ottawa in Darkness, Fearing Bomb-droppers." The story reflected the xenophobic paranoia that was building in the Dominion. Although many Canadians of non-British origin had volunteered to fight for the Empire, they were branded as "alien suspects" and sent home from the Salisbury training camp. Hundreds of German and Austro-Hungarian Canadians were now being rounded up and marched into internment camps. Canadians were also growing nervous of the eight million Germans who had settled in the U.S. and were said to sympathize with the Kaiser. In January, the British consul in Los Angeles had warned that German sympathizers were planning attacks on Port Arthur, Fort William, and Winnipeg. Then, the British consul general in New York claimed that German Americans in Chicago and Buffalo were preparing cross-border offensives. Vivid imaginations fed wild rumours, and Prime Minister Borden was so unsettled that he requested a report on the invasion stories from the Canadian police commissioner.

On that mild Monday morning, Toronto's paper boys discovered that the prospect of explosives raining down on the federal capital was almost as good for business as "Massey Murder!" The *Globe* article described "light balls" flying from the sky, the "unmistakable sounds" of a whirring motor over Brockville, and the distant outlines of at least three airplanes. Torontonians snapped up the story. Unfortunately, a couple of days later the paper had to explain that it had all been a false alarm, generated by toy balloons released by some rowdy young men in Gananoque. But the sense of panic lingered, along with anxiety that a distant threat had now become an imminent and real danger. The illuminations on Parliament's Victoria Tower remained switched off.

The three evening papers, on the other hand, dogged the Davies story. The *Toronto Daily News* was a Conservative newspaper with a declining circulation. Its newsroom was too small to dedicate a reporter to the story, so it uncritically repeated statements from the police and the Masseys. Five days after Bert Massey's death, a front-page item in the *News* announced, "The rumours of indiscretions on the part of the murdered man prior to the shooting are not credited by the majority of police officials." A "senior detective" (who had undoubtedly been treated graciously by Mary Ethel Massey) told the paper that Carrie had severe fits "every month" and that the shooting was the result of "the girl's state of mind."

The *Tely*'s publisher and editor paid closer attention to the *Toronto Daily Star*, which, as they had anticipated, showed more sympathy for the murdered Massey than for the woman who had held the gun. The *Star* had betrayed its bias from the start, when it described the eighteen-year-old in her first court appearance as resembling "the Slavic type more than the English" and suggested that her mouth showed a "capacity for resentment." Two days later, the *Star* reporter who had watched the funeral cortege leave Admiral Road noted, "Many beautiful floral tributes testified to the popularity and esteem in which the late Mr. Massey was held by a host of friends and acquaintances." The paper reported at length what Arthur Massey, Bert Massey's brother, had said before the funeral. Carrie's hysteria "on the Island when it took five men to pursue her, statements that she is alleged to have made to other domestics that are said to have been wild and irrational, and the apparent lack of motive for the shooting would all go to show that her condition was weak mentally." As far as the *Star* was concerned, the insanity defence made perfect sense: a reporter collared Mr. Maw to ask bluntly, "Will there be any suggestion that the girl is unsound?"

This was all very satisfactory for the *Evening Telegram*. The way was clear for Robertson to take a leaf out of his rival's book and launch a feel-good fundraising campaign. The beneficiary of this fund would be the penniless Carrie. The opening salvo came on Saturday, February 13. The *Tely* published a letter that, claimed the paper, came from "a lady living on Waverley Road," a residential street in the Beach, not far from the Fairchilds' home:

Dear Editor. I think that your sympathies must be with those of most people in Toronto with that poor child Carrie Davies, who is accused of murdering her employer. Don't you think it would be doing a charitable act to start a subscription to pay for her lawyer, and give her every help possible. I have heard so many people suggest ways of helping, but that seems the most practicable. Hoping you will interest yourself and others through the columns of your valuable paper on her behalf.

I am yours, FAIR PLAY.

{PART TWO}

The Law

CHAPTER 8

"With Malice Aforethought . . ."

MONDAY, FEBRUARY 15

Copenhagen: A large shipment of copper packed in casks which were labeled "sugar" and put aboard the steamship Carmen was seized here today. The copper was consigned to a German firm. The shipper and the captain of the vessel were arrested.
—*Evening Telegram*, Monday, February 15, 1915

Under the auspices of the Franco-British Aid Society, Professor Keys will give an illustrated lecture entitled "German Kultur and English Civilization" at Victoria College, Queen's Park, at 8.15 p.m. Prof. Keys, who has spent some time in Germany, is well-qualified to speak on his subject, and his point of view will be most interesting in the present crisis . . . The proceeds of these lectures are devoted to Belgian relief work.
—*Saturday Night*, February 13, 1915

Act II of the Massey murder drama began at 8 p.m. on Monday, February 15, when the coroner's inquest resumed in the dingy Lombard Street morgue and the same twelve men, led by foreman James Burford, filed in. It was exactly a week since Carrie had fired the revolver at her boss. This time, there was no body on a nearby mortuary slab, but the crowd of lawyers, witnesses, spectators, and reporters milling about the dimly lit courtroom was much bigger than the previous Tuesday's opening session. The lingering stench of death and disinfectant horrified those who had never been to the Lombard Street building before. A couple of women kept smelling salts close to their noses; other spectators gagged into handkerchiefs.

Carrie Davies sat quietly next to the jail matron at the back of the court, attracting stares and whispers. Newspaper reports of her behaviour continued to diverge. According to the *Toronto Daily News*, Carrie radiated a chilling indifference: "Her cheeks were fresh and her eyes showed no signs of weeping or distress, while her expression was one of slightly stolid unconcern." Elsewhere, however, reporters noticed the eighteen-year-old's habit of constantly wringing her hands and looking helplessly at Miss Carmichael, the sympathetic Scottish matron from Don Jail's hospital wing.

At the front of the room, next to Mr. Maw, sat Hartley Dewart, KC. This was the first time that lawyer and client had been in the same room:

all Dewart knew about the case came from what he had read in the newspapers and what Mr. Maw had been able to elicit in his chat with Carrie in the Don Jail. Dewart turned round and directed a reassuring smile at the silent Carrie—then noted with some surprise two figures sitting at the back of the room. The first was Mary Ethel Massey, in all her rustling finery. The second was a dark-coated figure who had slipped inconspicuously into the courtroom. This was Dr. Beemer, superintendent of the Hospital for the Insane at Mimico, a lakeshore town a few kilometres west of Toronto. Some of the reporters who recognized him wondered what he was doing here: Dr. Beemer did not usually attend coroners' inquests. Dewart could make a pretty good guess whose interests Dr. Beemer was representing. Dr. Beemer belonged to a new breed of physicians who specialized in mental disorders and were often known as "alienists." These early psychiatrists were starting to claim the ability to detect symptoms of madness that might underpin an insanity defence. His presence implied that the Masseys were still hoping to have Carrie judged insane, in the hope that the charge would be dropped and the scandal smothered.

The Dewart–Maw partnership was leaning in another direction. So far, despite pestering from reporters, Henry Maw had not divulged the defence strategy. But Saturday's *Star* had quoted Maw as saying he had visited Carrie in the Don and found her "a bright and good girl . . . I am not an alienist but she appears to be quite rational. I will see that the living are not injured for the sake of the dead."

⁕

The first witness to be sworn in was Joseph Pearson, a young man who had been reading on the third floor of his grandmother's house opposite the Masseys' on the night Bert Massey died. He dismissed the sound of the first shot as an automobile tire exploding; the noise of the second shot sent him to the window to see what was happening. When he saw a man fall to the ground on the sidewalk outside 169 Walmer Road, he ran down two flights of stairs and into the street.

Mr. Pearson introduced a new figure into the drama he had witnessed: "a foreigner," who was bending over Bert Massey's prone figure and who told Pearson that Massey had fainted. Dr. Arthur Jukes Johnson, the chief coroner, was surprised to hear about this man, who had not been mentioned in the police report. He asked Pearson whether he meant that the man was "not an English-speaking person," then enquired whether he had a beard, or a moustache, or was smooth-shaven. Pearson's reply reflected the deep-seated suspicion of strangers that prevailed among middle-class Torontonians. "He looked strange," he told the coroner. "He talked with a funny accent . . . He didn't seem to talk right . . . He disappeared." Perhaps such a man existed, and, fearing how the police might treat him, faded into the dusk as quickly as he could. He was never mentioned again. Pearson described how he had helped to carry Massey into a neighbour's house.

Most of Pearson's account (except the presence of the "foreigner") was confirmed by Ernest Pelletier, the newsboy who had come to deliver the *Star* and collect his twenty-five cents from 169 Walmer Road. Although Pelletier was only sixteen years old, his evidence was clear and unhesitating. Carrie Davies had opened the door to him and told him that her employer was not home yet. Ernest asked her if the man coming down the street was him. Carrie said it was, and Ernest could get the quarter from him there. After Ernest got his money, he had walked about five steps down Walmer Road " . . . when I heard the first shot. I turned around, and the door was half open. Mr. Massey was on the threshold. He had his hat and coat on. He jumped back. He said, 'Oh' and he turned around and ran down the steps and down the sidewalk kind of bewildered, as if he didn't know which way to run . . . I heard the second shot. I looked on the veranda and I saw a flash, and I saw a girl there. Mr. Massey staggered to the end of the sidewalk, and fell. . . . The girl turned around and walked into the house." The boy described how he ran to fetch Dr. Elliott, who lived on Spadina Road, and then watched Massey being carried into 171 Walmer Road and the police arriving.

At this stage, Richard Greer, the Crown attorney responsible for clarifying exactly what had happened, rose to question Ernest. At thirty-seven years old, Greer had held the job of Crown attorney for eight years, but none of his previous cases had attracted the kind of public scrutiny he now felt. He proceeded warily, establishing that the newsboy had seen Carrie several times before. He asked Ernest, "Was there anything in her attitude towards you to denote any excitement or nervousness?"

Hartley Dewart was immediately on his feet with an objection: "Is he a judge?" It was his first public move in defence of Carrie. But Ernest carried on unfazed: "She seemed pretty cool. She put out her hand and I gave her the *Star* and she took it." The newsboy had not observed any signs that the eighteen-year-old was overwrought. Greer then asked the coroner to allow Ernest to identify Carrie. Dr. Johnson summoned Carrie to the front of the court and Ernest pointed her out as the maid who had answered the door. Dewart requested that Carrie and Miss Carmichael, the prison matron, should be allowed to go and sit outside the courtroom. Once Carrie had left the room, her lawyer turned to cross-examine Ernest Pelletier, particularly as to whether he had actually seen Carrie fire the shots. For the first time, the newsboy stumbled. He became confused about how exactly Massey had fallen, and he admitted that the estimate of the time that he had given the police was wrong.

Inspector Kennedy then stepped forward to read the statement Carrie had made to him the night she shot Bert Massey. With some embarrassment, the policeman had to admit that there was a problem with it: he had forgotten to ask Carrie to sign it, which made it vulnerable to a challenge by Carrie's lawyer. This blunder exasperated Crown Attorney Greer. He knew that the information in Kennedy's statement was essential for the inquest's deliberations, so he told the policeman to go ahead and read it. Reporters leaned forward, eager to catch every word. It was the first time they would hear any firsthand details of what happened the previous Monday, and their editors would print this almost verbatim, if they could get it all down. Inspector Kennedy lowered his eyes to his notebook and began to read out his questions and Carrie's answers. The sound of scribbling pens accompanied the policeman's plodding recitation about Carrie's age, birthplace, employment with the Masseys, and actions that evening.

"Why did you shoot him?"

"I really shot him in self-defence."

"What do you mean, self-defence?"

"He took advantage of me yesterday, and I thought he was going to do the same today."

"What did he do yesterday?"

"He caught me Sunday afternoon and kissed me twice. I ran upstairs and then he called me to make his bed and I obeyed and as soon as I went into his bedroom, he said, 'This is a nice bed.' Then he caught me and I pushed him on one side and ran upstairs, locked my door while I dressed, and I then went out and told my sister who lives at 326 Morley Avenue."

"Were you alone in the house with Charles A. Massey when this took place?"

"Yes, I was."

"What did your sister say?"

"I cannot remember what my sister said but my brother-in-law told me I would have to be careful."

Kennedy's voice droned on, as those present tried to picture the events of eight days ago. There was an incongruity to the ritual: Carrie's words—words first uttered by a flustered eighteen-year-old female with a Bedfordshire accent—were now repeated in a monotone by a male Canadian twice her age. But the story was clear enough. Carrie had described how she returned to the Masseys' house at 11:30 on Sunday night, and did not speak to Mr. Massey when he came downstairs for breakfast the following morning. The son, she had told Kennedy, was a nice boy who had never molested her. And Mr. Massey had never done anything like this before, either. But she had shot him because, she explained, "I seemed to lose control of myself."

Kennedy continued to read the questions and answers:

"Did he ever attempt to indecently assault you before?"

"No."

"On Sunday did he succeed in having sexual intercourse with you?"

"No. He attempted but I pushed him aside."

In the Court Street police station that night, Inspector Kennedy had tried to get a sense of what kind of girl this frightened servant really was.

"Did any other person have improper relations with you since coming to Canada?"

"No, sir."

"Have you any gentleman friends in the city?"

"Yes, I have a friend to whom I was engaged before he went to the war. I don't want to mention his name."

There was a pause after the inspector finished reading his statement. Crown Attorney Greer asked the policeman about Carrie Davies's state of mind. "She seemed quite an intelligent little girl," Kennedy replied. "She was a little bit nervous apparently. She answered my questions freely."

Hartley Dewart then rose. He asked Inspector Kennedy, "She made no statement except as you have given us in answer to the particular questions you put to her?"

"Not to me," replied the policeman.

"And you didn't ask her to make any. You were the person who was interviewing her that evening?"

"Yes, sir."

"How long was she with you?" continued Dewart.

"Oh, she would be about half an hour, probably."

Dewart nodded, then asked, "You didn't ask her to give you her own story in her own way voluntarily, but you asked her these questions?"

"Yes," replied Kennedy. "And she gave me these answers."

Dewart nodded again. He did not challenge the unsigned statement; however, he did ask a question to which he knew the answer, but wanted everybody present to understand the point he was making. "She had no opportunity of giving a continuous story in her own words? You did not ask her to do that?"

"No," said the policeman.

The police inspector was followed onto the witness stand by Sergeant Brown, who had arrested Carrie, and two passersby who had seen Carrie fire the shots and Bert Massey fall to the ground. When Mrs. Edna Nesbitt, a particularly excited witness, said that she supposed the first shot hit Massey, Hartley Dewart snapped, "Don't suppose, please." Next, Dr. Elliott, the physician who had done the post-mortem on Bert Massey, took the stand. He explained how a bullet had struck the victim directly in the heart, puncturing the aorta and causing almost instant death. He produced the bullet, now in a glass bottle, that he had removed from Bert's body. It was noted as Exhibit A.

An hour had already passed, and it seemed that the jury had all the information it needed to answer the questions covered in a coroner's inquest: when, where, how, and by what means the deceased met his death. But Carrie's lawyer had not finished. Hartley Dewart knew that Toronto was buzzing about this case, and that, so far, the Massey version of events was winning the battle of public opinion. The eighteen-year-old servant was already being dismissed as unbalanced, and probably epileptic, by pro-Massey papers such as the *Star* and the *Toronto Daily News*. A.J. Thomson, the Masseys' lawyer, was widely quoted as saying, "There are but two people who knew anything [about the case]. One is dead and the other may be mentally deranged." The anonymous *News* reporter who attended the inquest took a swipe at Carrie's statement that she had killed her employer in "self-defence," given how little Bert had actually done. There had been no violent assault, no rape. "According to her statement, she had little difficulty in repelling [Massey's] alleged advances, and they had been confined entirely to the one occasion mentioned."

Dewart wanted to cross-examine Bert's imperious sister-in-law, Mary Ethel Massey, about Carrie's illness the previous summer on Toronto Island, which Mrs. Massey had described in such detail to the *Evening Telegram*. The coroner's inquest was the only chance he might get to do this before the case went to court. But evidence about Carrie's state of mind was not strictly relevant to a coroner's inquest, which was only concerned with the facts of Massey's death. And Dr. Arthur Jukes Johnson rarely allowed irrelevancies when he presided over inquests. Addressing the coroner with exaggerated deference, Dewart said, "No one is better acquainted with the details of medical jurisprudence than Your Honour. No one understands better the bearing that matters of this kind might have on the subsequent disposition of the case." Dewart's unctuous tone worked; Dr. Johnson gave permission for Mrs. Massey to be called. The fact that Bert Massey's sister-in-law was present suggests that she half-expected to be called, and was eager to promote the Massey version of events.

Mary Ethel Massey, dressed in black, bustled up to the witness stand and stared unblinkingly at the Crown attorney, who was conducting the examination of witnesses. As soon as Greer began his questions, she launched into an account of Carrie's behaviour on that hot July night of 1914 that was even more spectacular than the description she had given the *Tely*'s Archie Fisher. Carrie was "pulling at her hair, and trying to bite her hands, and scratching at her neck and tearing her clothes, and then she would be quiet for a little while, and then she would start up again, and she kept calling something about her father all the time . . . Sometimes she would have a queer look in her eyes, [a] sort of glassy stare in her eyes. Sometimes her eyes would close, then she would be quiet." This behaviour apparently continued for hours, Mrs. Massey told the court, adding that she herself had helped hold the maid down as Carrie tried to "tear with her hands and claw at her neck." A Dr. Harris from the Sick Children's Hospital was summoned, and he used a stomach pump. When Greer asked if Carrie had hurt herself, Mrs. Massey declared that "her neck was all marked, and she would pull out some of her hair."

Greer asked Mrs. Massey if there had been other occasions when she had noticed something peculiar about Carrie's behaviour. Hartley Dewart must have suppressed a smile as she made a statement that reeked of condescension. "I noticed once or twice a peculiar look in her face," the woman replied. "I thought, 'Oh well, probably some of these English girls look funny when they come out here.'" The effect of this dismissive answer on the crowded courtroom was noticeable.

The coroner thanked Mary Ethel Massey for appearing, and she sailed out of the room. The jury had not warmed to her. Dr. Norman MacLaurin, who had called at the Massey cottage the day after the incident, described how he found Carrie on her bed curled up in a tight little ball. Despite his efforts to turn her over, she refused to talk or be examined. As far as he could see, Carrie was in good health, with no abnormal symptoms. Two days later, she was a little more responsive, but only after extensive questioning did she mutter something about "worrying about her people in the Old Country." A member of the jury who had paid careful attention to Mrs. Massey's testimony asked, "I would like to know if the Doctor found any scratches on Miss Davies' chest? On the night, Mrs. Massey said she scratched her neck and chest. Was there any loose hair to be found?" Dr. MacLaurin shook his head. "No, I found no loose hair. As to the scratches, I'm afraid I do not remember actually that."

Dewart now called another witness—a witness that nobody was expecting and who was not happy to have been subpoenaed, although he had been a close friend of Bert's and had acted as a pallbearer four days earlier. A well-dressed man in his early forties, John L. Hynes lived at 106 Walmer Road, a few doors down from the Masseys. When he gave his name, the clerk spelled it "Heintz." Dewart asked him when he had last seen Mr. Massey; Hynes replied that Massey had been at a family dinner party at the Hynes's house on the Sunday prior to the shooting and hadn't gone home until 1:45 a.m. on the morning of Monday, the day he was shot. Asked if Massey had been drinking that evening, Hynes said he hadn't.

Then Dewart asked him about another party, two days earlier, at Massey's house—a dinner for ten people where Carrie had done all the serving. Fixing a cold eye on Hynes, the lawyer asked, "Was there any person who was conducting themselves abnormally that evening?" Hynes shrugged. "I would not say so."

Dewart pressed on. "Do you not recollect there were some persons who were under the influence of liquor whom Miss Davies had to serve that night?"

Dr. Johnson interrupted to question the relevance of this question to a coroner's inquest. Dewart replied, "I want to show that these conditions existed, because I want to show that this is the pivot around which this thing swings." When the coroner gave an impatient nod, Dewart turned back to Hynes and repeated the question. John Hynes tried to laugh it off. "It's a matter of what you mean by being under the influence of liquor."

Dr. Johnson immediately announced that this answer was enough, and Hynes walked back to his seat as fast as he could.

Carrie's lawyer had achieved exactly what he wanted. His questions to Inspector Kennedy had suggested that Carrie's statement was only part of the story: the girl had been given no opportunity to explain her conduct in her own words. In addition, Mary Ethel Massey's descriptions of Carrie's "fit" had sounded not only snobbish but also suspiciously exaggerated to make it sound like an epileptic seizure. And a whiff of dissipation now clung to Bert Massey after John Hynes's evasions. Dewart had raised doubts in the minds of spectators and reporters. Was there more to this story than simple, cold-blooded murder?

But Dr. Jukes Johnson was exasperated by what he considered extraneous information being dragged into his court. It was already after 10 p.m., and the temperature outside was rapidly falling below freezing. The courtroom door kept swinging open and shut, letting in drafts, as newspapermen left so they could file before deadline. The chief coroner could not have been clearer, or more impatient, as he instructed the jury.

He began his remarks by telling jurors to ignore all the stories about Carrie's "fit" the previous summer. "The matter is absolutely immaterial to you, whether these were attacks of smallpox or hysteria or insanity or hives or anything else. You have nothing to do with that. It does not matter what either her physical or her mental condition was at the time of shooting.

"You are to consider the evidence that you have heard, and you are to form out of that evidence the answer that you are to give, and that answer is as to when, where, how and by what means the deceased, Charles A. Massey, came to his death . . .

"There is no question as to when this occurred. There is no question as to where it occurred, and there is no question as to how and by what means it occurred. The evidence is perfectly plain. You may say to yourselves, 'What was the motive?' Well, I do not think that that need bother you. A person does not commit murder without a motive . . . It does not matter whether a person stood on his head and shot him, or stood on his feet and shot him. It does not matter whether they were sane or insane. Insane people commit murders, and sane people commit them. Therefore, take all that out of your mind, the question of sanity or insanity."

After such clear instructions, the jury did not take long to reach its decision. At 10:40 p.m., foreman James Burford led the jury back into the room, and then read the verdict. "We find that Charles A. Massey came to his death on February 8, 1915, as a result of a pistol shot which we, the jury, believe was fired by Carrie Davies, and that the aforesaid Carrie Davies did feloniously and with malice aforethought kill and slay the said Charles A. Massey."

"Feloniously and with malice . . ." The coroner's jury had decided that Bert Massey had been deliberately killed, and that Carrie Davies should be charged with the murder. Dewart and Maw knew this meant the police court would confirm the murder charge, which would then be heard in front of a different jury in Ontario's top trial court. Thanks to the *Toronto Daily Star* and the *Evening Telegram*, both Bert Massey and Carrie Davies would also be tried in the court of public opinion. But Carrie herself understood little of this as she was hustled across the Don River, back to the prison hospital.

CHAPTER 9

"Well-Dressed Women Who Might Find Better Things to Do . . ."

TUESDAY, FEBRUARY 16

———

SPECTER OF STARVATION STALKS IN KAISERLAND

PEOPLE ALREADY ON HALF RATIONS OF BREAD . . .

GERMANY GROWS DESPERATE THROUGH THE LACK OF FOOD

STRONG IN A MILITARY SENSE, BUT WEAK IN MEANS OF LIVING

MENINGITIS ATTACKS TWO SOLDIERS AT CAMP

. . . HAMILTON MAN DEAD

PATRICIAS IN ANOTHER FIGHT NEAR ST. ELOI?

—*Toronto Daily Star*, Tuesday, February 16, 1915

HAS THE GOVT. TAKEN HAND IN CARRIE DAVIES' CASE?

FROM THE CORONER'S REMARKS IT LOOKED AS THOUGH SHE MIGHT NEVER GET A TRIAL

DR. BEEMER OF MIMICO ASYLUM WAS "ALSO PRESENT"

BEDFORDSHIRE ASSOCIATION JOINS IN THE DEFENCE

WOMEN SWARM TO SEE GIRL

RECORD CROWD ALMOST STORMS CORRIDORS.

—*Evening Telegram*, Tuesday, February 16, 1915

The following morning, you couldn't see an inch of the terrazzo tiles on the floors of City Hall, the crowd was so thick. The police were furious. "Clear away that mob of women," ordered the sergeant. "You'd think it was a circus." He fought his way through the throng of hatless girls, furred and expensively gowned matrons, street urchins, and young male idlers who jammed the corridor from City Hall's main entrance, up the staircase, as far as the door to the Women's Court. Many of them had no idea where the case would be heard, and they called out to each other for directions, their voices producing a deafening roar that echoed through City Hall's lofty corridors. Three constables did their best to clear a path through the crowd as Magistrate Denison made his way up the marble stairs.

After a few hours' sleep, Carrie Davies was returned to the Women's Court to be formally charged. Today's furor made the excitement at City Hall the previous week look like a Quaker meeting. Court watchers had burst into the second-floor courtroom as soon as the solid wooden doors were opened, and then crammed onto the spectators' benches, many of them protesting that they were "so sorry for the poor girl." Denison, who could never resist an audience, announced he would admit another fifty women onlookers. These newcomers now stood behind the prisoners' bench.

At a table just below Magistrate Denison sat Hartley Dewart, along with his clerk, T.C. Robinette; they were among the few men allowed into the courtroom. Dewart affected an attitude of nonchalant confidence as he glanced through his papers. Carrie's sister Maud ("almost broken down over the affair," according to the *Tely*) was not present, nor were any members of the Massey family.

Crammed into a couple of benches on Denison's left sat a clutch of women reporters—an unusual sight, given that newspapers had only recently begun to employ women as anything other than secretaries to the editors. From the 1890s onwards, editors of big-city papers had grudgingly allowed a few women into their newsrooms. The reason for female hires was nothing to do with gender equality, and everything to do with economics; Eaton's and Simpsons department stores would buy half-page advertisements for household goods, fashions, and daily specials if they were placed opposite pages geared to a female readership. The *Globe*'s women's section was called "Women at Work and at Play," the *Evening Telegram*'s was "For the Woman of Today." Female journalists catalogued notices of weddings and society events and churned out articles on kitchen tips, fashions, and beauty treatments. The implicit message of the women's pages was that matching dishes and dainty linen were every reader's priority. "Sandwiches should always be made as short a time as possible before being used," was a typical tip. Fashion advice was equally lacklustre: "Many women will rejoice to hear that one of the smartest French dressmakers has advanced a new suit with skirt not more than two yards wide." Nevertheless, the number of women reporters crept up, and by 1911 sixty-nine women listed their occupation as "journalist" on the federal census.

Women in newsrooms knew that, almost to a man, their editors shared the general prejudice against women professionals. A few women elbowed their way into hard news; at Toronto's *Mail and Empire*, Marjory MacMurchy had a column called "Politics for Women." Even the old-fashioned *Tely* had a feisty and determined woman who had broken out of the pink ghetto: in 1912, Mary Dawson Snider managed to win an exclusive interview with the *Titanic* survivors. (It did not hurt that her husband, Jerry Snider, who encouraged her ambitions, was the *Tely's* city editor.) But most newspaperwomen found themselves in a peculiar position. While they themselves were adventurous and open-minded, their work required them to promote the idea that marriage and motherhood were a woman's true calling.

However, women like Kathleen Coleman from Toronto's *Mail and Empire*, Robertine Barry from *Le Journal de Françoise*, Grace Denison from *Saturday Night*, and the *Tely's* own Mary Dawson Snider, were forceful characters who were not going to let a few curmudgeons shut them out of political, business, and financial reporting. Coleman, Barry, Denison, and Dawson were among the sixteen Canadian women (eight writing in English, eight in French) who had been invited by the Canadian Pacific Railway to travel to the 1904 St. Louis World's Fair on the CPR so they could file reports home. George Ham, the CPR's jovial publicity director who organized the trip and travelled with them, nick-named the group the "Sweet Sixteen," although he acknowledged that some of them "didn't think they were [sweet]." On the journey home, the women decided to establish the Canadian Women's Press Club. Kit Coleman had remarked to a young reader a few weeks earlier that she thought women ought to form an association: "Why should Canadian men journalists have all the trips and banquets?"

But Coleman wrote in a more serious vein when she described the new association in a column: "The heart and object of the club is to bring together and make known to each other the women who are work-ing on various newspapers in the Dominion, that we may be friendly and helpful to one another in the work." The club grew and prospered: by 1915, membership stood at over three hundred and it included two bestselling authors—Lucy Maud Montgomery (a friend of Marjory

MacMurchy's) and Nellie McClung, a westerner preoccupied with the suffrage campaign. The club's constitution proclaimed its high-minded goals, which included "mutual sympathy" and a commitment to "maintain and improve the status of journalism as a profession for women." Marjory MacMurchy made the same point in a spirited address to the collected potentates of the Canadian Press Association, when she addressed their annual meeting in 1910: "The conduct of a social page, a beauty department or a section on home adornment did not exhaust the possibilities of a newspaper woman." The camaraderie was a welcome relief for club members, who had nowhere else to share the problems of being a small minority in newsrooms filled with competitive men, some of whom were the stereotypical foul-mouthed drinkers of popular culture, and many of whom resented the newcomers.

But there was one arena in which female reporters could monopolize a front-page story: the Toronto Women's Court. Thanks to the Women's Court ban on male onlookers, only women were welcome in the court's press box. This outraged reporters like Archie Fisher and Harry M. Wodson: Wodson spoke for many when he dismissed women reporters as "fluttering lady scribes." He accused them of writing maudlin and misleading reports in order to elicit reader sympathy for "the diseased figure of a fallen angel." Newspaper articles in this era, whether written by men or women, were usually anonymous. But on the day that Carrie made her second appearance in the Women's Court, Helen Ball of the *Toronto Daily News* was given a byline.

The turmoil at City Hall when Carrie Davies made her second appearance shocked Ball. "The scene in the court, and in the corridors leading to it, was one of the most disgusting in the history of Toronto," she wrote for that day's paper. "Mobs of curious men and women packed the passages . . . Many of the women were well-dressed and evidently of the 'upper' stratum of society: but they pushed and jostled with the rest, intent on satisfying a more or less morbid curiosity.

"It was an excessively unpleasant picture of women, well-dressed women who might find better things to do than fight to get in where they might see a girl who had shot a fellow-being, hoping to hear the unhappy story of what had led her to such extremities."

Denison banged his gavel ferociously. Once the hubbub had died down, he gave a brisk nod and the sturdy figure of Police Constable Minty entered the court, followed by a line of women. Carrie was third in line as the women shuffled along the prisoners' bench. Ball noted her shabby coat and battered black hat, "with its pink ostrich tips." But Ball remained the cold-blooded reporter as she marvelled that a girl so normal in appearance should be accused of such a "horrible crime." Although she had editorialized about the crush outside the court, and suspected there was an "unhappy story" that had compelled Carrie to shoot Bert Massey, once in the press box she simply recorded the proceedings. Back among the guys at the *News,* where the editorial line was already anti-Carrie, it would not do to look "soft" on the eighteen-year-old accused. The class barrier between educated women like Ball and servants like Carrie was an even higher hurdle than the gender barrier between male and female reporters. Ball would have jeopardized her own professional status if she crossed it.

Denison dealt quickly with the first two cases, and then a court official barked, "Carrie Davies." A buzz of excitement erupted: spectators craned forward as Carrie stepped towards the Beak's desk. She appeared composed, "but much whiter than on her first appearance, and her eyes had a look of terror in them." Clasping and unclasping her hands, from time to time she sent desperate looks of appeal to Miss Carmichael.

The proceedings were so routine that the eager mob of onlookers was bitterly frustrated. The salacious details of how Carrie was nearly "ruined," revealed the previous night at the coroner's inquest, were not mentioned. In the Women's Court, the verdict from the coroner's jury was read, and only two witnesses were called: Sergeant Brown, who had been first on the scene of the crime, and the paper boy Ernest Pelletier, who identified Carrie as the woman who had fired the gun. The Crown attorney briskly announced that this evidence, along with the decision from the coroner's inquest, was "all we need to commit her for trial." Mr. Maw announced that the prisoner would plead not guilty. Happy to proceed at his usual gallop, Colonel Denison snapped that there would be no bail: the prisoner would return to jail. Once again, Carrie was led out of court without having uttered a word. Disappointed onlookers edged towards the door. The case would now move to the Ontario Supreme Court, High Court Division (today's Ontario Superior Court), which sat on the ground floor of City Hall, in an imposing, high-ceilinged room. It could be days, weeks, or even months before Carrie was summoned to face the charge of murder.

But the publisher and editor of the *Evening Telegram* had no intention of letting the case languish. John Ross Robertson and Black Jack Robinson were busy on two different fronts on Carrie's behalf.

❧

The *Tely*'s first priority was to shoot holes in the Massey claim that Carrie was unbalanced. The Masseys' motives were obvious. If the court decided that the young woman was unfit to stand trial by reason of insanity, she would be locked away in an asylum until she became "fit" (if ever). In the unlikely event that she was declared fit, she might then have to go back and stand trial for murder. Meanwhile, Bert Massey's behaviour would not get a public airing.

The paper had already carried a story berating its competitors (particularly the *News*) for declaring that Carrie was subject to monthly fits of severe depression. The *Tely*'s headline over that story was "Slide to Asylum via Trial by Newspaper." Now, immediately after Carrie's appearance in the Women's Court, the *Tely* published an article with the headline "Has the Govt. Taken Hand in Carrie Davies' Case? From the Coroner's Remarks It Looked as Though She Might Never Get a Trial." As far as the *Tely* was concerned, Dr. Beemer's presence at the coroner's inquest was clear proof that the Masseys were pulling strings. The article claimed that Dr. Johnson had told the coroner's jury, "Before her trial is arranged, the Government will probably see fit to order some enquiry into her mental condition. It will largely depend on that investigation whether she will ever be tried."

The day after the coroner's inquest, the *Tely*'s Archie Fisher cornered Dr. Johnson and questioned him about this statement. Dr. Johnson denied making it (it does not appear in the official transcript, and no other paper reported such remarks). The coroner tried to shoulder aside the scruffy reporter, but Archie wasn't going to be brushed off. "Have you had any orders from the Government or spoken to the Attorney General concerning Carrie Davies's sanity?" Dr. Johnson insisted that no such conversation had taken place. He explained that it was normal practice for the government to appoint experts "in all cases where a person's sanity is questioned." Archie ostentatiously scribbled down every word in his dog-eared notebook as he persisted: "Did you know that Dr. Beemer of the Mimico Hospital for the Insane was present at the inquest?" Dr. Johnson admitted he saw him there, but denied that he represented the government. "I suppose he was there to get a line on the case." Whatever the coroner said, a *Tely* reader could not escape Archie's spin—that the government and the Masseys had ganged up on Carrie Davies in the interests of preserving the Massey reputation. Nor could the reader be satisfied that all the facts were on the table, because Archie made that clear, too. "It was clearly established that what the girl said was not her story of all that has happened. She only answered the questions asked her."

It was no coincidence that the *Evening Telegram*'s account of the coroner's inquest echoed all the points Hartley Dewart had made. Dewart had not spent twenty-eight years at the Canadian bar without knowing the importance of perception. He had a smart young law student named Arthur Roebuck working in his office, and he quietly instructed Roebuck to keep in close touch with the *Telegram*'s city editor, Jerry Snider. Snider, in turn, had daily meetings with Black Jack. A quiet word to a reporter . . . a quick note sent over to the *Tely* office on King Street . . . and a reply to Dewart's law office on Adelaide Street. Dewart and Black Jack were manipulating public opinion in unison. And Black Jack was not acting alone. "Nothing was ever done at *The Telegram* without Robertson's approval," according to Ron Poulton, John Ross Robertson's biographer. "He engineered Carrie Davies' defence because she was a lone figure against a member of The Establishment, just as he had been."

The *Tely*'s second tactic to save Carrie was the public fundraising campaign that Black Jack and Robertson had dreamed up a couple of days earlier. The letter from "Fair Play," the paper announced, "has produced many others of similar strain." The *Tely* orchestrated an outpouring of sympathy for Carrie, publishing every letter that offered support. "I can assure you in the east end district where the poor girl spent so many happy days, the public would be pleased to assist," wrote "Justice," who went on to describe the eighteen-year-old as "a very bright and cheerful girl, and at no time . . . ever known to have epileptic fits . . . I was in her company a good many times. We are ready to come forward to give any assistance it is possible to give."

Henry A. Ashmead of 16 Belmont Street was more explicit: "The suggestion of your correspondent 'Fair Play' that a subscription should be taken up to defray the expenses of counsel engaged in the defence of Carrie Davies is a very good one."

And an anonymous "Irish-Canadian" begged to know how he could help save the "poor orphan girl" from "the mad house." "I would be pleased to contribute to help this young girl, who is probably the sole support of her poor widowed mother in the old land in her efforts to keep the body and soul of her small family together, in her fight to obtain justice under the flag that her father fought and died for."

"Fair Play of Waverley Road" turned out to be a Mrs. J.W. Drummond, who dropped her *nom-de-plume* and told the *Tely* that "the girl was only eighteen years of age and it could hardly be expected that a girl at that age would use the mature judgement of a man of forty [*sic*], nor have the financial resources necessary to prove, first her sanity and second, her innocence of the crime with which she is charged . . . Every person I have been speaking to feels the same as I do and is willing to assist in any way they can towards helping her. I would be quite ready to start a fund myself among my own friends."

Were these letters real? Who knows. But thanks to the *Evening Telegram*, momentum built for a Carrie Davies Defence Fund. The main beneficiary of the fund would inevitably be Carrie's lawyer—and the *Tely*'s ally—Hartley Dewart. But the newspaper put more emphasis on other, more poignant uses—uses that might open sympathizers' purses. "May Have to Bring Mother to Save Girl from Gallows," read a headline in Monday morning's paper. But who should establish the fund? One correspondent suggested either Toronto veterans or the Sons of England, a benevolent society founded in Toronto in 1874 with goals dear to the hearts of the *Evening Telegram*'s owner and editor—to assist needy Protestants from England and to promote the British monarchy. Another correspondent urged the newspaper itself to organize the fund.

How much did Carrie's mother, back in Bedfordshire, know about the murder case gripping Toronto? Since she almost certainly did not have a telephone, and two weeks had elapsed since Bert Massey's death before news of the case was featured in the British press, the answer is probably nothing. No matter. What could be more wrenching for *Tely* readers than the image of the blind and grieving mother, helpless on the wrong side of the Atlantic?

The most surprising suggestion, however, was not promoted in the *Tely*'s columns. Although representatives of Toronto's Local Council of Women had been indifferent to Carrie Davies when she first appeared in the Women's Court, and had barely noticed her when they shared a City Hall elevator, the case had now caught the attention of Florence Huestis and her colleagues. A couple of days after Carrie's second appearance in the Women's Court, the LCW had its monthly meeting at the Margaret Eaton Studio, a progressive girls' school housed in an ersatz Greek temple on Bloor Street that Timothy Eaton's wife, Margaret, had financed. The fearless Florence Huestis was in the chair. At the end of the meeting on Wednesday, February 17, in a discussion of the Women's Court, Mrs. Huestis rose. Dignified and articulate, she clasped her hands in front of her and raised a question that she knew would provoke some discomfort in the room: Should the LCW take a position on the Massey case, or even contribute to the legal defence of the young English girl now in Don Jail?

There was a long silence. On the one hand, these women knew the vulnerability of young women in this city, and the frequency with which they were exploited. Hadn't the LCW already spoken out about the horrors of the white-slave trade? A donation to a public defence campaign would demonstrate the LCW's commitment to protecting women's interests. Unlike Helen Ball, these women were sufficiently secure socially to show sympathy for a member of the working class. One member reported that the Council was prepared to offer the unfortunate girl the services of one of Toronto's most prominent KCs (probably the husband of one of the women present).

On the other hand, many of these women would have found Carrie's actions more shocking than the accusations against Bert Massey. Men would be men, but did the submissive young women sweating away in their own kitchens harbour murderous thoughts about their employers? And surely it wasn't right that a member of one of Toronto's most prominent families now lay six feet under in Mount Pleasant Cemetery? Florence Huestis's own loyalties must have been torn. She instinctively sympathized with Carrie, but she herself had known the Massey family since she was a little girl and regularly visited Bert Massey's cousins at Dentonia, their handsome country estate east of Toronto.

Before discussion got much further, someone mentioned that the girl's sister had engaged Hartley Dewart, KC, and that the Bedfordshire Fraternal Association (a local branch of the Sons of England) was taking up subscriptions to pay his fees. The collective sigh of relief that the matter was taken out of LCW hands was almost audible. The minute-taker noted that, "It was felt by the Council that any interference in the case by the members would be an impertinence." Florence Huestis briefly moved the meeting on to the appointment of new conveners for a dozen standing committees, dealing with circulating Council literature; citizenship; conservation of national resources; education; employment for women; finance; immigration; laws affecting women and children; objectionable printed matter; press; equal moral standard and prevention of traffic in women; and public health.

Once the business was over, members enjoyed tea and sandwiches and heard a talk by Mrs. Horace Parsons on "Life in the North"—the North, in this case, being the new Ontario railway town of Cochrane.

CHAPTER 10

Deadly Bayonet Work

WEDNESDAY, FEBRUARY 17 TO FRIDAY, FEBRUARY 19

———

Members of the first Canadian contingent are likely to be under fire this week. If the enemy can locate the point in the line to which the Canadians are sent they are certain to pay them very special attention . . . The entire Canadian people will henceforth feel their hearts stirred as they read accounts of the fighting in Northern France and Belgium in which the men of their own blood are risking their lives in a great cause.
—*Toronto Daily Star*, Monday, February 15, 1915

CARRIE DAVIES SHOT WITH INTENT TO KILL
VERDICT OF CORONER'S JURY IN MASSEY MURDER
ALLEGES SELF-DEFENCE
STATEMENT TO POLICE AFTER THE SHOOTING ACCUSED MASSEY OF
IMPROPRIETY—MENTAL CONDITION TO BE EXAMINED.
—*Globe*, Tuesday, February 16, 1915

After Carrie's second appearance in the Women's Court, she temporarily disappeared from the headlines of Toronto's newspapers. Even the *Evening Telegram*, Carrie's staunch ally, relegated her to the back pages. Editors knew that public interest in the Massey murder would revive only when that wan, cheerless girl was back in court, in the prisoner's dock.

The weather turned bitter, with sharp winds and cold rain many days, coating the sidewalks in ice. Citizens pulled woollen scarves over their faces as they hurried past the recruitment posters in office windows. Up to now, the European conflict had seemed a long, long way away—which is why the previous week's story of a possible bombing raid in Ottawa had triggered unusual excitement. The war's most noticeable impact on Toronto was the cancellation of several events—Toronto's major military training camp, for example, had bumped the Automobile Trade Association's annual show from the Exhibition grounds. The mood amongst lawmakers was sombre. On Thursday, February 4, when the Dominion Parliament opened in Ottawa, "khaki and questions of war superseded the gold lace and scarlet and attendant social gaieties of other years," according to the weekly magazine *Saturday Night*. Two weeks later, when the Ontario Legislature opened a new session, the expected reception in Premier Sir William Hearst's offices was not held, out of respect for his predecessor, Sir James Whitney, who had died five months earlier. The session promised to be "unusually quiet socially," predicted *Saturday Night*.

Yet this was a critical week for Canadians. It was the week when the first contingent of the Canadian Expeditionary Force, which had spent the winter training on Salisbury Plain after being recruited the previous August, finally reached the battlefield. For the first time, an intensely personal commitment to events across the Atlantic hit newspaper readers. And the emotions aroused by the war, and those stirred up by the Massey killing, began to merge.

The first bulletin about troop movements appeared in a box on the *Globe*'s front page on Saturday, February 14, three days before Magistrate Denison committed Carrie for trial. "Canadians landed safely," the paper announced. The First Canadian Division, consisting of most of the men who had spent a bitter winter on Salisbury Plain, had been shipped across the English Channel. Once on French soil, they were loaded into cramped rail cars, labelled *40 hommes ou 8 chevaux*, for a forty-six-hour trip to the western front. With no seats or lavatories in the rail cars, it was a miserable journey. But the Canadians were welcomed at the front, where the core of the British Expeditionary Force had been wiped out in the war's early battles.

The contingent was made up of about nineteen thousand men—three infantry brigades of four thousand men each, plus artillery, cavalry, and supply columns. There were already Canadians in the trenches—a few hundred who were members of British regiments, and over a thousand members of the elite Princess Patricia's Canadian Light Infantry, a privately raised Canadian regiment of experienced soldiers (mainly British-born) that had been in France since December. But now there were more than ten times that number—over twenty thousand Canadians altogether within earshot of German guns. The four thousand volunteers who had left Toronto the previous August were among them, and on February 16, the *Star* ran the headline "Toronto men first to enter trenches."

In 1915, ties to Britain remained strong in Ontario, and Queen Victoria's birthday was an annual opportunity to flaunt them.

Until the outbreak of war in 1914, British immigrants streamed into Toronto, and 85 percent of the city's residents claimed British ancestry.

Joseph Atkinson was the young and ambitious editor of the *Toronto Star*.

During a typhoid outbreak in 1912, a girl called Beatrice Webb won a *Star*-sponsored "Swat the Fly" contest by trapping and swatting 543,360 flies.

Above, left: John Ross Robertson was proprietor of Toronto's *Evening Telegram*, which appealed to "the masses not the classes."

Below, left: The *Telegram* moved into a lavish new building on the corner of King and Bay Streets in 1900.

Below, right: Newsboys as young as nine called out the headlines at street corners.

Printers in the *Telegram*'s composing room set the type for stories of scandal and corruption.

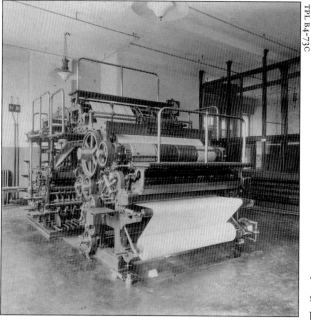

The *Telegram*'s state-of-the art printing presses.

Each evening, the unemployed desperately scanned the *Telegram*'s Want Ads.

On their return journey from the St. Louis World's Fair in 1904, sixteen women reporters founded the Canadian Women's Press Club and dedicated themselves to making journalism a more accessible profession for women. Mary Dawson Snider is standing fourth from left, their host George Ham fourth from right. Grace Denison and Kathleen Coleman missed the official photo session.

The back of City Hall directly overlooked the wretched slums of the Ward.

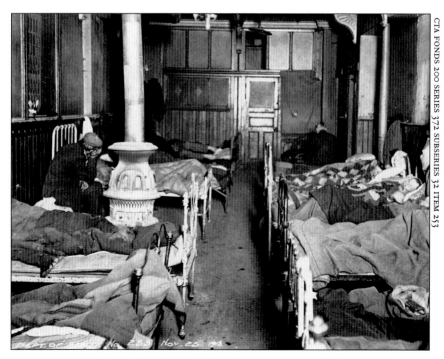

Immigrants from Eastern Europe crammed into the Ward's rooming houses.

Residents of the Ward lived in poverty and squalor, but they could expect no help from the city's health department.

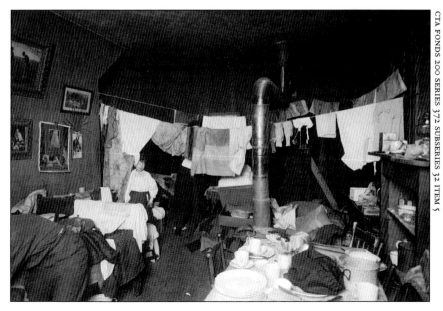

Diseases such as tuberculosis were rife in overcrowded family homes.

The south end of Morley Avenue boasted better housing than the north end, where the Fairchilds lived, but cars were no match for its mud after a downpour.

Toronto's policemen spent more time enforcing bylaws about public decency than chasing criminals.

Private George Bell of the 1st Battalion described in a memoir the troops' elation during their February crossing to France: "While we may have been a bit deficient in discipline and some of the finer points of military etiquette, our eagerness to get into the big show was not lacking." There was still a *Boy's Own Annual* tone to some of the war coverage. The same day that the *Globe* announced that the Canadians troops had landed safely in France, Claude Grahame-White, a daring British aviator, and his elegant wife, Ethel, appeared in a front-page photograph posed next to a flimsy canvas and plywood biplane. Grahame-White's plane was one of thirty-four little flying machines that had soared across the British Channel in the "Greatest Aeroplane Raid in All History" to bomb German military and submarine bases on the Belgian coast. "A Beautiful Flight," wrote the *Globe* correspondent, before explaining that Flight Commander Grahame-Wright had unfortunately fallen into the sea. Luckily, a nearby French vessel had scooped him out of the chilly water. The bombs had little effect.

But during Carrie Davies's ordeal, the rhetoric of war was shifting in Toronto. After the harsh German occupation of Belgium, notions of chivalry and honour had evaporated, along with respect for Germans as industrious, Christian, and sensible fellow immigrants with an endearing fondness for beer and children. A hazy romanticism about war had developed during the century since Britain fought its last major European battle, at Waterloo—a century during which the reality of butchery and death had been obliterated by tales of heroism and valour. The misery of the Crimean War in the 1850s was long forgotten. The previous August, Toronto Mayor Horatio Clarence Hocken had told one regiment, "You will have the proud privilege of fighting not only for the British Empire but for the cause of civilization." By February 1915, that kind of language had begun to sound hollow to some people, even though politicians continued to talk about "The Great War for Civilization." Lucy Maud Montgomery read the war news obsessively:

"The sufferings of the men everywhere in the trenches this winter must be dreadful," she confided to her journal. "I never go out on these cold dark nights without thinking of them miserably. I am ashamed that I am warmly clad and housed."

The four million–strong Imperial German Army had proved itself well armed, well drilled, and ruthless. Now, German gunsights were trained on Canadians, including the progeny of many of Toronto's best-known families. Colonel George Denison, for example, had already lost a nephew, Bertie Denison, who was in a British regiment during the fighting in France in September 1914, and had watched his own son George Taylor Denison, his grandson Alexander Kirkpatrick, and his nephew Edgar Denison volunteer for duty and disappear to France. Bert Massey's half-brother, Clifton Manbank Horsey, now a twenty-four-year-old engineer, had joined the 13th Battalion of the Canadian Infantry as soon as war was declared. He and Carrie's anonymous boyfriend were almost certainly in France, along with hundreds of British-born immigrants from working-class neighbourhoods like Cabbagetown and Leslieville who had returned to Europe to defend the Empire.

Anger against "the Hun" smouldered. A mob of Torontonians attacked the Liederkranz Club, the city's leading German institution, when it continued to fly the German flag. Soldiers' families were yet more unsettled by February's news from the eastern front, where the Germans, according to the *Globe* and other papers, resorted to "point-blank slaughter by rifle fire and bayonet" and "poisonous chemical smoke." Letters from individual soldiers started to appear in the evening papers: the *Star* printed one from a private in the 48th Highlanders who described seeing a little Belgian girl who "had no eyes; they had been gouged out by one of the Kaiser's officers. I know of many cases of outrage . . ." The rules had changed: while the British and French were sending cavalry into battle, the Germans were using brutal new methods of industrial warfare.

This was a different kind of combat—a gruelling war of attrition instead of a quick-fire, knockout blow. Its costs were going to be far greater than imagined, and the casualty lists longer. Toxic rumours abounded. In mid-February, Toronto editors had a welter of items from Europe to jigsaw together on their front pages. The same day that Carrie was returned to the hospital wing of the Don Jail, charged with murder, group portraits of men in uniform dominated newspaper front pages. The *Toronto Daily Star* featured twelve of the Toronto soldiers, sporting the moustaches required by army regulations, who had left the previous summer. The *Globe*'s gallery included officers of the Canadian Expeditionary Force, their names a roll call of Family Compact and United Empire Loyalist membership: Lieutenant-Colonel Macdonell, Lieutenant-Colonel Nasmith, Major Chisholm, Major Beatty, Colonel Heard, Lieutenant-Colonel Hamilton, Major Sutherland, Captain Clifford, and Brigadier-General E.A. Lawrence among them. "Most of the officers shown here are no doubt in France," read the caption. How many would return? On the same page of the *Globe*, another headline read, "Patricia's are paying their share of death toll." Three of the Princess Pats had been killed in a minor skirmish, one had subsequently died of wounds, and a fifth was seriously wounded. The Canadian force was moving ahead to relieve the division to which the Princess Pats were attached.

There was upsetting news everywhere. The naval war was in full swing, with German submarines scoring hits against the British navy, once thought invincible. Although civilian vessels from neutral countries were supposed to be exempt from hostilities, transatlantic shipping companies like the Cunard Line were concerned about the safety of their New York–bound liners. The United States had not yet joined the Allies, so captains quietly lowered the Union Jack and raised the Stars and Stripes when they were in danger zones. Now the German government announced that it intended to enforce a blockade around

Britain by sowing mines around the British Isles. The *Globe* described such an action as "nothing short of indiscriminate murder on the greatest scale ever attempted in the history of maritime warfare," since the floating mines would "strike blindly at both neutral and belligerent and destroy not only their ships but the peaceful and unsuspecting sailors on board." Part of the "warrior culture" that had once defined previous European conflicts had been respect for civilians, especially women and children, but once again, the Germans were showing no respect for civilian lives. Within days, German mines had sunk two American steamers, and a German torpedo struck a cross-Channel steamer from Boulogne to Folkestone. With war more dependent on the strength of an entire economy, the morale of civilians became a key target. Winston Churchill, then first lord of the admiralty, pronounced the German tactic "piracy" and promised active reprisals.

Soon after the Canadians arrived at the front, Torontonians began to learn of hand-to-hand fighting between German and British soldiers, and "deadly bayonet work," near the Belgian town of Ypres. Each day, newspaper readers on Toronto's streetcars, and in its taverns, clubs, and kitchens, absorbed increasingly ghastly bulletins from the front. There were heavy losses on both sides, with the Germans fighting "savagely and frantically," and few prisoners taken because "action was too hot for much activity in this direction." Farther down the line, Ontario battalions were "now experiencing active service conditions, eating bully beef and hard tack, and each man sleeping under one blanket." It was only a matter of time before they came under fire.

The new technology of warfare exerted a chilling fascination on Canadians because it could perpetrate so much damage. Germany was experimenting with zeppelins—giant airships nearly two football fields long, held aloft by huge bags of hydrogen within their steel frames. These airships had been developed around 1900 by Count Ferdinand von Zeppelin for reconnaissance and bombing missions. In 1915, the

German navy had two zeppelins patrolling continuously, regardless of the weather, under the personal command of Count Zeppelin. The lumbering dirigibles might lack the speed and manoeuvrability of Claude Grahame-White's biplane, but they could fly at higher altitudes, carry heavy machine guns and bombs, and had greater range and endurance. Count Zeppelin's nephew, Baron Gemmingen, had invented a zeppelin "observation car" that hung below the airship and allowed an observer to spot vessels, then relay navigation and bombing orders to aircraft flying above the clouds.

The Kaiser authorized bombing raids against England in January, causing a scramble in Britain to bolster air defences and prompting the *Star* to go after Count Zeppelin in a story headlined "Baby-killers' 'Father' Excuses Aero-Murders." Later in the war, the Allies would invent incendiary ammunition that destroyed zeppelins by setting them alight. But in this first year of fighting, German dominance of the skies unnerved the Allies and infuriated non-combatants. In some areas of London, crowds rioted after the first air raids, smashing the windows of merchants of German or Austrian origin. A locomotive of the London and North Western Railway named *Dachshund* was quickly rechristened *Bulldog*.

On Friday, February 19, the *Globe* printed a diagram of a zeppelin on its front page, with ominous news: "Germany now possesses about twelve first-class airships." Readers who studied the menacing, torpedo-shaped aircraft could draw a little comfort from the story that a zeppelin had foundered in the North Sea, off the coast of Jutland, due to the weight of snow. Three crew members had drowned in the icy waters, and the rest had been interned in Denmark. In Toronto's clubs, men found it easier to discuss novel airborne military machines than the stalemate on the ground.

But there was also news of confrontations on both the western and eastern fronts. In Poland, after the Battle of the Masurian Lakes,

German units continued to advance towards Warsaw. In northern France, the Germans had made a determined, though unsuccessful attempt to retake trenches lost the previous month. Casualties mounted on both sides: the *Globe* published the names of two more members of the Princess Pats killed in action, along with a list of Canadians who were wounded or who had died in hospital.

Toronto residents could no longer escape the pressure and proximity of war. On February 19, three days after Carrie Davies was indicted for murder, four thousand khaki-clad recruits, many of them mere boys, performed a route march from their camp on the Toronto exhibition grounds to Queen's Park. These men had responded to Prime Minister Robert Borden's January appeal for volunteers for another contingent of Canadian troops. Schools were closed for the day to allow children to cheer "the largest and most unique military parade this city has ever seen." The column was so long that when its leaders reached the Legislature, the column's tail was still at Bloor Street. Crowds lined the route, cheering fathers, brothers, sons, and friends who would soon leave homes and families far behind in Canada, in order to fight against a brutal enemy.

Meanwhile, pressure intensified on men below the age of forty to sign up. In London, England, women would soon be handing out white feathers, an ancient symbol of cowardice, to young men not in uniform. Rudyard Kipling, a hero of Colonel Denison's, asked, "What will be the position in years to come of the young man who has deliberately elected to outcast himself from this all-embracing brotherhood?" Bert Massey could claim that his responsibility for wife and son was reason enough to keep him in Toronto. But plenty of men his age and in similar circumstances were in the khaki column that day, making a citizen described as a "man about town" and accused of trying to "ruin" a maid look ignoble in contrast.

Amidst the war fever, Black Jack Robinson of the *Evening Telegram* was not going to let Carrie Davies be forgotten. Hartley Dewart had let him know, through their go-between Roebuck, that there was the promise of a good scandal when the Davies case came to court. And, like any good editor, he had a feel for the mood of his readership. Hunched and thoughtful, Robinson sat in his office surrounded by untidy piles of old papers, government reports, and proof sheets. He allowed himself a wolfish grin as he tapped a pencil on his cluttered desktop, cast a quick eye over the *Tely* newsroom, and then reread the menacing headlines from Europe. Events there were spawning outrage among *Evening Telegram* readers. The heartless German war machine was sideswiping innocent civilians, putting Canadians on edge, and making public opinion within Toronto easier to sway. The *Tely* could subtly suggest that Carrie Davies was simply a civilian who was trying to defend herself.

Carrie Davies's murder trial would be heard at the Supreme Court by one of the young Dominion's grand old men: the chief justice of Ontario, Sir William Mulock.

Like Colonel George Denison and John Ross Robertson, Chief Justice Mulock had watched the city of Toronto mushroom from a gossipy small town into a bustling metropolis. But unlike those anglophiles, and like Joe Atkinson, Imperial ties were less important to him than the task of constructing a nation. A white-bearded, cigar-chomping lawyer, Mulock had served as postmaster general and minister of labour in Sir Wilfrid Laurier's Liberal cabinet before moving to the Supreme Court of Ontario in 1905. *Saturday Night* contributor H.F. Gadsby lauded the chief justice as "broad-gauged, big-brained, high-thinking and greathearted." Prime Minister Laurier was blunter in his comment on his former colleague: "the best-hearted and worst-mannered man he knew."

In short, Mulock was both a man of vision and an abrasive personality who rode roughshod over everybody, including his own relations. Devoted to the interests of his city, his country, and the Liberal Party, he liked to get things done. As postmaster general in the 1890s, he had implemented the Imperial penny post, personally designed a new stamp that showed the extent of the British Empire, secured wireless telegraphy between Canada and London, and (perhaps most significant in the long term) brought an ambitious young Liberal called William Lyon Mackenzie King to Ottawa to work for him. There was barely an institution within Toronto in which Mulock did not play a role. Besides backing Joe Atkinson's relaunch of the *Toronto Star* in 1899, Mulock had helped make the University of Toronto a major educational establishment and was among the founders of the Dominion Bank, the Toronto General Trust (both part of the TD Bank Group today), and the Wellesley Hospital.

Although he came from a relatively humble Irish-Canadian background, the chief justice was now in his seventies and deeply entrenched in the Canadian establishment. Distantly related to the wealthy Cawthra family, which had been part of the Family Compact back in the 1830s, as a young man he had ridden Cawthra coattails until he himself was wealthy. He then made an advantageous marriage to the startlingly plain but well-connected Sarah Crowther. When Mulock's tall, spare figure strode through Osgoode Hall's vaulted library or into the velvet-curtained dining rooms of the Toronto or York Club in Toronto, or the Rideau Club in Ottawa, at least a dozen admirers would rise to shake his hand. He had been painted by both of the fashionable portrait artists of the period (J.W.L. Forster and Wyly Grier) and shared his time between a prosperous farm near Newmarket, where he raised prize cattle and Shetland ponies, and an elaborate mansion at 518 Jarvis Street, just down the road from the Masseys. (His son Cawthra lived close by, at 538 Jarvis Street.)

In 1914, Sir William was at the forefront of Toronto's response to the European conflict: he was co-creator and chair of the Toronto and York County Patriotic Fund, established to look after the families of Toronto volunteers. At the fund's launch in a crowded Massey Hall, nobody sang "God Save the King" louder. When former U.S. president

William Howard Taft came to speak at the University of Toronto the following February, while Bert Massey's cousin Vincent served as an usher on the floor of the hall, Mulock sat in the prime spot on the platform, next to the portly Taft. The following day, the former president lunched with Chief Justice Mulock.

(Other than the odds of America entering the war, what did they discuss? Sir William probably did not confide to the teetotalling Taft his current obsession: the threat of Prohibition in Ontario. The chief justice's drinking habits were as rough as his manners. In 1886, he had bought hundreds of gallons of the best rye available, at a cost of less than a dollar a gallon, and stored it in barrels in his Jarvis Street cellar. Now he was busy constructing special concrete closets in which to hide it, in the event that Prohibition should place limits on personal stockpiling.)

In court, Chief Justice Mulock was known as a no-nonsense judge who had much in common with Magistrate Denison. In the words of journalist and social commentator Augustus Bridle: "Impatient with counsel, impetuous and severe with witnesses, and heavy with admonishment to the depraved prisoner . . . he asserts himself with the trenchant emphasis of a bushwacker splitting rails." But if Mulock shared Denison's brusque impatience, he did not share the Beak's bigotry or rigid adherence to the status quo. Mulock was a go-getter, and having grown up poor, he felt no nostalgia about "the good old days." He had little time for United Empire Loyalist snobbery or anti-American feeling. For all his respect for King and Empire and pride in the knighthood that had been conferred upon him in 1902 by King Edward VII, he harboured no hostility towards Catholics or non-British immigrants. As a cabinet minister in Ottawa he took French lessons at 6:30 every morning so he could speak to Quebec colleagues in their own language. Most important for Carrie, he was a compassionate man, noted in his judgments for occasionally going (as Bridle put it) "wide of the mark in mere sentiment."

In general, Justice Mulock was considered to be lenient with the accused in criminal cases. Only one group of malefactors could expect no mercy: chicken thieves. So many of his own hens had been stolen from his Newmarket farm that the mere whisper of a missing Rhode Island Red or Leghorn would turn him purple with rage. One of his idiosyncracies was that he banned the use of brass clips to fasten court documents, because he had once torn his gown on one. (The rule prevailed for years after his death, long after the reason for the ban was forgotten.) Chief Justice Mulock's unpredictability could be the wild card in a sensational case involving a world-famous family, murder, and sex.

The *Tely*'s Ross Robertson and Jack Robinson knew that the chief justice probably wanted to clean out all cases pending before the Ontario Supreme Court rose at the end of February. Carrie's case might be heard within days. The *Evening Telegram* needed to keep interest in the case simmering so that donations for Carrie's defence would continue to roll in.

"Interest in Carrie Davies, Many Want To Help" was the headline on one article, which claimed that the paper was flooded with letters about the case. Apparently, almost all these writers warmly championed Carrie, although the *Tely* (which had published several such letters only days earlier) now announced that it would be inappropriate to publish them because the prisoner should not be "tried by newspaper." But it did mention that Mr. William Goldsmith of the Bedfordshire Fraternal Association was taking donations for a Carrie Davies Defence Fund, and that envelopes had arrived from "'An Englishman,' 'Funny Looking One,' 'East Toronto Sympathiser,' Henry Ashmead and others." Carrie's fellow worshippers at St. Monica's Anglican Church were said to be pressing cash on the Reverend Robert Gay, their rector, and he was going to pass it on to the Bedfordshire Association.

How accurate was the *Tely*'s reporting? Rumours and misinformation were flying around. The *Toronto Evening Star* told a completely different story. A couple of days after the *Tely* implied that money was pouring in for Carrie, the *Star* claimed that the Fund had only attracted $20 in donations, and that the Bedfordshire Fraternal Association had withdrawn its support for Carrie when it heard that the Local Council of Women had found her a lawyer who would give his services pro bono. President Hall of the Bedfordshire Fraternal Association, happy to hear of an offer that would take the burden of raising a large sum off his threadbare organization, was reported to have announced, "I shall strongly advise that the money which has been raised be returned to those who sent it." Given that a KC's fees for taking a murder case ran between $1,500 and $2,000, his reaction is understandable.

Such a possibility didn't suit the *Evening Telegram*'s publisher and editor at all. If Hartley Dewart did not handle the case, the *Tely* would no longer have advance notice of any scandalous revelations the court might hear. And if Mrs. Huestis and her middle-class do-gooders took over the case, *Tely* readers might lose interest, and that could hurt sales.

A new round began in the battle between the *Tely* and the *Star* to promote conflicting versions of events. The *Tely* took direct aim at the *Star* the following day, reprinting the story in full, then quoting President Hall as denying he had suggested that donations should be returned. "While argument goes on," asserted the *Tely* headline, "the Girl Stays in Jail, and Sympathy for Her Necessity is Shooed Away." The reporter (almost certainly Archie Fisher) accused the rival paper of "steer[ing] or veer[ing]" public opinion against "a poor English girl, two years out from 'ome, in a desperate scrape, with the gallows or asylum ahead of her . . . She needs help just as much as she did on the night of the shooting."

The *Tely* story went on to make outrageous claims about cutthroat competition triggered within the legal fraternity. Representatives from law offices "have camped on Carrie Davies's trail as though she were a missing heiress. Some got past the police and visited her in the cells—

so they boasted." The newspaper even managed to find a lawyer who insisted he had "been able to visit her at the jail in the guise of 'medical expert,' but he couldn't get in the place, possibly owing to the crush of other [lawyers] who wanted to get out." The vivid (and unlikely) account of legal rivalry ended on a note of bathos: "But while the Fairchilds are thus loaded with offers of counsel, nobody has come forward with very much cash."

Archie Fisher ended this particular article with a dramatic catalogue of questions that "had to be asked," for which expensive expert testimony would be required:

> Is Carrie Davies sane?
> Can she prove it?
> Is Carrie Davies innocent of the crime of murder?
> Can she prove it? . . .
> Quality rather than quantity in expert technical evidence
> counts, and quality costs.

The melodrama of Archie's defence of Carrie, "a poor English girl, two years out from 'ome, in a desperate scrape," was matched only by some appalling verse that appeared on the same page of the *Evening Telegram*, two columns away, that hit the same note of British solidarity and pluck. Written by a deservedly forgotten poet named Albert E. Sleighs, it was entitled "Queen's Own," a reference to one of the Toronto regiments seeing action in France for the first time that week.

> *O, listen to the bugle call that summons men to arms,*
> *Their King and country need them at the front;*
> *They leave the desk and factory, they leave the town and farms,*
> *To face the foe and bear the battle's brunt . . .*
> *Queen's Own, Queen's Own,*

Sure a finer lot of lads were never known.
You've a bonnie lot of laddies,
You'll be missed by Rose and Gladys,
When you're fighting at the front, Queen's Own.

They've made their wills and settled up and counted every cost,
Though most of them to give had only life,
But they'll give it, give it freely and count it cheaply lost,
To help the Empire triumph in the strife.
Queen's Own, Queen's Own,
When you're fighting in the cannon-roaring zone,
When you're charging with the bayonet
And the blood of foemen stain it,
Don't forget the slaughtered babes, Queen's Own.

How many *Tely* readers, slumped at kitchen tables with the paper and a cup of tea after a long day, could resist the sentimental appeal of two parallel stories—a young girl in trouble, and the Empire imperilled? Brave boys were defending the Empire, but who was looking after poor Carrie, who had tried to protect her virtue while her boyfriend was at the front? Was she really so different from "Rose and Gladys," who were missing their laddies at the front?

CHAPTER 11

Legal Circles

SATURDAY, FEBRUARY 20 TO
WEDNESDAY, FEBRUARY 24

———

The once vast armies of the Germans are melting away from day to day . . .
and their feverish activity and frightful sacrifice of life shows that they
know the desperate nature of their position.
—*Toronto Daily News,* Wednesday, February 24, 1915

DOCTORS TO SEE CARRIE DAVIES
SHE PLEADED NOT GUILTY WHEN CASE WAS OPENED THIS AFTERNOON
INDICATIONS ARE THAT THE DEFENCE OFFERED WILL BE INSANITY
—*Toronto Daily News,* Wednesday, February 24, 1915

C arrie would never fully appreciate how lucky she was to have Herbert Hartley Dewart, KC, as her defence counsel. She was fortunate not because Dewart was already a distinguished member of the Toronto bar, but because her high-profile case was particularly enticing for him.

It was pure chance that Dewart was Carrie's legal representative. When her brother-in-law Ed Fairchild heard from the *Tely*'s Archie Fisher that Carrie had been arrested, he was both horrified and helpless. What did a bricklayer know about the Ontario bar? Ed had gone to James Wickett, his employer, on the morning after the killing and asked him to recommend a lawyer. His employer scribbled down the address of a solicitor called Henry Wilberforce Maw, who handled the bread and butter of a busy legal partnership—house and land sales, wills, civil suits. Clutching the scrap of paper, Ed had then found his way to the Home Life Building, an imposing nine-storey brownstone building on the northwest corner of Adelaide and Victoria Streets, two blocks south of City Hall. There, he knocked on a door on which was painted in gold letters: "Dewart, Maw & Hodgson." A clerk opened the door, listened to the agitated bricklayer stutter out Carrie's sad tale, and invited Ed to wait in an outer office while he consulted Mr. Maw. After a short wait, the clerk returned and told Ed to follow him into Mr. Maw's office. Henry Maw asked the breathless, unhappy Ed to sit down and explain what this was all about. Ed Fairchild repeated his story as Henry Maw listened, nodding gravely and silently wondering who would pay for the young woman's defence. Nevertheless, after asking a few questions, he agreed to look into Carrie's case, though he couldn't make any promises.

That evening, Henry Maw had made his way to the city morgue on Lombard Street to hear Coroner Arthur Jukes Johnson open the inquest into Bert Massey's death. Once Maw had grasped the outlines of the Carrie Davies case, he knew that his partner, who handled all courtroom work, would love this case. It touched on two sensitive issues in Dewart's past.

Hartley Dewart was such a familiar figure around Toronto that even distant acquaintances referred to him as "Hartley." Born in 1861 and a graduate of Toronto's best public schools and the University of Toronto, he was shrewd enough to recognize that law was his ticket into the city's educated elite and the stepping stone to a political career. Up until the mid-1880s, legal education in Ontario had been rudimentary, consisting of office apprenticeships, rote learning, and slavish adherence to precedents. The Law Society of Upper Canada, housed since 1829 in Osgoode Hall, the elegant Queen Street building, had sometimes offered courses of lectures, but initially shied away from requiring Ontario's legal students to attend them. Only in 1889 was a formal three-year bachelor of laws (LL.B.) program for university graduates established. (The first school at which common law was taught in Canada was Dalhousie Law School in Halifax, which had opened in 1883.) Dewart had studied at Osgoode, but emerged from its library with sufficient qualifications to start practising two years earlier, in 1887, when he was twenty-six.

By the dawn of the twentieth century, many other ambitious young lawyers had followed Dewart's route into the tightly woven network of Toronto lawyers, where family connections were as important as they had been in the pre-Confederation days of the Family Compact. By 1915, when Hartley Dewart had been in practice for more than a quarter of a century, the city had over 660 lawyers, of whom about a third were in solo practice. It was a homogeneous profession, dominated by men of Scottish or English origin and including only a handful of Jews. The exclusiveness of the profession was most starkly illustrated by the fact that in the *Canadian Law List* for the City of Toronto in 1915 there was only one woman: Clara Brett Martin. When Martin first applied to Osgoode, an outraged and deeply conservative bencher harrumphed that her admission would prove "disastrous to the best interests of women," and that anyway, no self-respecting woman of fashion would want to wear the official robes of a litigator. It had taken a lot of courage for her to pry open Osgoode Hall's elaborate gates. "I was looked on as an interloper, if not a curiosity," she later wrote. She had been one of the women who lobbied for the Women's Court at City Hall.

The city's most prestigious lawyers had their offices in the multi-storey brownstones, built in the previous couple of decades within walking distance of City Hall, the courthouse, and the men's clubs. The building boom had been financed by the banks, investment houses, and insurance companies that were doing so well. There were twenty-two law firms in the handsome Confederation Life Building, for example, and ten in the Canada Life Building. Most partnerships included only two or three lawyers, but a handful of larger and more muscular ones were already emerging, and most included at least two generations of the same family. In the Dominion Bank Building, McCarthy, Osler, Hoskin & Harcourt numbered six KCs on its brass plate and included three McCarthys and two Oslers among the nine lawyers. In the Bank of Commerce Building, Blake, Lash, Anglin & Cassels boasted three KCs among its eleven lawyers, who included three Lashes and two Casselses. These lawyers were corporate advisers and governmental confidants: their powerful connections into the provincial and federal governments, the banks, trust companies, insurance companies, and brokerage and investment houses guaranteed a steady flow of clients. Outsiders, like the Jewish partnership of Abraham Cohen & Ephraim Sugarman in the Sun Life Building, or Clara Brett Martin on Adelaide Street, rarely got a whiff of this lucrative business.

In contrast, Hartley Dewart moved comfortably through this world. He had excellent contacts: like Sir William Mulock, he was a solid Liberal with an ardent admiration for Sir Wilfrid Laurier. As a student, he had helped establish and then run the Young Men's Liberal Club, and he had run unsuccessfully in two federal elections, in 1904 and 1911. He also shared the chief justice's impatience with United Empire Loyalist pretensions, a belief in Canada's future as an autonomous North American nation, and a vehement dislike of the Prohibition movement. Dewart often displayed an Irish skepticism about the benefits of the British Empire.

At social events, you always knew where Hartley was in the crowd— he was wherever people were chuckling. Now fifty-four, he was charming, with a jaunty youthfulness and dry humour. He remained active within his alma mater as an examiner in English and a member of the university senate. His name remained in play as a possible candidate for either the provincial legislature or the federal Parliament. Strangers liked him—he was once described in *Saturday Night* magazine as "one of the most genial and popular young men in Toronto."

Hartley Dewart's colleagues all agreed that he was a sharp-witted lawyer, and the partnership of Dewart, Maw & Hodgson thrived. Even by the standards of the period, its client list was particularly rich. Dewart, the senior partner, acted in both criminal and civil cases. He was counsel to several banks and insurance companies, and to both the Canadian Pacific Railway and the Toronto Railway Company. His success had allowed him to purchase a farm near Uxbridge and a spacious mansion at 5 Elmsley Place, close to the university and surrounded by elm trees. He and his wife, Emma, filled their homes with a magnificent collection of antiques, including several paintings by William Hogarth and a huge oak four-poster bed in which Queen Elizabeth I was said to have slept. The Toronto Golf Club, the Toronto Hunt Club, the Ontario Club, and the Toronto Club had all welcomed him as a member. It was a well-upholstered life.

Yet by 1915, unrealized ambitions and his fondness for the bottle were beginning to sour Dewart. Those closer to the tall, lean, elegantly dressed lawyer had always known he had an irascible streak under the boyish charm, and he could be ornery, especially when he had a drink in his hand and a bee in his bonnet. He refused to toe party lines when his party endorsed temperance, and his disdain for imperialism didn't sit well with fellow Liberals. In court or political debate, people pulled away from him when he became pugnacious and uncompromising. He and his wife were childless, almost certainly not by choice. And he had never escaped the shadow of a famous father—a controversial Methodist clergyman who had crossed swords with the mighty Methodist *extraordinaire*, Hart Massey.

Hartley's father, Edward Hartley Dewart, was an Irish-born convert to Methodism who had become an ordained preacher in Upper Canada when he was in his twenties. The Reverend Dewart epitomized nineteenth-century Methodism at its most rigid and repressive. Eyes blazing and broad forehead gleaming in the candlelight of small stone churches, he exhorted fellow Methodists to seek salvation and abjure free thinking, sin, and whiskey. He also promoted Canadian literature, publishing one of the very first anthologies of Canadian verse in 1864. Five years later, he was named editor of the official Methodist newspaper, the *Christian Guardian,* which was required reading in thousands of Canadian households. But his editorials grew increasingly grumpy and conservative over the next thirty years. Dewart Senior thundered against the insidious creep of modern thinking, which questioned Old

Testament prophets and Biblical certainties. One of his contemporaries described how Edward Hartley Dewart "rained sledge-hammer blows [of] argument" upon opponents. The young Herbert Hartley Dewart was a smoother debater than his father, and he had cast off the Reverend Dewart's aversion to alcohol. But he had inherited his father's rhetorical passion, as well as his desire to see Canada develop as an independent nation.

Dewart Senior's fight with Hart Massey erupted in 1888, over the future of Victoria College, Ontario's most important Methodist educational establishment. At the time, Victoria College occupied an elegant Greek Revival building in the middle of the little lakeside port of Cobourg, one hundred kilometres east of Toronto. Founded in 1836 as an egalitarian challenge to the Anglican upper crust of Toronto, it boasted celebrated divines such as Egerton Ryerson and Nathanael Burwash among its principals. But by the 1880s it had fallen on hard times, and in the *Christian Guardian* the Reverend Dewart argued that the college should move to Toronto and become part of the University of Toronto federation of colleges that William Mulock was then promoting. For Edward Dewart, the transfer would boost the Methodist crusade against immorality: Methodism would reinforce the right values in the dangerously open-minded atmosphere of university life. "No modern culture," Dewart argued, "can be safely substituted for the fire and faith of the early Methodists."

However, another faction of powerful Methodists, including Hart Massey, regarded the proposed move as an Anglican takeover of the school. The ruthless patriarch of the farm machinery business tried to block it by offering $250,000 ($7.5 million in today's currency) to keep Victoria College in Cobourg. Despite the dangled donation, the move went ahead—but not before the Toronto press had savaged all Methodists, including both Hart Massey and Hartley Dewart Senior. A vicious series in the *Toronto World* alleged that Dewart had supported

Massey in a ruthless stock deal years earlier, in the hope of receiving financial donations to the *Christian Guardian*. Dewart was outraged: he and the Masseys had been on opposing sides of the Victoria College battle, and now his name had been dragged through the mud. The Dewarts did not forget.

The Carrie Davies case offered Hartley Dewart, KC, a chance to settle an old score with the Masseys.

There was another reason why Carrie's case had a particular attraction for Hartley Dewart. It reminded him of a notorious murder case in which he had been involved twenty years earlier, when he was a junior Crown counsel and a brilliant defence lawyer called Ebenezer Forsyth Blackie Johnston had run rings around the Crown.

This was the case of Clara Ford, a sturdy black seamstress who in 1895 had confessed to killing the son of a wealthy Toronto family. Dewart had watched with astonishment as the senior Crown prosecutor, the well-regarded Britton Bath Osler, floundered on what everyone thought was an open-and-shut case. Osler was a hero in Anglo-Protestant Toronto: he was the lawyer who had successfully prosecuted Louis Riel a decade earlier. As the dignified, courteous Mr. Osler laid out the evidence against Clara Ford, her chances of avoiding the noose seemed slim. She pleaded not guilty, but she had confessed to the murder, and she shocked observers with her refusal to display the feminine delicacy expected of women. In fact, she was downright aggressive. Before her trial, rumours had spread about her penchant for wearing men's clothes, brandishing a gun, and getting into fights. One newspaper asserted that she jumped onto streetcars "like a man," another hinted that she liked eating raw meat, and racist and sexist innuendoes reverberated in references to her "African blood" and checkered past.

Yet Dewart saw the Crown's case slipping away in the face of Blackie Johnston's adroit performance. Despite Clara Ford's confession, Johnston made her the heroine of a powerful tale. Ford, in his version, was a poor girl who had been wronged by a rich villain, and then forced into a false confession by unscrupulous detectives who were only interested in advancing their own careers. Johnston demonstrated his own selflessness and chivalry by offering to represent her without fees. Clara's new image, as a penniless woman who had been mistreated by an upper-class rake and was now on trial for her life, excited a groundswell of sympathy amongst Toronto's working classes. Popular distaste for a cross-dressing immigrant who swore like a trooper was forgotten, and Clara became the victim, claiming that a big-city detective had "kept repeating I was in a net . . . The more I denied, the more he pressed me to confess. At last, I said I did it."

Osler struggled to make the charge stick, but Johnston was unstoppable. And then the inexperienced Dewart found himself taking on Blackie Johnston in person. Osler's wife suddenly died halfway through the trial, so Osler's junior had to stand up and conduct the case for the Crown. Dewart spent three hours cross-examining Clara in the hope of poking holes in the new story of the "forced" confession. But it was in vain. He was followed by Johnston at full throttle, the latter reminding the jury in his closing remarks that the jury must return a verdict of "murder or nothing." Johnston asked the twelve men if they were prepared to accept the awful responsibility of sending a poor, wronged woman to the gallows. The jury acquitted Clara.

People have always been fascinated by violent crimes. And Blackie Johnston was in the great tradition of barristers, on both sides of the Atlantic, who deliberately played into that public fascination.

For years, British barristers had charted the intersection of murder and popular culture and treated courtrooms as theatres in which they enacted dramas. Nineteenth-century lawyers had plenty of material to draw on, as real-life events morphed into crowd-pleasing melodrama. The story of Eliza Fenning, a cook in London, was a typical example. When Fenning was convicted of poisoning her employers and hanged in 1815, as many as forty-five thousand watched her execution outside Newgate prison. Eliza's story re-emerged in 1844 as a play entitled *The Maid, the Master and the Murderer.* In 1858, the outlines of Fenning's case reappeared in a story by Wilkie Collins published in Charles Dickens's magazine *Household Words.* Dickens himself, who frequently attended executions, titillated his readers with gruesome murders in short stories and in several of his novels, notably *Oliver Twist.* By the 1890s, readers were hooked on murders, especially when the villains were identified by fiendishly clever fictional detectives like Sherlock Holmes (who had made his first appearance in 1887). Fictional accounts of murders featured stock characters—innocent maidens, untrustworthy foreigners, helpless women, honest workmen, or wealthy cads. Defence lawyers used versions of these one-dimensional stereotypes in the narratives they shaped for juries.

Canadians shared the taste for murder: books by Dickens and Arthur Conan Doyle were bestsellers on this side of the Atlantic, especially among British immigrants. But by Carrie's day, a unique brand of crime fiction had evolved here, featuring two aspects of the country that enthralled outsiders: its wilderness, and its North West Mounted Police as incorruptible heroes. (The villain was often winter weather.) The first serial character in Canadian crime fiction was Corporal Cameron of the North West Mounted Police, launched in 1912 by the bestselling author Charles Gordon, a Presbyterian minister whose pen name was Ralph Connor. The same year, the Mounties' image got a jolt of hero-worship from the ballad "The Riders of the Plains" by Mohawk poet Pauline Johnson (Tekahionwake):

> For these are the kind whose muscle makes the power of
>   the Lion's jaw,
> And they keep the peace of our people and the honour
>   of British law.

All melodrama celebrates the triumph of virtue, but Canadians' glorification of the Mounties reflected respect for law and morality. Canadian readers enjoyed police procedurals even more than grisly murder mysteries, and they ate up black-and-white morality tales. The simplistic crime reporting from Toronto's police court provided by the *Tely*'s Harry Wodson and his colleagues fed this appetite.

Blackie Johnston knew all about the public taste for melodrama. His forte as a Canadian defence lawyer was to construct a convincing theory of innocence for his client, and then to tailor every question in his cross-examination to support his portrayal of Clara Ford as a wronged damsel and her victim as a debauched scoundrel. By the time he had finished his defence, jurors could almost hear the wicked cackle of the victim—now transformed into a villain.

Johnston had served a year as honorary president of the Canadian Bar Association in 1911, and Dewart (who was elected a bencher of the Law Society of Upper Canada the same year) had heard him discuss his methods. As the elderly lawyer liked to remind colleagues, he never asked a question to which he did not know the answer, and he never allowed a witness to lead him off in an unplanned direction. The job of a defence lawyer, insisted Johnston, was to weaken his opponent's arguments and win his client's acquittal, and his witnesses were carefully rehearsed. To expose truth or falsehood was not his job, and he rarely spoke directly to a client accused of murder. Instead, he wove together a compelling script from the facts gathered by his juniors, then treated the jury with Uriah Heep–like deference as he staged his storytelling magic. His case for the defence always captivated the popular imagination. There was little defence for Clara Ford in the letter of the law, but an appeal to the jury's hearts had overridden that technicality.

Hartley Dewart never forgot his defeat at Blackie Johnston's hands. Moreover, nervous little Carrie was a much more virtuous heroine than belligerent Clara Ford. Twenty years after Dewart had lost the Ford case, Carrie's case offered him the chance to prove himself the equal of the great Ebenezer Blackie Johnston in playing the coveted role of defender of wounded womanhood. If he won, he would be the envy of his peers and the talk of the town. All in all, the prospect of emerging as the victor in a David-and-Goliath battle against the mighty Masseys was irresistible.

But to win, Dewart had to develop a storyline for Carrie, and the clock was ticking. The winter session of the Ontario Supreme Court was due to wind up within days—it had already extended its sitting by two weeks. Nevertheless, both the Crown and Chief Justice Mulock had let it be known that they wanted to deal with Carrie this month, rather than letting the case and its attendant publicity fester for several weeks until the spring session opened in April. Carrie's case would be heard with a rapidity that was unusual in 1915 and would be unheard of today.

CHAPTER 12

Fallen Angels

WEDNESDAY, FEBRUARY 24 TO THURSDAY, FEBRUARY 25

German submersibles have scored again. The British steamer "Oakby,"
going "light" from London to Cardiff, Wales, was torpedoed and sunk and
the crew landed all safe today at Ramsgate. A Berlin report that a British transport
had been sunk probably referred to the government collier "Branksome Chine,"
destroyed off Beachy Head yesterday.
—*Toronto Daily News*, Wednesday, February 24, 1915

HEARST HEARS OLD STORY

PROMISES "CONSIDERATION"

PROSPECTS FOR VOTES FOR WOMEN AT A WAR SESSION NOT VERY

BRIGHT BUT THERE WAS NO ROW

Canada was rapidly becoming a nation, said Dr. Stowe Gullen. It was high time that
Canada recognized the rights of women . . . The war would not have occurred if women
had equal rights in the world and had a chance to direct affairs.
—*Evening Telegram*, Wednesday, February 24, 1915

At the second police court hearing, Dewart had entered a plea of not guilty on Carrie's behalf. But how could her defence team justify that plea? What were the choices facing Hartley Dewart, as he sat at his desk in the Home Life Building and started to map out his strategy to rescue Carrie from a murder rap?

Dewart was well aware that his options were limited. If Carrie were found guilty of murder, the only punishment in law was the mandatory death penalty. However, Dewart also knew that, even if his client was convicted, she was unlikely to hang. Since Confederation, close to half a century earlier, only twenty-one women, compared to 555 men, had been convicted of murder and had faced the death sentence. Most female convictions involved miserable stories of family abuse and social stigma, with violent husbands or unwanted children as the victims, and judges and juries had chosen to be lenient. Such women were more to be pitied than punished, in the eyes of the community if not the law. In the wake of all twenty-one murder convictions, petitions for clemency were sent to the governor general in Ottawa (although the minister of justice in fact made the decision): eighteen of the death sentences had been commuted to manslaughter and the women given prison sentences. Only three of the twenty-one women swung from the gallows.

But a woman who killed her employer in cold blood presented a different and more serious kind of challenge. The closest precedent to

Carrie's case augured ill for Carrie. Hilda Blake, a twenty-one-year-old English-born domestic servant in Brandon, Manitoba, shot and killed her employer's wife in July 1899. Local newspapers went over the top in their relish for bloody details. The *Western Sun* described the killing as "one of the most atrocious crimes in the annals of Manitoba's history and one of the most villainous that ever occurred in the Dominion of Canada." Although Hilda was an attractive woman who may have been seduced by her employer, she had allegedly destroyed the kind of Victorian marriage idealized in literature, and her crime left four young children motherless. She was sentenced to hang. In Ottawa, Prime Minister Laurier refused to commute the sentence to life imprisonment, despite arguments in her favour from no less an advocate than Governor General Lord Minto.

The outcome fit all the demands of melodrama. On December 27, 1899, before twenty-five ticket holders in a small enclosure just outside Brandon courthouse, Hilda was hanged. She put on a brave show, climbing the steps to the noose with "her head erect and her bearing that of a young lady going to an evening party, rather than the gallows," according to the *Winnipeg Morning Telegram*. The press revelled in the grim drama. "She was ashy pale, but completely composed and plucky to the end," intoned the *Winnipeg Free Press*. Nevertheless, the paper showed little sympathy for the penniless domestic.

Hilda Blake had refused legal counsel. Carrie Davies had one of the best barristers in Toronto. Could clever Hartley Dewart save her?

One option was for Dewart to offer a plea of not guilty on grounds of insanity—the plea that the Masseys would like to hear, so the story could be buried. The first comprehensive Canadian Criminal Code, passed by Parliament in 1892, made a specific provision for such a plea if the accused was "laboring under natural imbecility or disease of the mind." But what did this mean? The House of Commons committee that debated the new Criminal Code had spent more time struggling with a definition of insanity than with any other clause in the lengthy bill, and it remained controversial. Courts were notoriously leery of accepting that an individual was incapable of knowing the difference between right and wrong. Besides, the Don Jail's Dr. Owen Parry had already dismissed the suggestion that Carrie Davies was epileptic or obviously unstable. "I have her in the hospital ward and she is under observation," he told reporters. He considered her "perfectly rational so far as we can determine . . . She drinks a quart of milk every day and is in fine condition physically."

Dewart could suggest to his client that she make a plea to the reduced charge of manslaughter. Such a plea would eliminate even the possibility of the gallows, but if found guilty she likely faced a long stretch in jail. However, a manslaughter plea had none of the brio of Blackie Johnston's "murder or nothing" appeal to the jury in the Clara Ford case.

It was possible that the jury might come up with a third verdict: that she was not guilty because, in the jurors' minds, there were compelling extenuating circumstances. For this, Carrie would have to plead not guilty, despite all the evidence that she had deliberately fired the fatal shot. Only a not-guilty plea would generate the excitement that the Clara Ford case had enjoyed. Only a not-guilty plea would respond to all the different demands on this case—including the ambition of Hartley Dewart, the public sympathy for Carrie, and the crusading zeal of John Ross Robertson's *Evening Telegram*. Only a heroic defence would ramp up contributions to the Carrie Davies Defence Fund, increase the *Tely*'s circulation, and pay Dewart's fee.

The *Tely* continued to track donations to the fund, but William Goldsmith, secretary of the Bedfordshire Fraternal Association, acknowledged that the flow was sluggish. Most of the donations were tiny, and by Wednesday, February 24, only $249.05 had been collected. Contributors included "A Working Woman, $2; 'Justice' $2;

'Bedfordshire to Aid' 25 cents; 'Two Business Girls,' 50 cents; Mr. and Mrs. Hall, $2; two Englishmen, $2." A list of those who had contributed one dollar included "Another Funny-looking English Girl," "One of those Funny-looking English Girls," "An English Girl," "Every Little Helps," "Well-Wisher," "Canadian Girl," and "A Few Lovers of British Fair Play and Justice." Mr. Goldsmith fretted: "May we ask for a more generous and urgent response for this worthy case?" The amount raised was paltry compared to the $22,912 the Ontario branch of Grand Trunk Railway employees announced, on the same day, it had raised for Sir William Mulock's Patriotic Fund.

But on what grounds could Hartley Dewart make a not-guilty plea on Carrie's behalf? A recent Ontario case suggested that self-defence because of a fear of *future* violence was a shaky line of argument. In 1911 in Sault Ste. Marie, a pregnant Italian mother of four children had taken an axe to her sleeping husband. Twenty-eight-year-old Angelina Napolitano had been abused for years: six months earlier, her husband, Pietro, had stabbed her nine times, scarring her face, shoulder, and neck. Pietro had now demanded that she earn some money by selling her body so he could build a house. Angelina had apparently snapped. But when her case went to court, despite her scars and her trauma, she was found guilty because the judge ruled that "if anybody injured six months ago could give that as justification or excuse for slaying a person, it would be anarchy complete." She was sentenced to hang three months later—to allow her time to give birth. Only an international outcry persuaded the minister of justice in Ottawa to commute her sentence to life imprisonment.

Hartley Dewart carefully scrutinized the notes that Henry Maw had made of his conversations with Carrie Davies when he visited her in Don Jail. Undeterred by the Napolitano verdict, he and Maw began to sketch the outlines of a plea on the grounds of "self-defence," the words that Carrie had uttered when the police first arrested her immediately after the shooting. The arguments against the plea were strong. Carrie was not under attack when she shot Bert Massey; it had been close to thirty-six hours since her employer had pawed at her. Moreover, Bert had been unarmed, several feet away from her, and completely unaware of the danger when she fired. But Carrie was a timid British immigrant rather than an inarticulate Italian—a "hot-blooded foreigner," as the *Sault Star* had described Angelina Napolitano. Dewart had a plan.

~

At Don Jail, Carrie remained in the prison hospital, better fed and rested than she had been for most of her life. To Dr. Parry, she seemed curiously indifferent to her predicament. He told the reporters who clustered day and night around the Don's wooden gates, "She is in good spirits and chats with the nurses in the ward." She would have heard the whispered gossip among staff and fellow inmates about her case, although newspapers were not allowed in the jail. Her sister or brother-in-law visited her when they could, and perhaps their accounts of public donations to the Carrie Davies Defence Fund allowed her to believe that she would not be convicted.

But sixteen days after she was arrested, she had a jolting reminder of what lay ahead. On Wednesday, February 24, she and Miss Carmichael were bundled into a police wagon and she returned for the third time to City Hall. But this time, instead of facing Colonel Denison, whippet-thin in a dark business suit, she found herself in the larger presence of the chief justice, in crow-black robes, with a thick, trimmed beard almost as white as his starched cravat. Carrie's appearance today was a formality: it was her arraignment, in which Hartley Dewart entered a plea of not guilty on her behalf and declared that he needed a few days before the case was heard because he had made arrangements with "several medical men to examine his client." Chief Justice William Mulock watched over the top of his wire-framed glasses as Dewart negotiated a timetable with Crown prosecutor Edward Du Vernet, the lawyer who would make the case against Carrie. No one paid any attention to the accused herself, as she sat silently, watching three men debate her fate.

Dewart asked for the case to start the following Monday at the earliest, and assured the court that the case would be closed in two days. Dewart, Du Vernet, and Chief Justice Mulock were all eager to deal with Carrie as quickly as possible. Finally, in a deep, loud voice, the chief justice announced he would hear the case on Friday.

Dewart's talk of "medical men" suggested to observers that, once again, Carrie's sanity was going to be tested by "alienists," like Dr. Beemer from Mimico's Hospital for the Insane. The *Toronto Daily News* announced in a front-page headline, "Doctors to See Carrie Davies . . . Indications are That the Defence Offered Will be Insanity."

The *Daily News* was wrong. The two physicians who arrived at the Don Jail the following day to examine the eighteen-year-old were not looking for evidence of insanity. For Carrie Davies, the arrival of Dr. Andrew Harrington and Dr. Duncan Anderson was simply one more episode in her alarming experience with medical professionals. After being manhandled on Toronto Island the previous summer by the Masseys' doctor, then facing the Bertillon calipers after her first court appearance on February 8, she now underwent yet another intrusive examination. The two physicians, both well-established family doctors in Toronto, were met at the door of the jail by Dr. Parry and escorted through the jail's dank corridors up to the hospital wing, where Carrie was waiting in a windowless examination room.

Dr. Harrington asked Miss Carmichael and Dr. Parry to wait outside. Shutting the door behind him, the doctor told the eighteen-year-old to remove her underwear and lie on the iron cot with her legs apart. Then he took from his black bag an instrument that looked like a pair of blunt scissors with bent ends. He inserted this vaginal dilator into

Carrie's vagina and peered inside. He may also have examined her manually. Next, his colleague did exactly the same. Then they stood back, told her to get dressed, and left the room. Did they guard against contamination when they performed this unexpected procedure in the jail's filthy surrounds? Perhaps. Although rubber surgical gloves had been in widespread use for about twenty years, there was still resistance to them. Did they tell Carrie what they were checking for? Probably not. They did not tell the jail personnel, either. Instead, Dr. Harrington wrote a quick note to Hartley Dewart.

Dewart must have been elated when he opened the note and read the brief message inside. The doctors confirmed that Carrie Davies was a virgin.

Virginity defined a woman in Carrie's era. It was fetishized in a way that is hard to believe today—unless we look at some of the fundamentalist sects of Christianity or Islam. Virginity and purity were synonymous, and Toronto in 1915 was a society in which seams of hypocrisy and prudery ran deep. Only a few days earlier, the manager of the Toronto exhibition grounds had triggered outrage when he authorized a poster that featured the figure of a female angel taken from a painting by Raphael in the Sistine Chapel. The city's Moral Reform Association complained to Colonel Denison, the police magistrate, that the image was obscene since Raphael had given the angel only a pair of wings and a wreath of roses to hide her nakedness. Angels, in Carrie's day, had to be fully clad and unflinchingly demure—and the same was expected of decent women.

If a woman lost her virginity before marriage, she had forfeited the right to be considered "pure"; in fact, she had become a pariah or, in the euphemisms of the period, a "fallen angel" or a "soiled dove." Men could not be expected to control their natural impulses if a woman had lost her virtue, so a "fallen angel" was fair game for male seducers because she was already corrupted. This was true for unmarried women at all levels of society—for the daughters of Toronto's Fine Old Ontario Families as much as for servants like Carrie. It was the standard to which Carrie herself clung when she feared that an assault by her employer would lead to her "ruin" because she would be instantly transformed into little more than a prostitute.

Hartley Dewart knew exactly how to use this medical evidence. He would weave a story in which his client's purity made Bert Massey the pariah in this case.

Almost certainly, Dewart shared the contents of Dr. Harrington's note with young Arthur Roebuck in his office at the Home Life Building, knowing the news would be transmitted to John Ross Robertson at the *Evening Telegram*. The trial of Carrie Davies on a charge of murder would start within twenty-four hours, on Friday, February 26. Her counsel was ready.

PART THREE

The Trial

CHAPTER 13

"A Most Unpleasant Duty"

FRIDAY, FEBRUARY 26

9,000 CANADIANS INCLUDING ALL THE TORONTO REGIMENTS
IN ACTION SUNDAY
FIRST AND THIRD BRIGADES WERE IN TRENCHES ALL SUNDAY, AND
WERE ENGAGED PRACTICALLY ALL THE TIME THEY WERE THERE
PRINCESS PATS GRADUALLY DRIVING THE GERMANS BACK.
—*Toronto Daily Star*, Wednesday, February 24, 1915

WOMAN WEAK AND NERVOUS. FINDS HEALTH IN LYDIA E. PINKHAM'S
VEGETABLE COMPOUND . . .
*For forty years this famous root and herb medicine has been pre-eminently successful
in controlling the diseases of women. If you have the slightest doubt that Lydia E.
Pinkham's Vegetable Compound will help you, write for advice. Your letter will be
opened, read and answered by a woman, and held in strict confidence.*
—*Evening Telegram*, Friday, February 26, 1915

Police officers, lawyers, court officials, and clerks were braced for the crowd that converged on City Hall on the final Friday of February 1915. Nevertheless, there was an unholy hubbub outside the building for Act III of the Carrie Davies drama, in which her fate would be decided. No case in living memory had captured the public imagination and stirred up the city like the one due to be heard that day. Reporters from all six Toronto newspapers, representatives of various women's organizations, concerned citizens, and idle gawkers all crowded around the narrow wooden doorway into the courtroom where Chief Justice Mulock would hear the case. The sounds of various regional British accents and the smells of damp woollen coats and nervous sweat were suffocating.

At eleven o'clock, two policemen shouldered their way through the crowd, unlocked the door, and tried to control the surge of people. Carrie's sister Maud Fairchild was given a reserved seat behind the bar at the front of the court; her husband, Ed, was going to be called as a witness, so he did not join her. Reporters quickly crammed into the press box and searched the crowd for familiar faces. There appeared to be no Massey present: Rhoda Massey, Bert's widow, was still in seclusion in her brother-in-law's Admiral Road house. The smooth young lawyer, Arthur Thomson, was probably in court, but the press made no note of his presence. Proceedings were now out of Massey hands, and no Massey had been called as a witness.

Newspaper artists took out pads and pencils, ready to catch the likenesses of all the main players. As soon as the public benches were full, the police barred the way to everybody else. Once the crowd of three hundred spectators was settled, the prisoner was led to the dock from an entrance close to the judge's dais accompanied by two escorts: Miss Minty, from the Toronto Police, and a Salvation Army matron.

When Carrie Davies appeared, there was a crescendo of whispered comments; spectators close to the press box watched the newspaper artists sketching furiously. Next, the jury and the two legal teams filed in. Crown prosecutor Edward Du Vernet and Carrie's defence lawyer, Hartley Dewart, both tall, thin men with bony faces and bald heads, looked like a pair of vultures in their black silk robes. Du Vernet sat at the table facing the chief justice and the court reporter to the right of the dais; Dewart, accompanied by Henry Maw, sat to the judge's left. Before Dewart sat down, he smiled at his client, took her hand, and asked how she was. Carrie's reply was audible to reporters: "All right."

For Du Vernet and Dewart, the courtroom was as familiar as their offices and clubs. But for Carrie, this court was even more nerve-rackingly formal than either Colonel Denison's police court or the coroner's inquest. Spectators and lawyers rose to their feet as Chief Justice William Mulock, in flowing robes, swept in. Placing his hands on his elevated desk, he cast an unsmiling eye over the crowded courtroom as the clerk of the court read aloud the formulaic statement that had opened judicial hearings in English law courts for centuries: "Oyez, oyez, oyez. Anyone having business before the King's Justice of the Assize Court, attend now and you shall be heard. Long live the King!" Once the crowd was seated and hushed, Mulock called for the jury to be admitted.

The court clerk rose and read out the formal indictment. "Caroline Anne Davies, you are charged that on the eighth day of February this year, you murdered Charles Albert Massey. How say you, are you guilty or not guilty?"

Dewart sprung out of his chair: "Not guilty."

For the next two days, two different versions of Bert Massey's death, and the circumstances surrounding it, would be batted back and forth across the courtroom. Which was closest to the truth? Only the opinions of the twelve members of the jury mattered, but everybody watching the proceedings made their judgments. Reporters and editors played their role in spinning the story. The *Toronto Daily Star* and the *Toronto Daily News* paid closest attention to prosecution counsel Du Vernet's arguments, while the *Evening Telegram* devoted pages to defence counsel Hartley Dewart's questions and commentary. (An advance copy of Dewart's address to the jury was probably slipped to the *Tely*, since its coverage was so exhaustive.)

Initially, all observers agreed that Carrie looked anxious (who wouldn't be, facing a murder charge?), but while allies within the press saw a young woman at risk, others remarked on her composure. The *Star* noted, "When she was placed in the dock, a faint smile played about her mouth. She was pale and painfully nervous, but bore up with a perfectly blank expression in her eyes while the jurors were sworn in to take her fate in their hands." The *Globe* described her as "looking a trifle pale, but calm and self-possessed." The *Toronto Daily News* reported that she looked "anything but jaunty or confident . . . Her clothes were plain and not exactly up to the latest fashion, in fact she was far from being attractively dressed . . . She smiled only once."

Hartley Dewart had already shaped the jury he wanted during the jury selection process by objecting to eight of the men who had been called as potential jurors. On what grounds he objected, and whether Du Vernet made any objections, was never reported. But thanks to

Dewart's careful choices, most of those selected lived outside downtown Toronto and all were well into middle age. There were no Bert Massey clones—businessmen in their thirties—on the jury. The final list included George Robbins (gardener), John Oldham (farmer), Samuel Miller (farmer), George Foster (farmer), William Webster (plasterer), Newman Wagstaff (machinist), Fred W. Carter (farmer), John Molloy (farmer), Arthur Pherrill (farmer), Chauncey Walker (tailor), Jerome Campbell (farmer), and James Johnstone (farmer). There was a disproportionate number of farmers for a city trial—in fact, it could have been a roll call from a rural jury in Carrie's Bedfordshire hometown.

Dressed in their Sunday suits, and uncomfortable in the formality of the court, the men stared uneasily at the eager throng of spectators and the white-faced prisoner. They were Carrie's social peers—as opposed to the lawyers, magistrate, newspaper editors, and Masseys who had, until this minute, controlled Carrie's fate in both the legal system and the press. None of the jury members had studied together at Osgoode Hall, mingled with each other at the National or Toronto Club, met at society weddings at St. James' Cathedral or the Metropolitan Methodist Church, or visited each other's summer homes in Muskoka or the Kawarthas. The court rituals were as unfamiliar to them as they were to Carrie.

After the court clerk had read the murder charge, Carrie's lawyer rose and asked the chief justice if the prisoner might leave the dock and sit at the defence counsel's table. Dewart knew this would remind a sympathetic crowd of Carrie's youthful vulnerability, even though he also knew what the judge's answer would be. Sure enough, Mulock curtly replied that, because she was charged with a capital offence, "it cannot be done."

Next, Edward Du Vernet rose and opened the Crown's case against the accused. Like Hartley Dewart, Du Vernet had considered his arguments carefully. Extensive newspaper coverage and intense public interest meant he must tread a narrow line. He had to avoid any appearance of undue harshness towards the eighteen-year-old immigrant, all the while pressing the Crown's murder charge. She had, after all, killed a man. So he turned to the jury and informed them that this case was "the most unpleasant duty I have had to perform during my career, to prosecute this young girl for murder. But I must do my duty and you must do yours. I want you to take your impressions of the details of this case solely from the witnesses. I want you to be like pieces of white blotting paper which have had no imprint. You must put aside all the ideas of the case which you have already formed and you must forget the opinions you have heard outside. You must not think of the articles concerning this case which you have read in the newspapers."

Finally, Du Vernet pinpointed the question that he wanted the jury to answer: Was there sufficient justification for Carrie's act? "It is not a question whether Mr. Charles Albert Massey was killed or if Carrie Davies killed him." Like Dewart, Du Vernet knew the jury would shrink from sending Carrie to the gallows. He read out sections from the Criminal Code that permitted the charge to be reduced from murder to manslaughter if sudden provocation was proved, or in cases of self-defence. But he also declared, "Life is sacred, and the law says any person who takes another's life is always held accountable."

"Many men may go a certain distance and not want to break the law," the Crown prosecutor said. Carrie had fled 169 Walmer Road after Bert Massey had made his fumbling assault, but she had returned the same night. "It seems that Mr. Massey did her no physical injury. Nothing was accomplished by him. He did not really assault her. It was not a serious offence for him to kiss her, although he should not have done so."

After minimizing Bert's offence, Du Vernet suggested that Carrie had carefully planned her attack on him. "There was a great deal of deliberation in all this. The girl takes this weapon; she puts five bullets into it. She goes downstairs. The man has not yet come in. She sees him on the street. She fires and he says, 'Oh!' She's missed him. There wouldn't be much inclination for a man to enter the house after that. But apparently she's not satisfied. She fires a second shot, which kills him. The assault that the girl spoke of took place on the previous day: it took all that time to formulate the plan which ended in the alleged murder."

Du Vernet tried to dilute the salacious aspects of the case by pointing out that, if this case had involved two men, the jury would have no difficulty in deciding on the verdict—it was a cowardly murder because the killer was armed and had planned the assault, and the victim was unarmed and taken by surprise. But he acknowledged that this case was different. "You must judge whether the girl was insulted. It is too bad that Mr. Massey is not here to state his side of the case. He has been called to a Higher Judge."

The Crown counsel recognized that Carrie had been provoked. But she had not acted in the heat of the moment when she shot her employer. In Carrie's favour, she had sought outside advice from her brother-in-law, who had advised her to return to Walmer Road but to be careful. This was probably the wrong advice, Du Vernet suggested, but it didn't excuse the death.

"If all this is true," Du Vernet concluded, "it seems to me that the death sentence would be rather severe. Give the benefit of the doubt to this girl as far as you can under your oaths." Manslaughter, he implied, was the appropriate verdict. But the law was the law, and a man was dead.

Crown prosecutor Du Vernet then called eight witnesses to confirm the details of the shooting. Spectators fidgeted as the mundane details of Bert Massey's death and subsequent events, all of which had been reported after the coroner's inquest, were once again trotted out. The newsboy, Ernest Pelletier, described hearing the shots just after his encounter with Massey. Sergeant Lawrence Brown repeated his account of Carrie's arrest, and Mrs. Nesbitt and Miss Beatrice Dinnis, the two women who had been walking down Walmer Road, described what they had witnessed. The medical evidence was given by Dr. John Mitchell, the physician who had pronounced Bert dead, and by Dr. J.E. Elliott, who had performed the post-mortem. There was an upsurge of interest when Dr. Elliott produced the small glass bottle containing the bullet that had killed Bert Massey. The twelve jurors inspected it with intense curiosity while spectators craned forward to catch a glimpse of the macabre object.

Carrie's lawyer, Dewart, cross-examined Dr. Elliott, and asked him whether the first or second bullet would have killed Massey. "He must have been facing the direction the bullet came from," replied the doctor, leading him to believe it must have been the first bullet that entered the chest, then caused the rupture of Massey's heart. Du Vernet's assertion that Carrie had missed the first time, so continued firing, did not fit the medical evidence. Dr. Elliott explained, "I think he would probably have lived for ten seconds"—enough time, Dewart ascertained, for him to stumble back to the Walmer Road sidewalk. The second bullet must have gone wide and been lost in the street.

Justice Mulock announced the court would adjourn for lunch and meet again at two o'clock. Spectators reluctantly left their seats, and the court clerk locked the door. By five minutes to two, according to the *Evening Telegram,* a "throng of people . . . struggled and fought and resisted the police in their efforts to get admission to the Assize Court . . . the wide corridors outside were blocked with people. When the doors were opened, the rush to get seats almost overpowered the strong force of police on duty, and reinforcements had to be summoned to press back the throng."

The afternoon began with Crown prosecutor Du Vernet calling Inspector Kennedy as a witness, with the stolid policeman once again reading in a monotone the answers that Carrie had given him during the interview at Court Street police station on the night of Massey's death. The Crown's final witness was Joseph Pearson, who had been staying with his grandmother that evening and had been amongst the first to reach the body. The Crown spared fourteen-year-old Charlie, Bert and Rhoda's son, from the ordeal of giving evidence. The facts of Bert Massey's untimely death were not in dispute; Charlie could have added nothing. This closed the case for the Crown, and Edward Du Vernet sat down.

❧

When Hartley Dewart rose to give arguments for the defence, a ripple of excitement ran through the court as the lawyer adjusted his gown and leaned towards the judge. As yet, he had not shown his hand. So far, his client had been a sad, silent figure in a shabby coat who had uttered barely two words in public since she had killed a man. What evidence was Dewart going to produce to justify a plea of not guilty?

Dewart's first witness was Dr. A.J. Harrington. Nobody was surprised that the defence led off with medical evidence; the shock came when he gave evidence about Carrie's physical, and not her mental, state. Dr. Harrington told the court that he had examined the prisoner the previous day. With a grave face, and a theatrical sense of timing, Dewart asked him what he had found.

"I have no doubt that she is a virgin," Dr. Harrington replied.

Dewart pressed on: "Were you alone in the examination?"

"Dr. Duncan Anderson was associated with me," Dr. Harrington informed the court.

Hartley Dewart asked his witness if Dr. Anderson agreed with him that Carrie's hymen was intact.

"Quite," Dr. Harrington stated.

Today, such evidence would probably not be allowed in court. But in 1915, the evidence was a bombshell. As Dewart had anticipated,

Carrie's virginity elevated her to the moral high ground. Everybody in court that day knew immediately that Carrie's sexual innocence was as good as an alibi. Now, judge, jurors, and spectators would screen all subsequent evidence and argument through the lens of her purity.

Dewart piled on more evidence of Carrie's virtue. His next witness was Carrie's brother-in-law Ed Fairchild, who talked about Carrie's family.

"Did you know your wife and the little girl in the dock in their home in England?" Dewart asked Fairchild. When the latter said he did, Dewart asked a series of questions about Carrie's father, the army pensioner, and the discipline in the Davies home. Ed described how strictly the girls were supervised: they were not allowed to speak unless spoken to, they were allowed out only two nights a week, and they had to be home by nine o'clock.

Next, Dewart asked, "Did you know the little girl's mother?"

At this point, Justice Mulock himself spoke up. "Do you mean the prisoner?" he rebuked Dewart. Dewart agreed that the "little girl" was the woman accused of murder, then continued with his examination of Fairchild. Ed explained how Carrie had appeared on the Sunday night before the shooting when the Fairchilds had visitors. She had told Ed that her employer had given her a ring, and kissed her twice, but her sister had indicated she should not talk about this anymore in front of the visitors. "She only told me that Mr. Massey tried to kiss her, nothing else."

"It didn't occur to you not to let her go back?" Dewart pressed Carrie's brother-in-law.

"No," replied Ed Fairchild, shuffling uneasily in the witness box. He described how, the previous summer, he had gone to Toronto Island when Carrie was taken ill, and offered to take her away. Mr. Massey had told him it wasn't necessary as the Massey family doctor was looking after her and she was getting the best attention. Carrie had not asked to be taken away. The Fairchilds were predisposed to trust members of the distinguished Massey family; besides, their own house was already overcrowded. Now, in this latest crisis, Ed still couldn't believe that Bert Massey was a serious threat. "When she was sick at the island . . . Mr. Massey told me then that he was interested in that girl. He said he would look after her and that his wife would look after her, that she would see that Carrie did not keep bad company. That alone threw me off." He didn't think there was any danger if Carrie returned to Walmer Road. Carrie herself had suggested that Massey must have been drunk, and would regret his behaviour the following day. "She did not mention anything about upstairs in the bedroom."

Finally, the moment that the crowd had been waiting for arrived. Hartley Dewart called his client to the witness stand. This was the first time that reporters and public would hear the young woman's account in her own voice and could judge for themselves the accused murderer's credibility. Justice Mulock agreed that she could sit as she gave her evidence. She spoke, commented the *Globe*, "coherently, distinctly and without faltering."

Dewart began with a line of questioning that reinforced the picture of Carrie as a dutiful daughter. Carrie's eyes rarely strayed from her lawyer's face as she gave brief, informative answers to his questions. He nodded approvingly after each response. She had come to Canada in order to earn money to send back to her mother in England, she explained, because her father was dying and her mother was losing her sight. She had always sent money home, and since her father's death the previous summer, she had been sending five or ten dollars a month.

Next, Dewart asked Carrie about her illness the previous summer at Toronto Island. Carrie gave an answer that surprised those who had heard Mary Ethel Massey's dramatic account at the coroner's inquest of Carrie's hysteria. According to Carrie, her discomfort was nothing more than mild gastroenteritis: the doctor had told her that her "trouble was caused through not digesting her food properly."

Then Dewart embarked on the subject that the spectators were eager to hear about, and the *Evening Tely* reporter had been primed to listen for: the events of the weekend when Rhoda Massey was away, which had prompted Carrie to grab a gun and shoot her employer.

"Was there any special work you did at the house during the week [Mrs. Massey] was away?" Dewart asked.

"There was a dinner party," replied Carrie.

"When?"

"On the Friday night."

"Were there many there?"

"There were twelve."

"How did you know what to get for dinner?"

"Mr. Massey gave me a slip of paper with some things on. He told me he would leave the rest to me. He brought home several things."

Prompted by Dewart, Carrie described how she had cooked and served the dinner, but she did not have anything to do with the drinks. Then her lawyer asked, "Did anything strange happen at that dinner?"

"Ladies and gentlemen were drinking rather heavily," Carrie replied in a clear voice.

"Did it have any effect upon any of them?"

"Yes, sir, except Mr. Massey. I didn't notice that it affected him."

"How do you know liquors were served?'

"I knew there was liquor in the glasses and by the bottles that were sent out afterwards to be put down the cellar."

"Were there many courses of liquor?"

"Several."

"What time did the party break up?"

"I think it was after midnight. They gave Mr. Massey three cheers as they left the door. Mr. Massey came and thanked me for what I had done."

"Anything unusual on Saturday?"

"No."

"On Sunday what took place?" Dewart went on.

Carrie described how Bert Massey had spent much of the day wandering around the house in his bathrobe. His son had gone out, and Bert had found Carrie cleaning up the dining room. He had given her a ring to thank her for all her efforts on Friday night; when he tried to put it on her finger, it proved to be too small. He told her to take it to Eaton's (where he had likely purchased it) and get it enlarged.

The ring, a small gold circle with a shamrock picked out in pearls, was produced, and the jurors passed it from one large, callused hand to the next. Reporters craned forward for a glimpse. Despite the press of people, the courtroom was utterly silent as Dewart continued to lead Carrie through the next stage of her story. He asked Carrie what her employer had said next.

Carrie continued her story without hesitation: "He asked me if I noticed anything Friday night. Did I see a lady drop her table napkin so many times, and did I see him run his hand up and down the lady's stocking. I didn't answer him, but just looked hard at him."

"What else did he say?" continued the lawyer.

"He said that he had a lady friend of his own."

"Did he do or say anything further?"

Carrie hesitated, then said, "He asked me if I heard any kissing going on Friday, and if I did, not to say anything to [my friend] Mary Rooney or my sister."

"What did he do then?"

"He caught me by both hands around the waist and said he liked little girls. Then he kissed me and I struggled, but he kissed me again."

Behind the bar of the court, there was scarcely a movement amongst the spectators. In the jury box, the jurors turned their heads first to the tall figure of the defence lawyer as he prompted his client, then to the tense figure standing in the witness box, next to the judge.

"Did he do anything else?"

"No, he only kissed me."

"What was his physical condition?"

"He was trembling and very much excited."

"What happened when you got away?"

"I went into the kitchen and he went upstairs to his room. I heard him turn the water on in the bathroom and then he called me to go and make his bed. When I went up he was in his bedroom, but I had thought he was in the bathroom."

Dewart smiled encouragingly at Carrie as he led her gently through the story, and she, with her eyes focused only on his face, appeared oblivious to the breathless tension in the courtroom.

"What was he doing?" Dewart asked.

"He was looking through Mrs. Massey's bureau drawers . . . He caught me again and started talking. He brought out Mrs. Massey's underwear."

"What did he say?"

"He wanted me to put them on for him and then he came towards me and tried to throw me on the bed. I struggled and ran away from him. I got out of the room and went to my own room and locked the door, because I was frightened of him."

"How close was he when you got into the bedroom?"

"I was over near the bed and nearly had it made when he spoke to me. There was only a small passageway between me and the bed."

"What did you do when you got to your room?"

"I got dressed, and though it was not my afternoon out, I left the house. I crept downstairs quietly and went to my sister's . . . I started to tell my sister what happened, but there was a little boy there and she looked at me as much as to tell me to say nothing."

Carrie explained that she started playing with her sister's children and forgot to tell Maud the rest of the story about her employer's behaviour. And she hadn't wanted to give her brother-in-law the details—details that enthralled the crowd in the Ontario Supreme Court. She had returned to Walmer Road and slipped upstairs without seeing anybody. She thought Mr. Massey was out.

"Tell me about Monday," Dewart asked his witness. Carrie kept her eyes locked on his and spoke in a steady voice.

"I called Mr. Massey about 8:15 in the morning. Then I got his breakfast ready and put it on the table. Then I went down into the cellar."

"Why did you go there?"

"Because I was frightened of him."

Carrie described how she had stayed in the cellar until she heard the front door slam and, through a window, watched her employer walk down the front path. She was unable to do her work most of the day because "I was worried over what had happened on Sunday . . . He was my master and he kissed me and that worried me . . . I knew he was a man who meant to do it from what he said."

When the paper boy rang the doorbell at six o'clock that evening, she saw her employer sauntering down Walmer Road. "I guess it was then I lost control of myself, and I thought of what he was going to do, and it frightened me. Everything was misty before me."

"What were the thoughts in your mind?" Dewart asked.

"I could only think of him doing me harm, sir, and I knew that I would have to defend myself some way or other . . . I went for the revolver that was hanging in the little boy's room."

"Had you ever used it before?"

"Never before."

"Had you ever been shown anything in reference to it?"

"The boy had showed me how to use it and how to load it. He had fired it before and I had watched him fire it."

From the hush that fell over the court and the expressions on the jurors' faces, Hartley Dewart knew his client's story was having just the impact he hoped. Carrie was emerging as a dutiful young domestic servant with a dissolute employer. The graphic new details—about Bert Massey stroking a woman's leg and having a special "lady friend"—had provoked short, shocked murmurs. The story of Bert Massey asking Carrie to don his wife's underwear was as vivid as anything that appeared in silent films. The holes in Carrie's sad tale (Why had she not told her sister about these traumatic events? Why had she given her brother-in-law the impression that she found Massey's behaviour pathetic rather than menacing? Why had she returned to Walmer Road?) had been smoothed over. But Dewart still had to stamp out any suspicion that Carrie's actions had been premeditated.

"Was it after you had seen Mr. Massey outside that you only thought of going to get the revolver?" he pressed Carrie.

"Yes."

"Had you thought of getting it before that?"

"No."

"How do you account for it at all?"

"I could not tell you," replied Carrie, wide-eyed and clear-voiced, speaking directly to her lawyer as he smiled at her.

Prompted by Dewart, Carrie described how she took the revolver and six cartridges from Charles Junior's bedroom and loaded five of the cartridges into the gun as she returned downstairs, "thinking all the time how he would do me harm." She was almost at the front door when it opened, so she immediately fired. "Then I turned and ran. I was pulling the trigger all the time, but the revolver did not seem to work . . . I thought of him doing me harm, that was the only thought I had in my head." She saw her employer walk back down the outside steps, then fall on the sidewalk. "I thought he was just lying there to escape the bullets. I only saw his head; the other part of his body was behind some snow."

Dewart took her quickly through the rest of the story—how she had run up to her room, written letters to her sister and Mary Rooney, and then heard the police arrive. "I did not know what I had done until I got to the police station and until I heard some man say on the phone, 'The man is dead, all right.' That is the first time I knew what I had done."

Hartley Dewart concluded his questions by asking Carrie once again what she was thinking.

"That he was going to do me harm. That was my only thought."

"What kind of harm?"

"That he was going to disgrace me."

"What do you mean by that?" Dewart asked. Raising his voice and speaking quickly before the Crown prosecutor could object to leading questions and melodramatic language more appropriate for a penny thriller than a courtroom, he forged ahead: " . . . That he would forcibly have connection with you, that he would ravish you, and accomplish his purpose?"

"Yes," Carrie replied demurely.

❧

Crown Counsel Du Vernet rose to cross-examine the accused, but he knew that the spectators' sympathy was all on Carrie's side. He felt blindsided: both the evidence of Carrie's virginity and the titillating details about Massey's behaviour at and after the dinner party had come as a complete surprise. Du Vernet pulled out some points from Carrie's evidence that put the Masseys in a better light—that they had always treated her kindly, and that they had regularly increased her wages. He asked Carrie why she had returned to Walmer Road that Sunday night if she was so scared of her employer. Carrie replied the idea "simply didn't seem to go to my head." Then Du Vernet asked her why she didn't return to her sister's the following day, after she had hidden in the cellar until her employer had gone to work. Carrie answered, "It was my duty to stay in the house. I was expecting Mrs. Massey home."

"It was a contest, then, between fear and duty?'

"Yes."

"But Mrs. Massey told you that you could go?"

"Yes, but I had told her that I wouldn't go out unless Mr. Massey was home."

"Had you made up your mind to go out that night?"

"If Mr. Massey was in, yes. If not, I wouldn't."

Carrie's clear answers and composure belied her claims to vulnerability. Du Vernet wanted to raise doubts about Carrie's state of mind. Was she really as panic-stricken as she said? He pressed her: "You want the jury to understand that from what took place on Sunday you were frightened till you shot him?"

"Yes."

"That was at 2:30 p.m.?"

"Yes."

"And you shot him at 6:20 p.m. the next day?"

"I'm not sure of the time. It was about that."

"You knew all the time you could have gone to your sister's, but you felt you ought to stay?"

"Yes."

"There was nothing happened on Monday to cause you to be frightened?"

"No."

"There was a telephone in the house?"

"Yes."

"Had you any friends that you could have got on the other end?" asked Du Vernet.

"Only Mary Rooney," replied Carrie, "and she worked for his brother."

"You weren't more frightened as it got darker?"

"No. I was frightened all day Monday."

"Didn't you realize that Mrs. Massey would rather that you had left than that this should have occurred?"

"Yes," came the simple response.

Whatever question the Crown prosecutor asked, Carrie's answer repeated her obsessive fear that her employer was going to "ruin" her. Du Vernet approached the same issue from a different angle: Why did Carrie continue to pull the trigger, even after she had seen Mr. Massey turn and run away?

"I didn't realize what I was doing."

"You don't want the jury to think that you shot him because you were angry?"

"No, it was because I thought he might try what he had done the night before."

Du Vernet glanced at his notes and said he had no further questions. Carrie's lawyer, Dewart, said he had no further witnesses to call. He was ready to give his final address to the court.

It was now four o'clock in the afternoon, and the exhaustion on the faces of the jurors, who had paid careful attention to hours of evidence and cross-examination, was evident. Justice Mulock announced that the hearing would resume the following day at 9 a.m., an hour earlier than usual.

"Miss Davies," reported the *Evening Telegram,* "was led away through the crowded corridor. She was smiling as she entered a cab." It was the first time the *Tely* had ever mentioned a smile on the face of the newspaper's chosen victim; in its columns, Carrie was usually portrayed as a woebegone child. The reporter left it to readers to speculate on the cause of the smile. Was it relief that she had survived the ordeal? Was it because she had finally been permitted to tell her story in full? Or was it because she had followed to the letter the script that Hartley Dewart had written and rehearsed with her?

And did the reporter himself, who may or may not have been Archie Fisher, mention the unexpected smile as an editorial comment on Dewart's theatrical, effective—and perhaps creative—defence?

CHAPTER 14

Brutish Lust

SATURDAY, FEBRUARY 27

───

LADY HOLDS PATENT OF TRENCHING TOOL

The patent for the 25,000 combination entrenching shovel and bullet-proof shield with which the Canadian Expeditionary Force is equipped is held by Miss Eva Macadam [sic], Private Secretary to the Minister of Militia [General Sam Hughes] . . . Miss Macadam, as the "inventor" of the shovel, has not received any royalty . . . These were some of the interesting facts given to the Commons this afternoon by General Hughes.
—*Globe*, Friday, February 26, 1915

SLAYER OF MR. MASSEY GAVE EVIDENCE IN HER DEFENCE IN A CALM AND ERNEST MANNER, OCCASIONALLY ASKING IF IT WAS NECESSARY TO ANSWER QUESTIONS.
MR. DEWART LED HIS CLIENT SLOWLY UP TO THE CLIMAX OF THE SENSATIONAL EVIDENCE.
—*Toronto Daily News*, Saturday, February 27, 1915

The second, and final, day of Carrie Davies's murder trial would open with her lawyer's address to the jury. Hartley Dewart already knew that this trial was a glorious opportunity to shine—to demonstrate his skill with the jury and to put the Masseys in a poor light. Better still, after his client's performance the previous afternoon, he could feel, as only an experienced trial lawyer could, that it was going his way.

If he glanced at the newspapers while eating his breakfast that day, the headlines would have boosted his elation. For the past two days, the major news stories in the "quality" papers had all been about events in France, and they reinforced the anxiety amongst Toronto families with relatives at the front. On Friday, when the trial opened, the *Globe*'s main story ran under the headline "The Canadian Expeditionary Force in Action: Canadians Capture Some Trenches . . . Several Men are Reported Killed and Wounded in Recent Fights . . . Toronto Man Receives Notice That His Son Has Been Wounded." The *Globe* hit exactly the note of patriotic sacrifice Dewart wanted. "From this time forward, thousands of Canadians will watch with anxiety for news from the front," read the first item in the paper's front-page war summary. "Now many of the Dominion's sons are at the front, and are proving that Canadian valor will be of service in turning the invaders out of France and Belgium. In a very real sense now the war is ours. With the laurel will come pain and heartache, lessened by the assurance that those who fall die in defence of liberty."

Today, the *Globe*'s war coverage was equally dark. "Clearing Hospital for the Canadians" was the headline over a report that Surgeon General Jones, Director of Medical Services from Canada, had left for France to facilitate the transport of Canadian casualties back to England. There they would be treated at the Canadian Red Cross hospital set up at Cliveden House, the lavish Buckinghamshire estate belonging to the Astor family. The Red Cross was busy enlarging the hospital from 150 to 500 beds, to accommodate the expected wave of maimed, wounded, and dying soldiers. *Globe* readers with relatives at the front would not be able to stop themselves imagining their loved ones, swathed in bandages and groggy with pain, lying in those beds. The same story mentioned that three Canadians had been killed a couple of days earlier, although their names were not given. As newspaper reports told the story, they had died defending the honour of the British Empire, facing unequal odds and an enemy that, through brutal attacks on civilians, had proved itself to be immoral and treacherous.

Dewart stepped out of his comfortable house on Elmsley Place. A brisk wind followed him down Bay Street as he made his way a dozen blocks south to City Hall. The journey gave him the time to rehearse the case he would make once he reached his destination. Like any good trial lawyer, he had watched the faces of jury members carefully yesterday, and he knew that the Massey name did not cut much ice with them. Bert Massey's behaviour, like the events in Europe, was stirring up subcurrents of indignation, resentment, rage, helplessness, and unease in Toronto. The trick, he realized, would be to harness them all together.

It was unusual for the criminal courts to sit on a Saturday, and it was particularly unusual that the Assize Court was starting its session at nine o'clock. Once again, a predominantly British crowd surged into the courtroom as soon as the doors opened. When Carrie Davies was led in, just after the hour had struck, the previous evening's confidence appeared to have drained away: "She sat quietly in one corner of the box, furtively wiping her eyes from time to time," according to the *Toronto Daily Star*. Chief Justice Mulock swept into the room with frosty dignity, and the clerk of the court began his incantation, "Oyez, oyez, oyez . . ."

Hartley Dewart preened in the limelight from the moment he rose to address the jury. With exquisite courtesy, he acknowledged that the charge before the court was one of murder, for which the penalty was death. The jury might reduce the case to one of manslaughter. But there was a third alternative that the jury might consider, he continued—then paused, to hold the jurors' attention. With all eyes upon him, he uttered one crisp word: "Acquittal."

"Never in the history of Canadian courts," said Dewart, "has a charge of murder of so peculiar a character been presented—in which the alleged motive for the murder was of such a character as that which the Crown presented."

Dewart began with a grand *tour d'horizon* of typical murder cases, where motives and guilt were easily understood. "You are accustomed to cases of murder in which sheer brutality plays so important a part and in which the wife or some member of a family may be attacked by a husband whose brutish instincts have overcome him, where sordid motives and the love of gain have led men to take the lives of others. There are many cases where jealousy plays an important part and in which you can find the motive in the relationship. You are familiar with the class of case in which revenge and the outraged confidence or vengeful feelings of a woman who has been despoiled of her virtue is the motive that leads to murder."

But this case was different—this case, suggested the lawyer, was on an altogether different and more lofty plane. "Never before has an honourable and virtuous girl been charged with the crime of murder because she successfully resisted the attacks of her master upon her person, and where her only motive was the defence of her honour and virtue against unequal odds and a treacherous assailant."

Lowering his voice, Dewart went on, "I desire you to consider the girl herself—for she is still in her teens—who was charged before you. In every crime of murder, intention is a most important part; in every crime of intention you must look for a foundation in probability and consider the life, the character, the circumstances and the surroundings of the person charged. These are facts for your consideration quite as much as the sworn testimony of the witnesses." Otherwise, Dewart asked with a Shakespearian flourish, "Where lay the virtue of character?" The jury had heard all about Carrie's upbringing in Bedfordshire—her loving mother, her father ("a man of fighting blood"), the wholesome discipline in the home, where "daughters were brought up as daughters should be brought up." Carrie Davies had come to Canada because her family was impoverished and she wanted to earn money to help her family back in Bedfordshire. "We have placed upon ourselves as Canadians the duties of trustees and guardians for girls who come from homes such as this to Canada," intoned the lawyer. "We find her here in service, trusted, favoured and respected. We find her sending home from her scanty means all but what was needed for the barest necessities of her existence. Murderous intent is only found growing in a character filled with viciousness. It was not so in this case."

The crescendo to this portrait of Carrie as a virtuous, self-sacrificing daughter was a masterpiece of rhetoric. "In the first place," Dewart insisted, "as there was provocation, there was and could be no murder. In the second place, with the lack of murderous intent, there could be no murder. In the third place, I shall ask you to find that the circumstances of this case afforded to this worried girl a justification for the act she has done and that you should not find her guilty of any offence.

"Was her life to be ruined by a married man who was her master? Was she to bring disgrace into a family that never knew a stain of such a kind? Her safety lay in self-defence. She was no match for him, and she took the pistol to intimate to him that he could not pursue his course with impunity. She shot with aimless rapidity; she shot in the direction of the man, but there was no intent to cause the death of that man.

"This attack gave the girl only one alternative choice. If she did not defend herself against this man she would have been a fallen woman, an outcast, one more sacrifice to brutish lust."

The lawyer stopped speaking for a full minute, then walked towards the jury and continued with deadly emphasis: "Let that sink into your mind. It was not manslaughter, it was brute slaughter . . . she was defending herself against a man in whom all the principles of decency were dead as far as she was concerned."

What a phrase! "Not manslaughter, but brute slaughter"! Reporters scribbled as spectators hung on Dewart's every word. This was judicial drama at its most riveting. The contrast between the banality of Carrie's vocabulary and the theatrics of her lawyer's address underlined the gulf that yawned between an ill-educated servant and the legal elite.

Next, Dewart turned to the evidence that the Crown prosecutor had introduced the previous day. "To get at the facts of the attempts to debase and shame this young girl, we must go back to the supper party and the orgy of Friday night . . . Her mistress was away, and a party was given which exceeded all the bounds of decency and propriety. There were doings which outraged the feelings of this young girl in service. There were doings of which her master cautioned her to be silent. He complimented her. Then the ring was produced—a bauble to affect the young and untrained mind. She becomes the target for this person's fulsome attentions. Effusive attentions and flattery are often the beginning for a certain line of conduct. We find her the target for improper proposals . . ."

By now, despite the crowding, few people fidgeted on the public benches. Dewart's mentions of an orgy, a bauble, and brutish lust enthralled his listeners. The lawyer continued his seamy tale. "Take the interview downstairs on Sunday. The boy had gone out and the two were alone in the house. Every suggestion and appeal that could be calculated to arouse passion in the mind of a young girl was made to her. Reference was made to indelicate acts at the supper party . . . The suggestions were painful for her to refer to, but they were brought out in evidence only to show the depths to which the master went in order to bring suggestive thoughts to her mind—all these things from which she escaped, but which were coming with increasing pressure.

"She was called by him to make up his bed. And then still more increasing pressure is brought to bear on her by this man. He suggests that she don his wife's underwear to see how she would look in it. He tried to throw her on the bed . . . Though some may think it an easy matter to cast these things off, these are terrible things to a young and innocent girl." Dewart could not be too explicit in his lurid version of events, but he picked his euphemism carefully: "She felt the full weight of what was being forced upon her."

With silky ease, the lawyer went on with his gothic horror story. "Do you wonder that, alone in the house, all that day she brooded over this horrible thing that had come into her life? Can you wonder that, when night fell, when the darkness was coming on, when the mind is more susceptible and the feelings more wrought up—do you wonder that at the close of that terrible day she thought only that he was going to do her harm? That was the one thought she had in her mind. She was possessed with it. Then when evening came, and the shadows fell, she was still thinking that he would come again, and do her harm."

Du Vernet watched his opponent with a mix of admiration and exasperation. *Suggestive thoughts . . . ! The shadows fell . . . !* Dewart's polemic was a mesmerizing mix of penny-dreadful titillation and Biblical phraseology—a mix that was irresistible to the sensation-seeking, churchgoing residents of his city.

"Oh, how that echo rang through that young girl's brain! How it possessed her mind! When I asked her, in the witness box, why she acted as she did, her reply was that she knew her master to be a man who would do as he said. She knew he meant to accomplish his purpose. Do not these things constitute provocation? . . . She was in fear of a brutal attack, a horrible attack on herself, a fear she could not drive from her mind. Under the circumstances, don't you see how the very first sight of him revived every insult and emphasized every feeling? He seemed so near to her that it would seem as if his hot, passionate breath was again approaching her . . . The man was nothing to her except the one attacking force that had to be resisted.

"He was a strong man, against whom her weak strength could not avail. Her one thought was of defending herself. It was in self-defence that she did what she did. She has never wavered from that statement.

"She did not carry the revolver around with her. When she saw her master, then it was that she got the weapon. She did not even know that she had hit him. At the police station, she could only cry, 'Take me away.' Why? Because she still had the fear in her mind that he would do her harm."

Dewart only occasionally glanced at his notes as he stood at the defence counsel's table and directed his arguments to the jury and judge. He gave a scientific gloss to the narrative he was spinning. "Constant irritation on the mind," he said, "brought on a state when the limit of resistance was reduced and the sufferer was akin to one under delusions. This is not a story but a fact." He quoted from the Criminal Code a provision that allowed a "reasonable apprehension of bodily harm" to be grounds for acquittal in a murder trial, although that clause was usually applied to killings that occurred in the middle of a violent altercation. Speaking directly to the twelve middle-aged men in the jury box, he stated, "You have the power to make the law common sense by returning a verdict of 'not guilty.' Gentlemen, I wish to put it strongly, not to your sympathies but to your brains, your intelligence, your common sense and to point out where your road lies."

Jurors stared stoically at the lawyer. It was difficult to resist the passion of his arguments, especially if they coincided with a juror's own sympathies.

After drawing breath, Dewart continued. "Look at the prisoner! Is she a murderess? She is a heroine, a woman of strong character, of stamina, of strong principles. Faithful to her duties as a servant, standing fast by the inherited principles of her family, true to her soldier lover, this girl is not of the stuff of which murderers are made." The jurors turned their eyes to the hunched, scared figure in the prisoner's dock. No one could look *less* like a murderess.

Dewart had been speaking for close to an hour, but he was now reaching the point in his address where he knew he was skating on thin ice. He was going to appeal to British patriotism, Imperial loyalties and class solidarity—sentiments that, privately, made him feel queasy. But he had watched events for the past three weeks. He had seen the emotions ripple through his city, whipped up by British propaganda, ambitious newspaper owners, and family fears. He knew how powerful such an appeal would be in a Toronto jumpy with war nerves.

"What are British troops fighting for at the present moment?" he asked, his voice ringing with passion. "Why has Canada sent 30,000 men to aid them, being prepared to send, if necessary, thirty times as many? It was the honour of Britain for which they fought. If honour was the principle for which British troops and the prisoner's soldier lover were fighting, was not the prisoner herself fighting similarly? The honour of the individual made for the upholding of the honour of England. In repelling an insidious attack from an unexpected enemy, the girl has not committed murder.

"When you look at the way the working classes view these questions of honour and morality, it makes us proud of the stamina that goes to make the people of the Empire. When you contrast some so-called society people with those in lowlier walks of life, we can see that it is the stamina, the principle and the conduct of the so-called working classes that make for the greatness and the continued greatness of the Empire."

It was a tour de force. But Hartley Dewart had not finished yet. He was going to bind generic British pride and a naked appeal to class sentiment with a pathetic scene that might have been taken straight out of a Charles Dickens novel. "Over in Bedfordshire there is a little home where a widowed mother is sitting today," he continued, lowering his voice and shaking his head as if in sorrow. "Her eyes are dimmed, and she is going blind and cannot pursue her work. She was depending upon her little girl. There are five other little children there. That mother has nurtured her daughter and instilled into her the principle that is exemplified in her conduct here. What will your verdict be? What will be the message that you are going to send across the sea? Will you say the girl is guilty because she defended herself from a fate she felt was worse than death? Nay verily, gentlemen.

"Look the facts in the face. You have a wife, a daughter or perhaps a sister at home. You are married men and have children. Can you look them squarely in the face and with a clear conscience say that you had done your duty in the case if you leave a stain upon this girl by your verdict? . . . Put someone near and dear to you in her position. Would you feel that ten or twelve men had treated you fairly if one of your dear ones was on the same set of facts found guilty?

"Our Sovereign Lord the King has tens of thousands of soldiers at the front, fighting and defending the honour of the Empire. None of them more faithfully defended the honour of the Empire than this girl defended her own honour.

"Never in recent years has so much interest been taken in any case as has been taken in this. The eyes of all Canada are upon you, so are the eyes of the people of Bedfordshire and the eyes of the people of England. A verdict of acquittal means that the standard of morality stands high in the county of York.

"Gentlemen of the jury, the issue is with you. You cannot shirk it."

For several minutes after Hartley Dewart finished speaking, the courtroom remained completely silent, with all eyes fixed on him.

{CHAPTER 15}

A Bleeding Corpse

SATURDAY, FEBRUARY 27

GERMAN CORPSES THICK IN FRONT TRENCHES
"EVERYWHERE STILL GREY FIGURES CAN BE SEEN LYING"
EXTENSIVE CAPTURE OF THE GERMAN HAND
BOMBS PROVE VERY USEFUL, AS THEY ARE TURNED
AGAINST THE ENEMY WITH GREAT EFFECT.
—*Globe*, Saturday, February 27, 1915

EATON'S DAILY STORE NEWS
DAINTY UNDERWEAR THAT THE FASTIDIOUS WOMAN LOVES
A SPECIAL DISPLAY IN THE FRENCH ROOMS ON MONDAY
*La Grecque Tailored Drawers, in envelope style, of extra good quality white nainsook,
made to fit neatly at the waist without fullness, finished with pearl buttons, trimmed with
dainty Valenciennes lace insertion and edging of lace. All sizes, price, each, $1.25*
—Toronto Daily Star, Saturday, February 27, 1915

Hartley Dewart's bravura performance had lasted an hour and a half. Even the chief justice, who could have intervened several times to reprimand the defence counsel for introducing points that were irrelevant or inadmissible, seemed spellbound.

A handful of reporters scrambled towards the door in order to telephone their newsrooms and relay Dewart's speech to their editors. As they left, replacement reporters from the same papers arrived to take their places and stay abreast of the drama. Meanwhile, Dewart sat down, a satisfied smile on his thin lips, while everyone else in the courtroom absorbed his powerful challenge to the jury. He had done what every courtroom lawyer wants to do: he had shaped a compelling narrative to hook the jury. He had put Bert Massey on a par with the vicious Huns, and he had made Carrie Davies's trial all about duty—the duty of Carrie to protect her honour after a wanton attack, the duty of Canadian lads in the trenches to defend the Empire, the jury's duty to acquit Carrie in order to prove that purity and honour were more valuable than life itself. The acquittal of his client would be tantamount to a patriotic act. He had used the fact that Bert Massey had *not* raped Carrie to prove that she had just cause to kill. He had argued that Bert Massey *deserved* to be killed.

Edward Du Vernet felt himself drowning in the emotion of his colleague's address. He knew exactly what Hartley Dewart had done:

without actually using the phrase "unwritten law," Dewart had made an implicit appeal to the American doctrine that said a murder was justified when committed in defence of a woman's honour. In lawless American cities and on the gunslinging frontier, the idea that a man was justified in avenging the seduction of a woman for whom he was responsible had proved an effective legal defence. Women, as the weaker sex, required a man's protection, according to this notion, and if a man killed an evil seducer, the latter only had himself to blame. In the American West, several men had beaten murder raps by invoking this "unwritten law" as a defence of their actions in shooting a sister's, wife's, or daughter's lover. The notion had crept north, and courts in British Columbia were also sympathetic to the idea that a man who tried to steal another's wife "deserved to die," and the man who killed him was simply doing what any "real man" would do. In a 1906 case in Vancouver, a man called Charles Johnson was found near the dead body of his lodger, yelling, according to a witness, that he would "learn somebody to come around to try and fuck his wife." Johnson was acquitted of murder.

But vigilante justice was not a concept that carried weight in central Canada—in fact, it is unlikely that Toronto's lawyers even knew much about judicial rulings from the other side of the Rockies. Moreover, the idea that a killing might be justified when an individual's honour was in jeopardy only came into play when the killer was a man. It is unlikely that it had ever been used in a case like Carrie's, where the female victim of the attempted seduction had later turned a gun on her seducer. Carrie might be just a frightened eighteen-year-old, but her actions did not fit the "weaker sex" stereotype.

Du Vernet had watched the forcefulness of Dewart's fanciful oratory overwhelm Chief Justice Mulock and the packed and sympathetic audience. Yet the Crown prosecutor had raised no objections: Dewart's address had been gripping. Du Vernet's heart must have sunk. He knew that the prosecution case was far more firmly grounded in facts and law than Dewart's heated rhetoric, but it lacked the passion: his own summing-up would sound Gradgrindishly pedantic. In the prisoner's dock, Carrie Davies's huddled figure reinforced her lawyer's brilliant depiction of her as a helpless victim, fighting with the same courage as the boys in France. Her very passivity bespoke an innocent victim, although she certainly had not been passive when she pulled the trigger. Had her lawyer *told* her to keep dabbing at her eyes like that?

All the jury could see was a frightened girl who had faced a terrifying, brutal attacker—although this image was a distortion of the story that she herself had told the previous day. Could he persuade these twelve stolid Canadians to see Massey's death from a different point of view? Could he pull them out of the emotional tsunami in which Dewart had engulfed them and explain that there was no provision in Canadian law to excuse a cold-blooded killing with no immediate provocation? Could he remind them that a slimly built man in galoshes who had just exchanged a cheery word with a newsboy was *not* the moral equivalent of a German soldier who bayonetted babies? Could he make the jurors identify with Bert Massey, family man, rather than with Carrie Davies, helpless immigrant?

Du Vernet rose, walked over to the jury, adjusted his glasses, and began to speak in a quiet, reasonable tone. "There is nobody in this court—bench, lawyers, or jury—whose sympathy does not go out to this young girl." However, he went on, sympathy should not be allowed to interfere with the course of justice. Canadians should be proud that they live in a country where men's differences are not settled with pistols. "How many men and husbands have suffered, but they have let the law deal with the offender. If they did not, where would we stop? It is very necessary for you to get at the truth and justice of this case. You are the judges of the facts. My only duty is to assist you in this difficult case. I have endeavoured simply to point out what the law says and what might be an excuse to reduce the charge. When human life is taken, it is the duty of the country to see who is responsible. That must be done to the satisfaction of the jury. If there is any reasonable doubt, it must be given to the prisoner.

"My learned friend has read you nothing that suggests killing can take place in this way and no offence be committed. You are the makers of the law, and hundreds of homes might be demolished if the bars were let down. Has there been any lack of sympathy in this court?

"The killing of a defenceless man who is not making an assault, but is on the street, not armed, would come within the definition of culpable homicide."

It was hard for the lawyer to tell if he was making any headway with the jury. The twelve men listened carefully, occasionally glancing over at Carrie as if to measure whether the prosecution's story fit better than her lawyer's.

Du Vernet began the slow process of undermining Dewart's version. "My learned friend has made a fierce attack on this man Massey. The Crown is not here to justify his conduct. If what the girl says is true, many men have been punished in this court for what the girl said was done to her.

"There was not a suggestion of improper conduct until Friday. They had encouraged the girl to go to church and increased her wages from time to time. Mr. Massey is not here. If this offence was committed, this man would have got six months." Instead, Du Vernet insisted, the jury was hearing only one side of the story: Carrie's. "The other side is not here to answer the attacks made upon him." Moreover, Hartley Dewart's defence had been over the top in its gothic flourishes and lurid suggestions. "Evidence was permitted that should not have been. Indulgence was given that almost became licence."

Detail by detail, the Crown Prosecutor unpicked the defence case. The prisoner had said nothing on the witness stand to show that Massey was a man without feeling or remorse, or that he would be guilty of criminal conduct. Quite the reverse. What had Carrie told her brother-in-law when she ran to her relatives after the bedroom incident? "She said that she thought he must have been drunk. Her own words are, 'I guess he'll look like two cents tomorrow morning.' He wasn't the heartless, worthless brute he has been said to be! Did that expression of hers indicate to your minds that the man was without feeling, without remorse? Was it not apparent that the girl did not think so? Was not the judgment placed on the man by Carrie Davies at this time a common-sense judgment? For two years she had lived in the same house with him and in that time he had been absolutely straight."

Speaking with careful precision, Du Vernet reminded the jurors that Carrie had told Ed Fairchild that she expected her boss would come to his senses. "Next day, [Bert Massey] hurries through his breakfast and gets out. Does that not indicate that he was ashamed? He comes back to his house probably feeling that he has done wrong and ought to apologize. Here was an unprotected man coming up the street, and the girl comes down the steps and as he opens the door she fires. He says, 'Oh don't.' But she comes forward and fires again. To plead that she was in actual danger of her life at that time was not possible." That she might have lost control of herself was quite another matter, continued Du Vernet in the same quiet, reasonable tone, but he was only pointing out that there could be no justification in the eyes of the law in this case.

Du Vernet pushed a little further, suggesting to the jury that Carrie's defence had been carefully embroidered. "When the girl goes to her brother-in-law, she tells a story of the man taking hold of her and kissing her. When she comes before the detectives, she tells about the kissing and then adds that upstairs in his room he made improper remarks to her and she pushed him away. Now, when she comes before you, she tells a third story, quite a different one. She adds to her previous stories, not improperly, I admit, but nevertheless, the stories are different."

The prosecutor turned to other weaknesses in the Dewart version. Carrie had returned to Walmer Road, from her sister's house, on the Sunday night after Massey had harassed her. "Did that show fear or terror of death or anything more than that the man had done a foolish thing that he would be sorry for? . . . There is no suggestion that anything improper took place when the boy was in the house. It is not a case of a girl fighting for her life and honor. There is nothing of that kind here.

"Doesn't it look as though he had merely forgotten himself on that one occasion? He may, perhaps, have had a few drinks. Only taking the girl's story as she tells it to you, without its being possible to hear the other side of the case, these are the facts. And do you think that this man intended to render himself liable to the death penalty or life imprisonment, punishments that may be meted out for the offence she says she feared he would commit?"

Du Vernet paused again, before beginning his summation. He had done his best to strip Bert Massey's death of Dewart's melodramatic embroidery, and even to suggest that Carrie had herself known that Massey's clumsy fumbles were not really much of a threat. But had he convinced the jury, or were its members still awash in pity for a weeping virgin? Along with Chief Justice Mulock, the jurors were poker-faced. Perhaps the prosecution should try and put Carrie in a new light . . .

"She did not seem to show any remorse for taking this man's life," Du Vernet mused, staring hard at the foreman of the jury. "A man strong and healthy at one moment, coming to his home, and the next moment, a bleeding corpse. It is a serious matter, and it is not this man you must consider. It is the rights of the community. Look at the deliberation; look at the way she puts it herself. She goes upstairs, and one of the most pathetic things in this case is that the unfortunate man probably owes his death to the fact that [his own son] taught her how to shoot. She gets [the gun] and six cartridges, but finds five enough. She loads it and goes downstairs. Her own story is, 'He opened the door and I fired a shot . . . I knew I didn't kill him, as he ran out on the sidewalk. I ran to the verandah and fired from there and he fell.'

"What danger is she in of her life?"

How difficult it was to remind jurors that, despite a trial's dramatic overtones, this was about the law rather than rival scripts. Carrie Davies had shot an unarmed man, and the Canadian Criminal Code specified penalties for such actions. Du Vernet drew breath for one final appeal to logic and law, rather than emotion.

"If you can say honestly that she lost control, the law allows you to say so. But let us brush aside all this nonsense about justification. No man is bound to surrender his life, and force may be repelled with force, but that does not apply to this case. We must not let down the bars of law and order, and we must do our duty, even if it is hard. The jury has realized that the law, in its efforts to be fair and reasonable, has a merciful side, but it must protect the public."

Edward Du Vernet had been on his feet for almost an hour, and Hartley Dewart gave him a courteous nod as the prosecution counsel gathered his robes around him and returned to his seat. Once again, some reporters shot out of the room to dictate the gist of Du Vernet's address to editors, and another shift took their places. It was now time for Chief Justice Mulock's charge to the jury. The judge's role was to remind jurors of the law, and the choices before them, but his instructions would reveal whose side the canny old politician took. In the prisoner's dock, Carrie Davies slumped helplessly, as twelve men prepared to mull over the arguments they had heard.

CHAPTER 16

"Order! Order!"

SATURDAY, FEBRUARY 27

No Peace Until Germans Have Been Crushed

. . . Britain has promised to fight to the last ship and the last man to secure complete reparation for Belgium's wrong, and France, which is suffering infinitely more from the war than England, is equally determined.
—*Toronto Daily Star*, Saturday, February 27, 1915

Constant irritation on the mind, said Mr. Dewart, brought on a state when the limit of resistance was reduced and the sufferer was akin to one under delusions. This was not a story but a fact. This state would deprive one of self-control . . . Was hers a heart story wrung from a burdened soul, or was it merely a girl's story?
—*Toronto Daily Star*, Saturday, February 27, 1915

T he case which you are considering is a serious one," began Chief Justice Sir William Mulock at 11:20, as he embarked on his charge to the jury. "I am sure it will cause you, as it does the Court and everyone concerned in it, very serious thought. You are all, I am sure, impressed with the gravity of the issue, and the vital importance to the community that you should reach a conclusion in harmony with the facts and in accordance with the law."

Listening attentively from the Crown prosecutor's table, Edward Du Vernet could be forgiven for hoping that His Lordship had been unmoved by Hartley Dewart's colourful defence. Looking as stern as Moses, Sir William seemed in no mood for bodice-ripping sensationalism as he reminded the twelve jurors of the alternatives before them. Despite all the emotion whipped up by the newspapers, perhaps the chief justice would stick to the letter of the law, and Carrie would be sent down.

"The case admits of three different verdicts at your hands," Mulock went on to explain. "One, that of murder; the second, that of manslaughter; and the third, not guilty. I will endeavour to make clear to you what circumstances in connection with the case give it the legal character of murder, what of manslaughter, and what would excuse the act of killing. Then, with those instructions in your minds, when you retire you will have to determine in which class of those three cases this one belongs—murder, manslaughter, or excusable homicide."

So far, so balanced. The judge's authoritative tones, honed by his twenty-three years as an MP and cabinet minister in Ottawa, held listeners in thrall. Hartley Dewart sat impassively across the court from Du Vernet, his face portraying not a quiver of concern that the case might not go his way. All eyes were on the chief justice, and almost none on Carrie, who seemed to have shrunk to nothing in her old brown coat.

Justice Mulock continued: "The word 'homicide' simply means the act of one person killing another. Homicide is of two kinds, wrongful and punishable, or innocent. A person is either guilty of murder—the most serious form of homicide—or guilty of the lesser homicide, manslaughter, or is only guilty of excusable homicide, which means not guilty. The prisoner admits the killing and therefore we have not to commence with what caused the death."

The chief justice spent a further ten minutes explaining the nuances of a murder charge—the requirement that there should be "malice aforethought," the legal definition of malice, the need for evidence to demonstrate absence of malice, the burden on the accused to justify and explain away the offence.

"The malice of which I am speaking," continued the judge, "is not that understood in common conversation. I am using it in its legal sense. What does it mean? It means a wrongful act done intentionally, without just cause or excuse."

A smile tugged at Hartley Dewart's lips. As the Old Boy tied himself in knots while exhaustively demonstrating his grasp of the law, expressions of confusion and boredom flitted across some jurors' faces. It was difficult to untangle the meaning of some of his pronouncements. It was certainly beyond the ability of the *Evening Telegram* reporter, who quoted him as saying, "For this case it may be assumed that either the killing was malicious and consequently amounts to murder until the contrary appears from excuse or justification and unless such circumstances appear in the evidence of the prosecution it is incumbent upon the prisoner to establish such alleviating circumstances to the satisfaction of the court and the jury, failing which the homicide retains the character presumed by the law, namely that of murder."

Next, Justice Mulock moved on to manslaughter. He read out loud the Criminal Code clauses dealing with manslaughter, and then dealt with the concept of self-defence in words that can only have confused the jurors further: "If the person assaulted can successfully retreat from the assailant, he should adopt that course instead of killing him. If instead of retreating he kills him, the plea of self-defence will not excuse the act. Everyone who is unlawfully assaulted is justified [in] repelling force by force, and he would be justified even though he causes death or grievous bodily harm if he causes it under reasonable apprehension of death or of grievously bodily harm from the violence with which the assault was originally made." Would any juror see through this tangle of verbiage a template on which to judge a woman who, when she fired the gun, was not "repelling force by force"?

However, the judge was clearer when he turned to the case before him. "If you find that . . . there was no premeditation, and that [the prisoner] acted on the spur of the moment . . . then you would say there was no murder in her heart." Mulock also dismissed the suggestion that Carrie's story had been embellished with every telling—that Dewart had inflated her tale with suspect salacious details. "It was stated by one of the counsel that she gave a more elaborate story here than at the inquest. I do not discover any substantial variation of the story the prisoner told on each occasion."

This was the point at which the two KCs must have realized where Sir William was heading. As he continued with his instructions to the jury, he emphasized all the elements in the case most favourable to Carrie. The evidence of virginity had obviously had the desired impact, although he never mentioned it. "She was a refined girl," he intoned from the bench, "with refined, pure ideas. Evidently she is a person of a supersensitive, conscientious nature. Her pledge to her mistress not to absent herself from the house when the master was absent was a pledge she felt bound to keep, and in this age I think it is an encouraging and pleasant thing to find some person so devoted to respecting one's promises as the prisoner seems to have been.

"Left alone with her thoughts," Mulock continued, "she brooded over the events of the day before, which she regarded as a terrible distress to her, added to, perhaps, by her idea of the fidelity she owed to her lover."

Several people behind the bar nodded their heads emphatically at this portrayal of Carrie Davies as the epitome of obedient womanhood, who kept her word and remained true to her soldier lover facing the enemy in France. Carrie's own passivity in court and the conflation of her plight with that of her mystery fiancé underlined the image. Yet Sir William Mulock had gone way beyond the conventional role filled by a Canadian judge in a jury trial. He had not stuck to the provisions of the Canadian Criminal Code, or unpicked Hartley Dewart's subtle appeal to an "unwritten law" that justified Carrie's behaviour. He did not tell jurors that Dewart's appeal to them was inappropriate, because however persuasive it might be, it made a mockery of the law's specific provisions. And now, in his instructions to the jury, he had implicitly endorsed the idea that Carrie was justified in defending her honour.

At 11:45 a.m., the jury retired to their room to decide on their verdict. Twelve men too old for war debated whether they should defend a young British girl's honour and offer her their paternal protection. In the meantime, Chief Justice Mulock and the two lawyers retired to their separate chambers, and Carrie was taken to one of the basement cells. A subdued murmur rose in the courtroom, as spectators tried to second-guess what the jury would decide, and how long it would take.

꧁

The chief justice had barely had time to take a fortifying mouthful of whisky before his clerk told him that the jurors had made their decision. It had taken them a mere half hour. At 12:15 p.m., the judge, lawyers, and prisoner all returned to the court. Then, twelve men filed back into the jury box as reporters and spectators watched in rapt silence. Maud Fairchild's hands were clenched tightly together; Ed Fairchild had a protective arm around his wife as he stared at the jurors' faces, trying to discern their intentions. The hush was, suggested the *Evening Telegram,* "the stillness that precedes a summer storm."

Chief Justice Mulock relished the drama: ever the politician, he loved a captive audience. He waited until the very last fidget, throat-clearing, and whisper had been stilled. Then his voice rang out across the court: "Gentlemen of the jury, is your verdict 'guilty' or 'not guilty'?" Samuel Miller, a farmer from East Gwillimbury who was jury foreman, rose, glanced at Carrie, and addressed the judge: "Not guilty."

The storm broke as, noted the *Globe,* "all the pent-up and nervous anxiety of the past two days poured out in sympathy with the forlorn figure huddled in the prisoners dock, sobbing and shaking violently." The *Evening Telegram* reported that pandemonium erupted: "From three hundred throats came one tremendous cheer such as never rang through a Canadian courtroom before." Reporters rushed out to telephone their editors and urge that special editions be published. The *Tely* had no misgivings about declaring that the crowd was a homogeneous "cheering mass of Britishers" who were "clapping and shouting and surging forward towards the railing near the prisoner's box." One man whooped so exuberantly that two court constables leapt over the railing that separated the public from the court officers, seized the loudmouth, and hustled him out of the room. Chief Justice Mulock, appalled at the noise, half-rose from his chair with "amazement on his face" as court clerks shouted, "Order! Order!"

In the middle of the mayhem, Carrie Davies seemed stunned.

When the Salvation Army matron leaned into the prisoner's box, hugged Carrie, and, with a broad smile, told her that the ordeal was now over, Carrie almost fainted. Only with the support of both Miss Minty and the matron was she able to stand upright while Sir William Mulock spoke to her.

"Carrie Davies," began the chief justice, in far warmer tones than he had hitherto allowed himself to use, "you have heard the verdict?"

Carrie recovered her poise. "Yes," she replied, drying her eyes and perking up. Mulock announced that the verdict was one "in which I concur, if that is any comfort to you." He admitted that perhaps the jury had taken a view of the case "not absolutely in conformity with strict rules, but they have rendered substantial justice. They found that when you killed Mr. Massey you lost control of yourself and at that moment had no murderous intent.

"You have had a strict bringing up and the influence of your parents upon you has fallen upon good grounds. You have had the highest regard for morality and honour. Those qualities caused you to take a stronger view of what Mr. Massey would have done than the facts warranted, but nevertheless your education, training and nature were such as to fill you with alarm of the possible consequences of meeting him again, unprotected, and so, from the very highest motives, you did a thing which you will regret perhaps all your life. It was a mistaken sense of duty."

By now, the crowd was starting to hum with excitement and eagerness to celebrate Carrie's release, but the chief justice raised his voice above the noise. "The proper thing for you to have done was not to have returned. Respect for your duty caused you to go back. Your mental training seems to have made it your bounden duty to go back to Mr. Massey's. You were between two forces—your promise to Mrs. Massey that you would not leave and your fear of Mr. Massey."

The chief justice's face softened as he looked over his glasses at Carrie. He had three daughters of his own: although some years older than the prisoner, they still seemed like children to him. Although he had earlier reprimanded Dewart for referring to his client as a "little girl," he now nodded at Carrie: "You are now a free girl."

Sir William Mulock's sentimentality (and perhaps that of the *Tely* correspondent) then got the better of him. "Tears were welling in the judge's eyes as he made his parting homily to the girl in the dock," the *Tely* reported, "and before he had finished his voice had failed him . . . There were few dry eyes in the courtroom."

For Hartley Dewart, the verdict was the triumph he had craved. Carrie had been declared not guilty by a jury of her peers. His impassioned defence—"Brute slaughter, not manslaughter!"—had been as effective as Blackie Johnston's twenty years earlier in the Clara Ford case. Twelve men had weighed the law against their own sense of natural justice and decided in favour of the latter. They had accepted the notion of "unwritten law" in order to protect an innocent against a sexual predator.

For Edward Du Vernet, the verdict was a defeat. He had always known that he did not have the public on his side, but now he discovered that even the judge had bought into the luridly melodramatic defence. With a not-guilty verdict, the Crown had no avenue of appeal, although the verdict was a clear contravention of Canadian law, which the judge had failed to explain in his instructions to the jury. Twelve unassuming men had collectively decided that, in this case, the law was oppressive— that Carrie Davies's behaviour was excusable. And now the courtroom crowd was behaving as though the jury had won a victory in Europe. Du Vernet could merely shrug and marvel that a woman who had taken the law into her own hands had got away with it.

For both lawyers, the Carrie Davies case had been a professional challenge. Now that the verdict was rendered, each would move swiftly on to his next case. They shook hands cordially, and barely cast a glance at Carrie as they gathered up their papers.

But for Carrie Davies, the verdict meant she dared to think about tomorrow, next month, next year. Clutching the Salvation Army matron's arms, she looked up at Chief Justice Mulock and stammered through her sobs, "I thank you, your Lordship." Then she turned to the jury box: "I thank the jury which has tried me." Once again, the *Tely* reporter revelled in the drama: "Even strong men not much given to sentimentality surreptitiously pulled handkerchiefs from their pockets and applied them to their eyes."

The clerk unlatched the gate of the prisoner's dock, and Carrie was helped over to where her sister sat. The two sisters fell into each other's arms, weeping with relief. The sight was irresistible for both reporters and spectators. "Several hundred spectators refused to leave the corridor when the court adjourned, and hovered around waiting to get a glimpse of the girl," reported the *Toronto Daily Star*. The *Tely*'s Archie Fisher managed to exchange a few words with the sisters. Carrie told him, "I was nervous at first, but now . . ." Then Maud Fairchild broke in: "I didn't sleep last night thinking of it. Carrie will go right home with me and stay. She needs the rest." She tugged at her sister's arm, but Carrie still had something to say as the Fairchilds and friends hustled her towards a waiting car: "They have treated me very kindly down there [in the Don Jail]. I didn't care much about the exercise I got down there. It was like a lot of soldiers marching. The bed that I had to sleep on was rather hard, but I have nothing to complain of."

Chief Justice Mulock told his hangers-on that he had never experienced such emotional scenes in a courtroom. He was obviously fired up by both the verdict and the excitement.

It was late afternoon before the last spectator finally left the building and court officials were able to lock the doors of the room where the Supreme Court sat. But by then, Carrie Davies and the Fairchilds were safely installed back in the little house on Morley Avenue. How the Massey family, which had steered well clear of proceedings, took the news was not recorded.

❧

Editors of Toronto's three evening papers had held the printing presses until they heard the outcome of the trial: none of them could afford to miss a story that the city would chew over all weekend. Two days later, the verdict was still a sufficiently hot news item to be on the front page of the morning *Globe*. "As the slight, pathetic figure supported by two women moved out of the courtroom, which she had entered that morning with a dark shadow hanging over her young life, the curtain rang down on what was probably the most dramatic scene ever enacted in a local court of justice. It was a sensational finish to a sensational case, a felicitous ending to a pitiful human drama that was full of bitterness and tears."

Emotions ran high in Toronto for the next few days. In her own way, Carrie Davies had become a reality show celebrity before reality shows were invented or the cult of celebrity understood. Reporters besieged the Fairchilds' house in the east end of the city, where she was staying.

The *Toronto Star* managed the biggest scoop—a long interview with Carrie, under a front-page headline: "Carrie Davies Says She Did a Terrible Thing." Carrie spoke of her treatment at Don Jail: "I was given good food and allowed to walk and talk with the matrons. They were awfully kind and I will never forget it." The reporter asked her what she was going to do now. "I would like to go home—to go home and see my mother, but I know I cannot do that, at least at present," she replied. "I want to work and work and work until I have saved up enough money to go back to my home and live in comfort. I want to go to work right away but my sister wants me to stay here with her for two or three weeks so that I may forget just what happened. I want to forget it and I know that I will, but it will be hard—that is, at least for a while. People don't forget those things very easily, do they?"

Finally, Carrie Davies's own spontaneous voice can be heard. On the only other occasions on which her words were captured—in her initial statement to Inspector Kennedy on the night of Massey's death, and during her appearance in front of Chief Justice Mulock—she answered questions, but never volunteered information. Interpretations of the eighteen-year-old's feelings and actions were projected onto her by lawyers, reporters, witnesses, and members of the Massey family. And her voice in this *Toronto Star* interview is the guileless voice that convinced the twelve members of the jury to acquit her, although she had shot dead an unsuspecting man. Carrie really was the meek, vulnerable "little girl" that her lawyer, the newspapers, and the onlookers wanted. Her naivety had protected her from the traumatic consequences of her action. She spoke of how good the Masseys had been to her when she worked for them, adding, "I always kept my place. I knew I was only a domestic— just a servant. I did what I was told and didn't think, like many other girls do, that I was as good as the people who were employing me."

A wistful note crept into the young woman's voice as she noted, "I have not heard a word from the Masseys since it all happened." She seemed unable to comprehend the damage she had done to the family, and the grief she had caused fourteen-year-old Charlie and his mother, Rhoda.

Would she return to domestic service, asked the reporter?

"Why yes, but not to the kind of domestic service that I have been in," Carrie replied, revealing her lack of imagination about the future. In a world of widening opportunities for women, Carrie wanted to continue in "her place"—the bottom rung of the socio-economic ladder. Her ambition was to become a parlour maid "or something like that. Some kind of light service where I will not be left alone or where I will

Toronto Star, Friday, February 26, 1915: At her murder trial, Carrie told a new story (*see top-right column*).

Canadian soldiers spent the winter in ankle-deep mud. An epidemic of spinal meningitis broke out.

Each Sunday, the Canadian troops attended a church service close to Stonehenge.

In February 1915, the next contingent of Canadian soldiers marched through downtown Toronto, before their departure for Europe.

News of the dreadful Canadian casualties in France dampened morale back home.

As fear of enemy saboteurs mounted, sentries were posted around Toronto's key buildings.

Women flocked into new jobs in munitions factories, as well as into traditional occupations like nursing. Munitions workers wore coveralls, like male mechanics.

Bobsledding in High Park: Women with factory jobs could enjoy themselves all weekend, unlike domestic servants, who had only one or two afternoons off a week.

Swimming in the Humber River, in all-too-revealing costumes, was another favourite occupation for Toronto's "good-time girls."

The carnage of the Great War, as it was known, meant that many young girls like these would never achieve the old-fashioned dream of home, husband, and family.

Department stores employed increasing numbers of female sales assistants.

SKETCHED BY A STAR ARTIST AT THE CARRIE DAVIES TRIAL

A GLIMPSE OF THE JURY.

MISS DAVIES
HER BROTHER-IN-LAW MR. FAIRCHILD
AND ERNEST PELLETIER

NO PEACE UNTIL GERMANS HAVE BEEN CRUSHED

Enemy Must Pay Belgium and France for the Damage

Court drawings from the *Toronto Star*, Saturday, February 27, 1915.

Bert Massey worked in a booming industry: Toronto's annual automobile show was a glamorous occasion.

"THOUGHT OF HIS DOING ME HARM MADE ME RUN FOR REVOLVER"

Carrie Davies Says She Feared What Would Happen Her When Massey Came Home

CARRIE DAVIES

FIRED AS SHE RAN

Girl Says She Had Never Used the Revolver Before—Knew Massey Would Carry Out What He Planned—He Had Given Her a Ring—Crown Closed Case Against Girl Early This Afternoon

Evening Telegram, Saturday, February 27, 1915: The surprise end of Carrie Davies's ordeal.

not have too much responsibility. That is where the trouble was at the Masseys. I was left alone too much." She was locked into the subservient role assigned to her.

Carrie's sister Maud Fairchild shooed the reporters away. Maud was astonished to discover that Carrie's remarks about staying in service prompted job offers from people who had been following the case. Maud scotched any suggestion that her sister was ready to return to work. "There is plenty of time yet," Maud told the *Star*. "Carrie will rest for a while until she has recovered from the shock before she decides what she will do."

Two days after the trial had ended, a rumour erupted that the young woman was in a downtown Royal Bank branch office at the corner of Richmond and Yonge Streets. Immediately, people massed in front of the bank, peering through the glass windows and crowding through the doors. The frazzled manager sent a clerk out to find a policeman, but the sidewalk and intersection were so congested that the policeman had to call for backup. In the end, it took three sturdy Toronto police officers to clear the crowd. Carrie had never been near the bank.

The verdict triggered furious debate in pulpits and the press, as people tried to understand what had actually happened in the courtroom. The day after the verdict, the *New York Times* carried an article that reflected shock at the outcome. Describing Massey as a "wealthy clubman," the article's author pointed out in his first paragraph that the grounds for the acquittal were "something almost unknown to Canadian jurisprudence." The headline was "Unwritten Law In Canada: It Saves Carrie Davies, Slayer of 'Bert' Massey at Toronto." In London, England, the *Daily Sketch* also headlined its report "'Unwritten Law' Trial," but the tone of the subsequent article ("Bedfordshire Girl Acquitted of Murder in Canada") was more sympathetic to Carrie. As if loyalty to Empire might justify everything, the article's final line read, "She has a sweetheart, who is now with the Canadian contingency of the Expeditionary Force."

It was all very well to talk about "unwritten law" or "substantial justice . . . not strictly in accord with the rules," but how far might such a pliable concept be pushed? Had old-fashioned notions of chivalry towards a weak and defenceless woman swamped the rule of law? In Wesley Methodist Church the day after the verdict, the Reverend Dr. J.A. Rankin pronounced, "Justice miscarried. I believe every word the girl said. But no man can say that what that man did deserved the death penalty." A week later, at Bond Street Congregational Church, the Reverend Byron Stauffer deplored Canadian overuse of clemency. Citing the Carrie Davies verdict, he said, "We are becoming so lenient that we are apt to be swept off our feet at times."

A "prominent Toronto lawyer" sounded off in an article headlined "Has the Carrie Davies Verdict of 'Murder No Crime' Created Dangerous Precedent?" The article (so sympathetic to the Masseys that they could have commissioned it) was carried in the *Star Weekly*, the Saturday supplement to the daily paper that had been most skeptical about Carrie's story in early February. Insisting that the verdict was deplorable, despite its popularity, the lawyer suggested that the chief justice's instructions to the jury were completely inadequate, that Hartley Dewart's defence "extolled his client as a heroine in a language that would have been effusive if applied to Joan of Arc," and that the newspapers' treatment of the case was exploitative.

Newspapers' correspondence columns were filled with passionate letters on both sides of the argument. "A father of four girls and two boys" told the *Star* that he admired Carrie's "keen sense of honour. We may yet hope that a girl or woman could go through her life in Canada at least, in office, factory, or domestic life, without that fear of man that I fear too often rightfully exists at the present time." Such sentiments enraged another *Star* reader: "It is a blot on Christian justice to so glorify this girl's act . . . There is a home broken up, a widow, a boy left fatherless. No sympathy for them is spoken of. What honor was there in staying in the house till her mistress came back, if it was only to remain and shoot the husband dead?" In the *Daily News*, John Simpson of Avonmore suggested the decision had "brought Canada into disrepute as a British country," and he accused the jury of being "carried away by the twaddle served up by the lawyer for the defence."

Critics of the verdict were particularly angered by the way donations rolled into the Bedfordshire Fraternal Association's Carrie Davies Defence Fund, which the *Evening Telegram* continued to promote. Donors put their sense of solidarity with the young servant on display: accompanying the dollars, dimes, and quarters were notes signed by "Another funny-looking English girl," "A few English working girls," "English integrity," "A young Englishman," "Mother of six," "Five sympathizers," "A Yorkshire woman," "Another English Carrie," "A mother of twelve," "Defender of Faith," "Another Funny-looking one," "Employees, Prince George Hotel dining-rooms," "English Sympathizers at Ottawa," "Polson Ironworks Machine Shop," "Girls' Ideal Women's Wear," and "A few box makers." One hundred and eighteen captains and privates from an unnamed regiment contributed twenty-five cents each.

By March 1, there was close to $1,000 in the kitty. "Who is getting this money?" "C.H.J." wrote to the *Star*. "Can it be that a public testimonial is being raised to reward Miss Davies for her courageous act in shooting in cold blood the man who some thirty-six hours before had made improper proposals to her? Has it come to this? That we regard murder as an act to be applauded and raise funds to enrich the one who kills? . . . Bah! The whole performance is sickening, and the sooner the newspapers of Toronto stop allowing themselves to be exploited, the sooner will one section of the public, at any rate, be satisfied."

When the Bedfordshire Fraternal Association finally closed the fund on March 16, $1,100 had been collected. But even if this wasn't enough to pay Hartley Dewart's fee, it seems likely that the canny lawyer secured the balance from the *Toronto Evening Star*. J.H. Cranston, who had been city editor at the *Star* in 1915, commissioned a reporter to write a story about women who had walked away from murder charges—a story reflecting Joe Atkinson's views of the Carrie Davies case. According to a memoir Cranston wrote several years later, the article was fine, "but the heading I put on it all wrong." The headline, "Ontario is Easy on Murderesses," immediately attracted a libel suit. Hartley Dewart, recalled Cranston, "had had no chance of collecting fees for the defence of his client [and now] jumped at the chance to make the Star Publishing Co. pay the shot." Since Carrie had been found not guilty of murder, there was nothing for the *Star* to do but negotiate an out-of-court settlement.

Disquiet about the jury's verdict on Carrie Davies has lingered through the years, although nobody ever suggested that she might resort to such behaviour again. It is tempting to assume that those twelve rural Ontario stalwarts on the jury were appalled by sexual harassment. But that is wishful thinking: the term had not even been coined yet. Did Bert Massey's lecherous behaviour really justify his death? Carrie successfully repelled his advances. Had she really brooded for a day and a half about his behaviour, and then, in a panic, grabbed a gun and shot him point-blank? Today, although the idea that a man might be shot dead for trying to kiss a young woman is shocking, we might admire Carrie for sticking up for herself and asserting her rights. In 1915, such concepts were unknown.

Looked at through a twenty-first-century North American lens, it is hard to imagine a situation where a woman's virginity is widely considered her most precious possession, where an eighteen-year-old has few legal protections, where a penniless girl who has "sinned" is as good as ruined. Today, it is unlikely that Carrie would be acquitted, given that she shot Bert Massey in cold blood. Today, we are more likely to be shocked by notions of "unwritten laws" or "honour killings." But today, Carrie would have had more places to turn for domestic and legal protection.

More likely, it was a combination of chivalry and patriotism that shaped the jury's decision. In the febrile wartime atmosphere, Dewart had managed to procure an unwritten gentlemen's agreement that Carrie was a heroine because she had defended "British" values. "Character," not facts, had determined the outcome. The hundreds of "Britishers" who cheered her and contributed to her defence were expressing a wider unease, to do with unspoken racial and class assumptions—rage against German brutes in the trenches, anger against wealthy employers who mistreated servants, frustration at the "foreigners" flooding into Canada and competing for blue-collar jobs in a booming city. Working-class wage-earning British men defended Carrie's honour because, in doing so, they reaffirmed their own status. A nasty current of xenophobia underpinned the judgment.

There were plenty of women at the time, however, who looked at the case from a different angle. They knew that the only people women could trust in 1915 to look after their interests were themselves: vigilantism was the most effective defence against would-be rapists. Despite Du Vernet's assertion, in his closing address, that Bert Massey could have been penalized in a court of law for his offence, since 1880, not a single Toronto domestic who had laid a complaint of indecent assault or rape against her employer had seen him punished. The law was an unreliable defender of their interests, and it took courage to challenge the status quo.

Mrs. Florence Huestis, with her knowledge of stigma, was one woman who knew this. The National Council of Women immediately began discussions on how to protect servants like Carrie from predatory employers. At the request of the Dominion conference of a moral reform group called the Canadian Vigilance Association, it floated the idea that there should be an office where domestics might bring complaints about their employers. The Vigilance Association had even made the start-ling suggestion that domestics be entitled to ask for testimonials of their employers' characters, as well as being required to produce testimonials about themselves. There is no evidence that this suggestion went any-where, but the notion of employment rights, even for the most defence-less of employees, began to gain ground.

Working-class women were more explicit about their attitude to Carrie, as demonstrated in a letter to the *Star*. "I am a married woman of 30 years," wrote someone signing herself "F. L. M." "At the age of 18 I was a Carrie Davies, and though there was no weapon in my favour, I sent my adversary down a flight of stairs, and he picked himself up with great difficulty. I presume if he had been killed [Carrie's critics] would have cried: 'Down with her! Hang her!' There are only too few Carrie Davies in this world . . . As for the financial side of it, God bless the donors: there are heaps of charitable subscriptions not half so worthy."

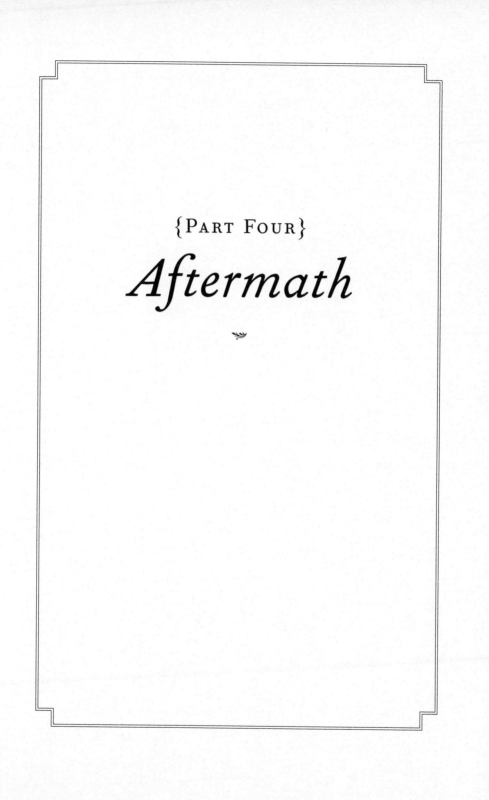

{PART FOUR}

Aftermath

{CHAPTER 17}

Total War

MARCH 1915 TO NOVEMBER 1918

═══════

The military strength of Germany is now at its maximum. Her troops are not now so disciplined as the highly-trained soldiers first put into the field, but they are more numerous. She probably has a million more men on both fronts than she had in September last when her tide of victory reached its crest. But the allies have made even larger additions to their forces and have overcome nearly every disadvantage that told against them in the first two months of the struggle. And as nations now neutral are certain to join the allies during the next two months, the outlook for Germany is eminently black.
—*Toronto Daily Star,* Monday, March 1, 1915

SUFFRAGETS [SIC] AFTER PREMIER HEARST.
Open letter written by Canadian Suffrage Association to the Ontario Government . . .
"It cannot be gainsaid that in social and moral reform work in which all good women are actively interested that valuable time is wasted, to say nothing of discouragement and defeat, when in order to bring about the desired results, Councils, Governments etc have to be 'influenced' by the indirect and frittering method of pleading, instead of by the direct method of the ballot, and thinking people feel that our country is the loser thereby."
—*Evening Telegram,* Wednesday, March 3, 1915

The international story soon swamped the local story, and interest in Carrie Davies evaporated as the war in France gathered momentum. Canadians were now within range of German guns. The first few days on the Franco-Belgian border, in early March, were nerve-racking for the newly arrived soldiers. "Come out, you Canadians! Come out and fight!" Germans yelled at them across no man's land; machine guns clattered during the chilly days and flares exploded at night; German snipers picked off several men who unwisely stuck their heads above the trenches. The front-line trenches were soggy ditches with inadequate latrines and crumbling walls that offered little protection from shrapnel. The rats were large, vicious, and ubiquitous. Lieutenant Colonel John J. Creelman from Toronto confided in his diary, "I expect that a lot of men will lose their minds out here and others their hearing because the noise made by a shell bursting alongside is terrific."

In the early days of the month, there was no large-scale Allied offensive, so casualties were intermittent, but the *Globe* began to list the dead and wounded on its front page. "Private Nugent of Toronto Wounded," read a sober headline on March 1. "Official Casualty List Shows The First Expeditionary Force Has Been Under Fire. No Particulars Are Given."

The *Evening Telegram* rang a different note in its war coverage: it echoed the euphoria of the "Britishers" at Carrie's trial. "Canucks' Warm Reception," read the newspaper's March 1 headline. "Union Jacks All Over." The article quoted a letter from Percy Buttery, a former reporter from the *Hamilton Spectator*. Percy was still elated by the adventure. "We met with a great reception [from the French] and it was evident that the Dominion troops had established themselves in the affections of the French people, particularly the female portion thereof." For families left in neighbourhoods like Cabbagetown and Islington, Percy Buttery's cheerful account was a reassuring boost to Imperial triumphalism.

But even the jingoistic *Tely* couldn't erase the horrors. Percy's letter went on to mention, "We can hear the daily booming of the guns, while at night rockets are used by both sides . . . In the very field in which our horses are now picketed, nineteen Germans are buried and large numbers of others are in different places round about." A few days later, *Tely* readers found in their papers an alarming letter from an English soldier to his brother in Toronto. "You cannot realize how it feels to have the shrapnel bursting in our trenches and whizzing past our heads. I have been hit three times . . . Our battalion has lost three hundred and twenty men in ten weeks out of fourteen hundred."

In the field, Canadian soldiers kept their spirits up with songs like "Mademoiselle from Armentières," "Keep Your Head Down, Fritzie Boy," and "Take Me Back to Dear Old Blighty." Their first major engagement occurred on March 10, when they were on the flank of a large attack by British and Indian troops at a small village called Neuve-Chapelle. For three hours, the Canadians kept up a heavy rate of fire from their trenches against the German trenches only two hundred feet away. The Canadians lost a hundred men: more worrying, several soldiers complained that their Canadian-made Ross rifles had jammed during the rapid-firing exercise. But Neuve-Chapelle was merely a preliminary taste of battle horrors: the Canadian Division was soon moved into the Ypres Salient. Now Canadians were firmly on the front lines, sandwiched between a British division to the right and an Algerian division to the left, and with the medieval market town of Ypres behind them.

Nervous anticipation of German brutality proved justified on April 22, when the Germans began pounding the city of Ypres with enormous shells from large-calibre siege guns. Then a menacing green cloud seeped out from enemy lines. The gas cloud was formed from 160 tonnes of chlorine liquid, released from canisters via rubber hoses. The Allies had been warned that the Germans planned to use poison gas, but nobody knew exactly what kind. Once the cloud drifted into Allied trenches, its true effects were obvious. It smothered the Algerian line first, and soon Algerian soldiers were stumbling away from the front, choking, screaming, and dying of asphyxiation. The Canadians missed the full brunt of the gas cloud and fought on, trying to fill the gap on their left flank, even as the poisonous fumes triggered streaming eyes and hacking coughs. "Piss on your handkerchiefs and tie them over your faces," yelled an officer at George Bell, a young Canadian soldier. Those who didn't use handkerchiefs or strips from their puttees "rolled about, gasping for breath." Bell's comrades fought for two solid days "with no sleep, not even a chance to nod, feeling that every minute is our last, and with nothing to eat or drink."

News of the battle that came to be called "Second Ypres," and this horrific new weapon, appeared in Toronto newspapers a couple of days later. At first, the extraordinary courage of Canadian soldiers was treated with enthusiasm. "This contingent, out-numbered and forced to give way, covered themselves with glory and apparently saved the day," commented the *Star* on April 24. The *Globe* was equally enthusiastic: "Every single evening newspaper [in London] contains the word 'Canada.'" But bravery came at tremendous cost. Two hundred officers (one in six from Toronto) and almost six thousand other ranks were killed, wounded, or missing—almost one-third of the total Canadian Division. Colonel Denison lost both a nephew and a grandson in the terrible mayhem—among the dead were thirty-six-year-old Lance Corporal Edgar Denison of the 16th Battalion (Canadian Scottish Regiment), and twenty-four-year-old Lieutenant Alexander Kirkpatrick of the 3rd Battalion CEF. It is likely that this was the battle in which Carrie's sweetheart fell, too. He would almost certainly have been at the front, along with other youngsters who had once demonstrated their marksmanship at the shooting gallery on Toronto Island.

Back home, spring had finally arrived: magnolia trees in Rosedale backyards bloomed, chestnut trees along University Avenue were in bud, and the days were lengthening. But the families crowded outside newspaper offices on King Street, waiting for casualty lists to be posted, were filled with feverish anxiety and dread. Week after week, in Anglican churches throughout the city, organists led the congregation in the hymn "O God, Our Help in Ages Past."

Second Ypres was only the beginning, and for the next three and a half years the war roared on like a pitiless meat grinder. Canadian troops were involved in the battles of Festubert (May 1915), Givenchy (mid-June 1915), St. Eloi Craters (April 1916), Mount Sorrel (June 1916), and Courcelette (September 1916). After months of anxious speculation, the Americans finally entered the war in April 1917, but the carnage continued. Each engagement spawned its own grim casualty list; the five-and-a-half-month Battle of the Somme, conducted in a slough of clinging, caramel-coloured mud, was a glimpse of hell for the troops. According to a French corporal, the battlefield "resembled in places a rubbish dump in which there had accumulated shreds of clothing, smashed weapons, shattered helmets, rotting rations, bleached bones and putrescent flesh." Back home, power brokers within Ottawa and Toronto were unnerved by the erratic behaviour of Sir Sam Hughes, the man who had run Canada's war effort for the first two and a half years as minister of militia and defence. The famous Canadian trenching tool invented by Ena MacAdam, Hughes's secretary, proved useless, as did the boots he had ordered from Canadian factories and the Ross rifle with which he had insisted that Canadian troops be equipped. Yet the Canadian soldiers gradually established a battlefield reputation as "elite shock troops," as Great War historian Tim Cook has put it, and the British High Command repeatedly turned to them to deliver victory.

In public, most Canadians clung to the belief that they were involved in an Imperial crusade against evil, that the hideous sacrifice of lives was justified, and that victory was just around the corner. At a giant rally in Massey Hall in January 1917, hundreds of Torontonians celebrated a Patriotic Fund drive that had yielded an astonishing $3.2 million (about $64 million in today's currency)—an average of nearly ten dollars for every man, woman, and child. The *World* caught the mood: "For sheer patriotic, selfless, spontaneous, exuberant enthusiasm, . . . there never has been such another meeting in Toronto . . . They sang 'Jolly Good Fellow,' whenever they got the chance, and 'God Save the King,' 'Rule Britannia,' 'Keep the Home Fires Burning' . . ." For this audience, links to the mother country had never felt closer. The shared euphoria at such crowded occasions was similar to the mood two years earlier, in the City Hall courtroom when Carrie Davies was acquitted.

Carrie herself, however, had effectively disappeared. Who cared about the timid young woman who had shot a ne'er-do-well on Walmer Road, when real heroes were dying in France? The *Evening Telegram* had got everything it wanted out of her story, and Archie Fisher had moved on to other scandals.

Toronto men of all social classes continued to sign up. Two of Colonel George Denison's sons volunteered. Bert Massey's cousin Vincent Massey was in uniform by 1916, although he never went overseas: he served as a staff officer in Canada and ultimately worked for the war cabinet in Ottawa. Bert Massey's nephew Arnold, son of Arthur and Mary Ethel Massey, volunteered for the Canadian Field Artillery in 1916, when he was nineteen, and after training in England he served in the Royal Naval Air Service.

However, rousing public choruses of Imperial solidarity could not drown out private grief: the shocking slaughter and grim hopelessness of trench warfare ate away at the romantic view of warfare as a stage for gallantry and heroism. In April 1917, nearly 11,000 Canadians were mown down (3,598 fatally) over the course of the four-day battle at Vimy Ridge. Families lived in dread of the knock on the door and the telegram that began, "Regret to inform . . ." Mothers realized they would be raising their children alone. Farmers' wives wondered who would help them keep the farms going. Single women looked around them and realized that, with a whole generation of young men lost, they themselves would be left adrift, their traditional dreams of marriage and children out of reach forever. They were condemned to lives as "spinsters" or "old maids"—the derogatory labels routinely applied to unattached women.

A new note of Canadian nationalism seeped into the thinking of both soldiers and politicians. In France, the commander of the Canadian Corps after June 1917, Lieutenant General Sir Arthur Currie, was ordered by General Haig, the British commander-in-chief, to move his divisions north to fight in the Passchendaele campaign. Currie did not trust Haig's strategic judgment and objected to his foolhardy battle plan. Haig insisted on sticking to the plan, although Currie managed to secure additional heavy guns to support his troops. Against the odds, the Canadian Corps captured what was left of the ridge and established a reputation within the German military command as the Allies' most effective troops. But once again, the cost in lives was appalling: 16,041 casualties, including 3,042 killed.

By now, even the mild-mannered Canadian prime minister had had enough. Sir Robert Borden was no longer prepared to give unquestioned deference to the mother country's needs and was increasingly exasperated by the lack of Canadian input into British military strategy. Did Westminster regard colonials as simply cannon fodder in the desolate landscapes of northern France? Borden expressed Canadian frustration at a meeting of the Imperial War Cabinet in London in June 1918. After a furious description of the ineptitude of British generals, he strode across the room and announced that no more Canadian soldiers would cross the Atlantic if such incompetence continued. When peace came five months later, Borden insisted that Canada sign the Treaty of Versailles in her own right, and take her own seat at both the new League of Nations and the International Labour Organization.

The war had been transformational: a different country was emerging in the northern half of North America. Thousands of families had lost loved ones: more than sixty thousand Canadian soldiers, airmen, and nursing sisters were dead. Every third man in uniform had been mutilated in mind or body: every tenth man had been killed. Bert Massey's half-brother, Lieutenant Clifton Manbank Horsey, was killed in 1916 at St. Eloi and was buried in a military cemetery in Belgium. George Taylor Denison Jr., the forty-eight-year-old son of Colonel George Denison, died on May 8, 1917, after being wounded a month earlier at Vimy Ridge. There was no sudden "Birth of a Nation" moment, as the troops went over the top at St. Eloi, or Vimy, or Passchendaele. There was no suggestion that Canada was still anything but the most loyal as well as the oldest dominion in the British Empire. But there was now daylight between Ottawa and Westminster.

People whose families had crossed the Atlantic from the British Isles began to rethink their identity and define themselves as "Canadians." The survivors of the bloodbaths of the Somme or Vimy Ridge came home with a new pride in their own as well as the mother country.

Raw-boned Canadian lads, working alongside British troops as they tunnelled, charged, fired, bayonetted, or flew, had discovered that Canadians *were* different and were just as good on the battlefield as more experienced men. Harold Innis, who would become one of the country's most renowned historians, wrote a thesis on "The Returned Soldier" while recovering in Surrey from wounds sustained at Vimy. He stammered out his personal mission and his burgeoning Canadian nationalism: "Work, work of brain and of brawn, co-operation, organization and determination to heal the sores . . . and to start again along the lines of sound national progress, is the hope of the Canadian people . . . that she may take her place among the nations of the world for the privilege of which her best blood had been shed."

Even in Toronto, the centre of Canada's Anglo-Celtic culture, a new generation began to feel the stirrings of a pro-Canadian sentiment. Such sentiment did not translate into greater tolerance of immigrants from non-British backgrounds: in August 1918, returned soldiers smashed fifteen restaurants in downtown Toronto that were suspected of employing enemy aliens rather than veterans. For seven days, there were repeated clashes between police and civilians, and although there were many arrests, most charges were dismissed. Nevertheless, the "Britishers" who had cheered the little girl from Sandy were now starting to define Canada as home and were eager to inject their own values into their country. They wanted a Canada where a wealthy elite could not expect unquestioning deference, and where men with diamond stick pins did not take advantage of eighteen-year-old servants.

❧

At the same time, another seismic shift in attitudes was occurring close to the surface of Toronto society. For four years on the home front, women had played a vigorous and visible part in the war effort. In the early months of the war, the first duty of women was to allow loved ones to serve the Empire, but that soon ramped up into a fever of knitting to provide soldiers with socks, gloves, and scarves. The Toronto Patriotic League reported: "Lonely women on farms are knitting long into the night. Society women take their knitting to theatres and concert halls. Everywhere women have got back to their needles."

Soon, women's participation in the war effort took them into less traditional activities. Campaigns to increase recruitment of able-bodied men became increasingly aggressive: by 1918, approximately three out of every four Toronto men had offered to serve. Women from all walks of life began fundraising not just for hospital ships and motor ambulances, but for front-line weaponry. While hundreds of working-class servants braver than Carrie untied their aprons and signed up to work in munitions and aircraft factories, middle-class women slid into typically male white-collar jobs, such as bank clerks. The women shared a sense of public purpose they had never felt before.

In July 1916, three and a half thousand women crowded into Massey Hall for a rally to discuss how much more they might do to support the war effort. As knitting needles clicked throughout the hall, representatives of women's organizations urged the audience to set free every available man. One of the most inspiring speakers was the Toronto Council of Women's Mrs. Florence Huestis. "We are not looking for women to replace men permanently; we are not looking for a position that a returned soldier could fill; we are not looking for a position that an unfit man holds; but we are looking for positions that are held by men who ought to be in khaki."

At the 1918 Canadian National Exhibition, on the shores of Lake Ontario, women gave demonstrations of handling tractors, lathing fence posts, and operating heavy machinery. A model tent field hospital had been set up, and, undeterred by drenching rain, nurses and female ambulance drivers displayed their medical competence. The

News reporter caught the novelty of the show, as he described how the women "seemed to typify the spirit of the new age . . . They did not seem like the same women of a year or two ago . . . To many a man in the audience it was a new phase of womanly character which might never have been seen had it not been for the war."

The campaign to give Canadian women the vote had begun well before the outbreak of war. The fiery orator Nellie McClung had led the fight in the west, and by 1916 women in all three Prairie provinces had won the right to vote in provincial elections. However, activists in the Ontario capital had to deal with more entrenched resistance. In 1909, Ontario Premier Sir James Whitney brushed aside a petition for female suffrage signed by a hundred thousand women with a dismissive "Not now." Once Canada was at war, politicians were not alone in continuing to say, "Not now." In 1916, the Women's Patriotic League announced that efforts to win the vote for women should wait until the end of hostilities.

Leaders like Mrs. Huestis refused to be deterred. Why should women *not* be treated as equals when the war efforts depended on their labour outside the home and their formidable organizational achievements in fundraising and recruitment campaigns? Out in Alberta, McClung put the issue most concisely: "After you have driven your own car, will you be content to drive an ox in a Red River cart?" Finally, in 1917, nurses serving at the front and those with close relatives in the forces were given the right to vote. Prime Minister Sir Robert Borden had made this concession for Machiavellian rather than feminist reasons. He calculated that these women would vote in favour of his commitment to conscription and outweigh the votes of conscription critics in Quebec. But once the door was open, there was no turning back. The following year, the right to vote in federal elections was widened to include most Canadian women.

By war's end, the balance of power between men and women had shifted, and women of all classes were no longer content to stay at the margins of public life. Returning soldiers found that most working-class women clung to factory jobs when they could, rather than return to dark basement kitchens, dirty fireplaces, and derisory wages. Women had proved they were more than helpless creatures in need of protection. They were not "little girls," and they began to demand rights, not simple chivalry. It would take three-quarters of a century and a revolution in social attitudes before abused women were given explicit protection in the law, but Carrie Davies's acquittal had hinted at the changes to come.

{CHAPTER 18}

The Later Years

What of Carrie Davies herself, in this social turmoil? Did she take a new position as a parlour maid? Did she risk German torpedoes and cross the Atlantic to visit her mother in the Bedfordshire village of Sandy? The Toronto newspapers were too busy following the horrors of war to keep track of her. Within a few days of the trial, she had slipped back into the shadows that envelope women like her. There is no trace of her in Toronto street directories, newspaper libraries, or obituaries.

However, in the early 1980s, an energetic *Toronto Star* reporter managed to track Carrie Davies down. Frank Jones had decided to write a novel about the case, and an acquaintance suggested he contact a Carrie Brown of Huttonville, a farming community a few kilometres west of Brampton, a city about fifty kilometres to the northwest of Toronto. It was the same Carrie, but when Jones called the number he had been given, he discovered that she had died two decades earlier, leaving a son and a daughter, Margaret Grainger. He arrived at the daughter's door with some trepidation. "Death can cast a long shadow," he recalls thinking. He was right to tread carefully. To his surprise, he discovered that Carrie had never told her children what had happened when she was eighteen. Jones described to an astonished Margaret the events of 1915 and showed her photocopies of all the newspaper stories. After Margaret had taken it all in, she quietly wept. "She had such a hard, hard life," she told Jones.

Margaret was able to fill in some of the blanks, although she said her mother had never talked much about the war years. Carrie had returned to England and tried nursing, but found the sight of blood too upsetting to continue. By 1917, she was back in Canada, where she met and married Charles Brown, an Englishman a few years older than she was. The Browns struggled to make a living from a succession of farms in the Huttonville area, but the wolf was never far from the door. Charles tried to get a roofing business established, while Carrie cared for a market garden and worked as a school caretaker.

As Margaret described her mother to Frank Jones, she emphasized Carrie's constant effort to help others, particularly young girls in a jam. "My girlfriend's sister was always getting into trouble and Mother was always so sympathetic towards her . . . And I never understood why." One of Carrie's final jobs before her death was as a house mother at the Cedarvale Home for Wayward Girls in nearby Georgetown.

Carrie kept her secret. But Frank Jones's revelation did explain to her daughter one anomaly in the life that the former domestic servant had fashioned for herself. After Carrie's death, her children checked the brief trail of paperwork she had left. She had always said that her birthdate was April 28, 1900—the date on her passport. But her birth certificate showed she was born April 28, 1897. She had quietly eradicated three years from her life—probably her first three years in Toronto.

Thirty years later, with Frank Jones's generous help, I reached out to Margaret, who was now ninety-one years old and living with her own daughter, a teacher in the Toronto area. I explained to Margaret's daughter what I was doing, and asked if I might speak to Carrie's daughter. I was told that Margaret had been unable to bring herself to read Frank Jones's novel, *Master and Maid: The Charles Massey Murder*, and she did not want to speak to me.

Some stories are too painful—even after nearly a century.

The Massey family continued to regard the verdict rendered on February 27, 1915, as a miscarriage of justice. Shocked to see the Massey name linked with depravity rather than philanthropy, in the years ahead they rarely mentioned the violent death on Walmer Road. When they did, Bert's death was firmly labelled a "murder." But the two branches of the family—the descendants of Charles Albert, Hart Massey's eldest son, and the wealthier descendants of Hart's younger sons, Chester and Walter—went their separate ways.

In the short term, Bert's widow, Rhoda, faced a difficult issue: How long could she afford to continue living on Walmer Road? Her husband had taken out some life insurance, but when the will was read, she discovered she and young Charlie had only $8,441.20 in the world. And she knew that the more illustrious Masseys, in their Yonge Street mansions, were unlikely to extend a helping hand.

Rhoda Massey never remarried. Sometime after her death in 1957, a simple marble monument marking the "other" Massey grave was finally erected in Mount Pleasant Cemetery. The inscription reads, "In Loving Memory," and on the left-hand side, "Charles Albert Massey, Aug. 5, 1880–Feb. 8, 1915 / His Wife Frances Rhoda Vandegrift, Jan. 17, 1880–Jan. 19, 1957." On the right-hand side lie Bert's older brother, "Arthur Lyman Massey, Feb. 6, 1874–Feb. 17, 1936 / His Wife Mary Ethel Bonnell, May 21, 1875–Nov. 7, 1951."

Bert and Rhoda's son, Charles Albert Massey, emerged apparently unscathed from the family scandal that had erupted when he was fourteen. Seven years later, after attending the University of Toronto, he graduated at the head of his class at Osgoode Law School and won the Chancellor Van Koughnet Scholarship and gold medal. The *Toronto Star* noted that the good-looking young man, dark hair swept straight back from his broad brow, was "son of the late C.A. Massey and great grandson of the late Hart A. Massey." Two years later, Charles Massey married into hockey royalty in a lavish ceremony at St. Paul's Anglican Church, Bloor Street. The bride, Audrey Hewitt, was the daughter of William Hewitt, sports editor of the *Star* and "very well known in the sporting world [who] managed the victorious Canadian Olympic hockey team." Charles's new brother-in-law was Foster Hewitt, who became the Ron MacLean of his day—a CBC hockey commentator with an instantly recognizable voice.

Charles Massey practised law for only five years. He would later tell a reporter that, every time he had a court case, he suffered from nervous indigestion and ringing in his ears. "I couldn't make a living as a lawyer," he admitted; he found the courtroom experience too stressful. He went on to become president of Lever Brothers of Canada, one of Canada's "youngest and most successful top executives." The *Tely* reporter who wrote the glowing profile of this successful businessman did not mention the Massey family history, nor the court case that had sullied the Massey reputation and perhaps triggered Charles Massey's panic. It was all too long ago.

In 1950, Charles Massey (now tagged "Canada's soap king") joined the board of Lever Brothers U.S. A member of the Conservative Party, the Toronto Club, the Toronto Hunt Club, and the Royal Canadian Yacht Club, he had been quietly absorbed into the Canadian establishment. His cousin (and lifelong Liberal) Vincent Massey served as the country's first Canadian-born governor general between 1952 and 1959, but no correspondence between the two men has survived in Vincent Massey's papers.

❧

The other individuals involved in the Carrie Davies case all continued on the trajectories on which they were already set in 1915.

Hartley Dewart finally won a Liberal seat in the Ontario legislature in a by-election in August 1916. At first, he seemed bound for political prominence: his eloquence and debating skills were unparalleled. But he was just too ornery. He opposed both conscription and Prohibition, causing splits within his party, and his withering wit offended colleagues. Although he took the helm of the Ontario Liberals in 1919, as Opposition leader, he was denounced by the *Toronto Star* (usually a rock-solid supporter of all Liberals) and by his own MPPs. His abstemious Methodist father would have been appalled to read the *Christian Guardian*'s description of the younger Dewart as the "chief representative of the liquor interests in the legislature."

The *Star* supported Prohibition, so perhaps that is why the newspaper turned against Dewart. But in his memoirs, newspaperman J.H. Cranston gives another reason. Joe Atkinson was furious that Dewart had successfully sued the *Star* for libel after the careless reference to a "murderess" in a headline. Cranston admitted that Dewart's libel suit was a cunning tactic to pay Carrie's legal bill. "But it is doubtful if his cleverness paid off in the long run. Atkinson gave orders that Dewart's name was henceforth to be kept out of the *Star* newspapers, and politicians live on publicity."

After Dewart lost the provincial election of 1923, he returned to private practice and lobbied Prime Minister Mackenzie King to be put on the Supreme Court of Canada. But the abstemious and prim King disapproved of Dewart's drinking, and the only federal bone Dewart was thrown was a seat on a commission charged with producing a new consolidation of the statutes of Canada. In 1924, Dewart died at the age of sixty-two of overwork, according to his obituaries. Prime Minister King was one of the honorary pallbearers at his funeral.

In contrast, William Mulock, already known as the "Grand Old Man" in 1915, became an increasingly revered figure in the Canadian pantheon, called upon to grace endless official occasions with his venerable presence. He lived for another twenty-nine years. He remained chief justice of Ontario until he was ninety-three years old, a record in Canadian courts (and, given the unpredictability of some of his later judgments, perhaps part of the reason that judges today must retire at age seventy-five). During the Second World War, when he was ninety-nine, he chaired the Canadian Committee of the International YMCA, which supervised enemy prisoners in Canada. Appointed chancellor of the University of Toronto in 1924, he still held that office when he died, aged 101, in 1944.

At a luncheon in his honour shortly after his eighty-seventh birthday, Mulock described his attitude to growing old: "I'm still at work with my hand to the plough and my face to the future. The shadows of evening . . . lengthen about me but morning is in my heart. . . . [T]he testimony I bear is this: that the castle of enchantment is not yet behind me, it is before me still and daily I catch glimpses of its battlements and towers. The best of life is always further on. The real lure is hidden from our eyes, somewhere behind the hills of time."

His stockpile of rye whiskey lasted him all his life, and in later years it was black—about 120 proof. This suited the old man fine: he would shake a single drop of water into a full tumbler so he could honestly claim that he never drank it neat.

Colonel George Denison III was another old soldier who stayed long in harness: he continued to gallop through police court hearings as Toronto's chief magistrate until his retirement, aged eighty-two, in 1921. The same year, he presided at the unveiling of the cenotaph commemorating nine members of the extended Denison family killed in the war. His belief in the nobility of military service was undimmed: "There is nothing that so much indicates the virile spirit of a nation as the habit of friends and relatives raising memorials to the memory of those . . . who have lost their lives in the service of their country," he said. Colonel Denison died in 1925. Harry Wodson wrote in his obituary in the *Evening Telegram*, "No city in the world has ever seen his like on the Bench, and it is improbable that such a man in that position will ever be seen again." To the relief of Ontario court officials, Wodson was right.

Arthur Roebuck, the young articling clerk in the offices of Dewart, Maw & Hodgson who was the go-between with the *Evening Telegram*, achieved the career success that had eluded his mentor, Hartley Dewart. Like Dewart, he was a Laurier Liberal who often clashed with party orthodoxy. However, this did not impede his ascent. He served as attorney general of Ontario from 1934 to 1937, and was active in promoting the rights of trade unions and defending Jews from the virulent anti-Semitism that characterized the province. He then moved into federal politics, as Liberal MP for the Toronto riding of Trinity. In 1945, Prime Minister Mackenzie King appointed him to the Senate, and he remained a senator until his death, aged ninety-three, in 1971. In his family memoir, *The Roebuck Story* (published in 1963), he does not mention the Carrie Davies case.

Mrs. Florence Huestis served an unprecedented nine years as president of the Toronto Local Council of Women. During these years, she continued to straddle the gulf between women who wanted to be in the centre of the political action, as voters and elected officials themselves, and those who preferred "maternal feminism," promoting more traditional welfare reforms. Under her adroit leadership, TLCW successfully lobbied for pasteurized milk, postnatal education for new mothers, purification of the water system, and allowances for widows and deserted mothers. She spearheaded the campaigns for medical and dental care for children and the provision of playgrounds in the city. Premier William Hearst must have got to know well the sound of her soft, persuasive, but insistent voice: she was constantly in his office, arguing for women to be appointed as school inspectors, for female householders to receive the same tax breaks as men did, and for more spending on health facilities.

Women like Florence Huestis made a remarkable difference to their communities across Canada, through their local organizations and the National Council of Women of Canada. Unelected and unpaid, their lives have too easily been dismissed as an unimportant reflection of their husbands' and fathers' status. There is no oil painting of Mrs. Huestis at Queen's Park, nor is there any monument to the TLCW's achievements. "She did so much, but there are few records— just a couple of old newspaper and magazine articles," observes her great-granddaughter Kathy Weekes Southee. Florence Huestis died in 1955. The National Council of Women of Canada, which in 2013 celebrates its 120th birthday, continues to work on a wide range of issues, including violence against women, assistance for immigrant women, and proportional representation.

Joe Atkinson and the *Star* won the press war. In 1971, the *Evening Telegram* folded, because the *Toronto Daily Star,* now known simply as the *Toronto Star,* had outsold it for years. John Ross Robertson, the *Tely*'s pugnacious proprietor, died in 1918; "Black Jack" Robinson remained as editor until his death in 1928. In 1971, many of the *Tely*'s employees moved to the newly launched *Toronto Sun,* which shared the *Tely*'s Conservative politics; however, the *Star* bought the *Tely*'s subscriber list.

Today, the *Star* is Canada's largest-circulation newspaper and largest online news source. Its politics remain true to the Atkinson vision: a nationalist voice on the left of the political spectrum. During its existence, its editors have seen Toronto become the largest city in Canada, with a population of 2.8 million that is more diverse than anybody might have imagined in 1915. Over 140 languages and dialects are spoken there today, and just over 30 percent of Toronto residents speak a language other than French or English at home. It is a very different city from the one where Masseys, Denisons, Dewarts, and Mulocks held sway. Fewer than one in five Torontonians have British backgrounds.

Yet vestiges of the Anglo-Celtic ascendancy remain. Many of Canada's largest law firms, with dozens of partners ensconced in glass towers in major cities, grew out of the small, powerful partnerships that existed in 1915. So far, the diversity of people on Toronto's streets is not reflected in the hierarchies in its politics or its law courts. And most of the buildings mentioned here remain. The old Don Jail has been transformed and now houses a health administration centre, and the Lombard Street morgue is a dilapidated music rehearsal space. But Old City Hall still houses the police courts, and 169 Walmer Street remains an unassuming house (now divided into three small apartments) on a quiet residential street.

❧

When Carrie Davies fired the shot on February 8, 1915, the impact on her victim and his family were shattering. Carrie herself must have been traumatized, and she seems to have spent the rest of her life in denial that it had ever happened.

Yet Carrie's case had surprisingly little impact on the law at the time. There is no evidence that the Davies case was ever cited in subsequent murder trials—because no decision was made on a point of law, it was never reported in any volume of law reports. To the 1915 editor of the *Ontario Law Reports,* it would have had no value as a precedent to guide future trials. Indeed, there was nothing to report because Justice Mulock gave no ruling from the bench. For the legal professionals involved, the acquittal was probably seen as a dangerous aberration—the right decision for this case, perhaps, but not the kind of thing that ought to happen other than in very exceptional circumstances. It certainly did *not* establish a tradition of judicial chivalry, let alone an assumption that a woman had the right to defend herself against sexual abuse. In fact, there was no mention of the case in law books for the next six decades, and Canadian law continued to treat women as dependants of their fathers, husbands, or brothers. Even the enthusiasm of early feminists for special legal protections for women fizzled out. Once women had the vote, Toronto's Women's Court was increasingly regarded as an anachronism: it was disbanded in 1934.

But some of the emotions and concerns that Carrie's case aroused flowed on through the twentieth century, as women entered universities, professions, and politics, and lobbied for equality.

It took a resurgence of feminism—the so-called Second Wave of the 1960s—to prompt a rediscovery of the Carrie Davies case. Feminist lawyers like Constance Backhouse and historians including Carolyn Strange wrote about the case as an example of the gender biases built into implementation of the law.

These were also the years in which Dr. Henry Morgentaler was challenging anti-abortion laws across Canada and was repeatedly prosecuted. In Quebec, on three occasions the jurors did exactly what their counterparts in the Carrie Davies case had done fifty years earlier in Ontario: they refused to apply the law and convict him. The jurors decided that the law was unfair: they deemed the rights of women worthy of precedence over legal rules that reflected the community standards of a previous era. The term "jury nullification" entered the Canadian legal lexicon.

The Supreme Court of Canada reversed the jury acquittals of Dr. Morgentaler and ordered new trials. But once the Charter of Rights became the supreme law of the land in 1984, the Supreme Court struck down the abortion law on procedural grounds. Justice Bertha Wilson, the first woman to sit on the Supreme Court, added to this decision a minority opinion that the issue also involved women's rights. "The right to reproduce or not to reproduce . . . is properly perceived as an integral part of modern women's struggle to assert her dignity and worth as a human being."

At the same time, increasing concern about domestic violence against women culminated in another important Supreme Court decision in 1990, the Lavallee decision. Canada's highest court upheld the acquittal of a woman called Angelique Lavallee, who had shot her abusive common-law husband in the back of the head during a fight. Like Hartley Dewart, Lavallee's lawyer had argued that his client was not guilty on grounds of self-defence. This was a much broader definition of self-defence within a relationship than had hitherto been accepted by the Canadian judiciary. Angelique Lavallee won her acquittal not because a group of men felt a chivalrous instinct to show mercy to a defenceless young virgin, but because the court recognized that a woman had a right to defend herself from a physically abusive partner. Lavallee had committed neither murder nor manslaughter: she was a battered wife who was in fear for her life.

The Lavallee decision enshrined the principle that a woman in fear of her life was justified in defending herself against an aggressor, even to the point of killing. Carrie Davies would never have passed what lawyers call "the Lavallee test": she was not in imminent danger of assault when she killed Bert Massey with his own gun on that chilly February evening. But under today's laws, Charles Albert Massey would have known that he harassed a young woman at his peril.

A frightened maid shot and killed her employer. Thousands of men fought and died on faraway battlefields. Day-to-day life for most Canadians went on: the generation that remembered Confederation Day in July 1867 died, and a new generation that would watch Canadian troops ship off to another European war was born. There was no dramatic change of direction: the Carrie Davies case and the Battle of Vimy Ridge were both symptoms of a larger reality—Canada's evolution into a prosperous, autonomous country. As the country developed, so Canada's laws, lawyers, and citizens adapted to its shifting values.

Sources

There is no transcript of Carrie Davies's criminal trial, with supporting documentation, because she was acquitted. Nor are there any notes from Toronto's police magistrate George Denison or Ontario's chief justice, Sir William Mulock: neither man collected or preserved many professional or personal papers. The only official records of Carrie's progress through the Ontario justice system are notices of her hearing in the police court on February 9, the transcript of evidence heard before the coroner at the inquest on February 15, and the notice filed on February 22 for her appearance in the Supreme Court of Ontario on a murder charge. These records are in the Ontario Archives (RG 22–392–0-9029 MS 8564). I am particularly grateful to Justice Robert Sharpe for passing on this reference to me.

However, newspaper accounts of the case are extensive. I spent hours poring over microfilm of the *Toronto Daily Star,* the *Evening Telegram,* the *Globe,* the *Toronto Daily News,* as well as the bimonthly magazine *Saturday Night,* piecing together the story and discerning the accuracy and biases of their reports. In most chapters, I have given attributions within the text for most quotations from newspapers: only in the trial, where differences were minimal, have I amalgamated the coverage.

There are several other reference books on which I relied for information about key figures in the case and background events. Chief among them is the *Dictionary of Canadian Biography (DCB),* a consistently accurate and lively online resource for researchers. I also turned to some of the wonderfully portentous catalogues of eminent men dating from this period, including John A. Cooper's *Men of Canada* (Toronto: Canadian Historical Company, 1901–02) and Geo. Maclean Rose, ed., *A Cyclopaedia of Canadian Biography: Being Chiefly Men of the Time* (Toronto: Rose Publishing, 1886).

For information about the First World War, I turned to Tim Cook's masterly two-volume account of Canadian contributions to the war effort: *At the Sharp End* (Toronto: Viking, 2007) and *Shock Troops* (Toronto: Viking, 2008). I also enjoyed Correlli Barnett's *The Great War* (London: Penguin, 1979, 2000) and Adam Hochschild's *To End All Wars* (London: Macmillan, 2011). There was much useful material in Ian Hugh Maclean Miller's *Our Glory and Our Grief: Torontonians and the Great War* (Toronto: University of Toronto Press, 2002).

On my website (www.charlottegray.ca), I provide a selected bibliography and the precise footnotes required by more exacting readers. But for general readers, here are some broad indications of where I found my material.

CHAPTER I

All the details of Bert Massey's death and how the police arrested and questioned Carrie Davies come from the transcript of evidence given at the coroner's inquest. Information about the new age of the automobile in Canada is mainly drawn from Richard White's *Making Cars in Canada: A Brief History of the Canadian Automobile Industry, 1900–*

1980 (Ottawa: Canada Science and Technology Museum, 2007), and Heather Robertson's *Driving Force: The McLaughlin Family and the Age of the Car* (Toronto: McClelland & Stewart, 1995).

CHAPTER 2

Colonel George Denison and the Toronto Women's Court attracted so much attention in their day that it is hardly credible that they are almost forgotten today. The journalist Harry M. Wodson wrote an admiring account of the Beak, *The Whirlpool: Scenes from Toronto Police Court* (Toronto, 1917). More recently, Carl Berger examined the origins of Denison's attitudes in *The Sense of Power: Studies in the Ideas of Canadian Imperialism, 1867–1914* (Toronto: University of Toronto Press, 1970), and Gene Howard Homel explored Denison's record in "Denison's Law: Criminal Justice and the Police Court in Toronto, 1877–1921" in *Ontario History* 73, no. 3 (1981). Amanda Glasbeek looked at the Women's Court in her article "Maternalism Meets the Criminal Law: The Case of the Toronto Women's Court," in *Canadian Journal of Women and the Law* 10, no. 2 (1998). I also drew on her book *Feminized Justice: The Toronto Women's Court, 1913–1934* (Vancouver: UBC Press, 2009).

CHAPTER 3

There is no authoritative history of policing in Toronto, but several scholarly articles, including Greg M. Marquis, "Working Men in Uniform: The Early Twentieth-Century Toronto Police" in *Histoire Social—Social History* 20, no. 40 (November 1987), and Bill Rawling, "Technology and Innovation in the Toronto Police Force, 1875–1925" in *Ontario History* 80, no. 1, March 1988.

Keith Walden describes the rituals of women's lives in "Tea in Toronto and the Liberal Order, 1880–1914," *Canadian Historical Review*, 93, no. 1 (March 2012). The early years of the feminist movement and women's social activism are covered in N.E.S. Griffiths, *The Splendid Vision:*

Centennial History of the National Council of Women of Canada, 1893–1993 (Ottawa: Carleton University Press, 1993); Helen Caister Robinson, *Decades of Caring: The Big Sister Story* (Toronto: Dundurn, 1979); and *Nothing New Under The Sun: A History of the Toronto Council of Women* (Toronto: Local Council of Women of Toronto, 1978). Kathy Southee shared with me details of her great-grandmother Florence Huestis, which she researched for her unpublished 2009 paper, "Christianity in Canada: The Story of Florence Gooderham Hamilton Huestis."

CHAPTER 4

The Massey Archives at the University of Toronto include Hart Massey's day book for 1888 (B87–0082/Box 142 [02]) and Vincent Massey's diary for this period (B87–0082/Box 302). Neither is extensive, but each gives a sense of the man. Eliza Hart's will is also in the archives (B87–0082/Box 121 [22]). The only family history is Mollie Gillen's *The Masseys: Founding Family* (Toronto: Ryerson Press, 1965). I also drew on Merrill Denison's *Harvest Triumphant: The Story of Massey-Harris* (Toronto: McClelland & Stewart, 1948) and Claude Bissell's *The Young Vincent Massey* (Toronto: University of Toronto Press, 1981).

CHAPTER 5

The Selected Journals of L.M. Montgomery, Volume II: 1910–1921 (Toronto: Oxford University Press, 1987), edited by Mary Rubio and Elizabeth Waterston, reveal the novelist's obsession with war news and her despair as young men in her husband's parish are wounded and killed at the front.

CHAPTER 6

Information about the lives of young women who worked as domestic servants is painfully scanty: few had time to record their experiences, and as they were considered amongst the least important members of society, little information was collected about them. I found two books particularly illuminating as background for this chapter: Alison Light's *Mrs. Woolf and the Servants* (London: Fig Tree, 2007) reveals much about existence downstairs in Edwardian households in England, and Carolyn Strange's *Toronto's Girl Problem: The Perils and Pleasures of the City, 1880–1930* (Toronto: University of Toronto Press, 1995) traces the shifting occupation patterns for working-class women in the British Empire's primmest city. For details about Carrie's early years in England, I turned to Brenda Fraser-Newstead's *Bedfordshire's Yesteryears, Volume 1: The Family, Childhood and Schooldays* (Dunstable, U.K.: Book Castle, 1993.)

Life in the Ward is put under the spotlight in *Immigrants: A Portrait of the Urban Experience, 1890–1930* by Robert F. Harney and Harold Troper (Toronto: Van Nostrand Reinhold, 1975).

Morley Avenue is today known as Woodfield Road.

CHAPTER 7
Predictably, the two towering press barons of 1915 Toronto both merited hefty biographies. Ron Poulton's *The Paper Tyrant: John Ross Robertson of the Toronto Telegram* (Toronto: Clarke, Irwin, 1971) and Ross Harkness's *J.E. Atkinson of The Star* (Toronto: University of Toronto Press, 1963) were invaluable sources for this chapter. I also drew on *From Politics to Profit: The Commercialization of Canadian Daily Newspapers, 1890–1920* by Minko Sotiron (Montreal: McGill-Queen's University Press, 1997) and an unpublished 1983 doctoral dissertation by Thomas Walkom, "The Daily Newspaper Industry in Ontario's Developing Capitalistic Economy: Toronto and Ottawa, 1871–1911." J.H. Cranston's memoir, *Ink on My Fingers* (Toronto: Ryerson Press, 1953) gave an exuberant account of the early days of the *Toronto Star*.

CHAPTER 8
The material in this chapter is drawn from the inquest transcript, plus commentary from the *Globe* and the *Evening Telegram* of February 17, 1915.

CHAPTER 9

There are two excellent books about the feisty women reporters in Toronto newsrooms: Marjory Lang's *Women Who Made the News: Female Journalists in Canada 1880–1945* (Montreal: McGill-Queen's University Press, 1999) and Linda Kay's *The Sweet Sixteen: The Journey That Inspired the Canadian Women's Press Club* (Montreal: McGill-Queen's University Press, 2012).

CHAPTER 10

My chief sources for this chapter were the February 1915 issues of *Saturday Night* magazine and Tim Cook's *At the Sharp End*. Information about Sir William Mulock came from several sources, including Augustus Bridle's *Sons of Canada: Short Studies of Characteristic Canadians* (Toronto: Dent, 1916) and John Honsberger's *Osgoode Hall: An Illustrated History* (Toronto: Dundurn, 2004.)

CHAPTER 11

I found material on Hartley Dewart, KC, in the *DCB*, and a discussion of his handling of the Carrie Davies case in Carolyn Strange's article "Wounded Womanhood and Dead Men: Chivalry and the Trials of Clara Ford and Carrie Davies," in *Gender Conflicts: New Essays in Women's History* (Toronto: University of Toronto Press, 1992), edited by Franca Iacovetta and Mariana Valverde. Information about legal education comes from Christopher Moore's *The Law Society of Upper Canada and Ontario's Lawyers, 1797–1997* (Toronto: University of Toronto Press, 1997), amongst other publications.

Judith Flanders gives an excellent overview of murder in popular British culture in *The Invention of Murder: How the Victorians Revelled in Death and Detection and Created Modern Crime* (London: HarperPress, 2011).

CHAPTERS 12 THROUGH 16

Material on Dewart's defence strategy and the two-day hearing in court is drawn from contemporary newspaper accounts, particularly the *Evening Telegram*. On particular points of law and use of precedent, I referred to Simon Verdun-Jones's article "'Not Guilty by Reason of Insanity': The Historical Roots of the Canadian Insanity Defence, 1843–1920," in *Crime and Criminal Justice in Europe and Canada* (Waterloo, Ont.: Wilfrid Laurier University Press, 1981), edited by Louis A. Knafia; Jim Phillips and Rosemary Gartner's *Murdering Holiness: The Trials of Franz Creffield and George Mitchell* (Vancouver: UBC Press, 2003); and Angus McLaren's *The Trials of Masculinity: Policing Sexual Boundaries, 1870–1930* (Chicago: University of Chicago Press, 1997).

The case of Hilda Blake is described in Reinhold Kramer and Tom Mitchell's *Walk Towards the Gallows: The Tragedy of Hilda Blake, Hanged 1899* (Toronto: Oxford University Press, 2002).

CHAPTER 17

Sandra Gwyn's *Tapestry of War: A Private View of Canadians in the Great War* (Toronto: HarperCollins, 1992) dealt movingly with the impact of the war on Canadians, and the quotation for Harold Innis is taken from her book. Another poignant discussion of the long shadow cast by the bloodbath is *My Grandfather's War: Canadians Remember the First World War, 1914–1918* (Toronto: Macmillan, 1981) by William D. Mathieson.

CHAPTER 18

Frank Jones discussed his encounter with Carrie's descendants in his novel, *Master and Maid* (Toronto: Irwin, 1985), pp. 333–337.

Acknowledgements

Time travel back to the Toronto of 1915 was a fascinating challenge, as I walked along old streets lined with new buildings and tried to visualize the smaller, less confident but unassailably smug city of Bert Massey and Carrie Davies. Several people were immensely helpful: Rachel Young and Jacob Bakan (lay-out of Old City Hall); Thomas Klatt (history of the Lombard Street morgue, today shuttered and covered in graffiti); David Wencer (information about Toronto streets and buildings); Elise Brais (library researcher *extraordinaire*). Paul Leatherdale, archivist at the Law Society of Upper Canada, helped with information about the lawyers involved in the case. At the *Toronto Star,* John Honderich gave me a sense of the *Star*'s continuing commitment to progressive values and opened the doors to the newspaper's archives, where Astrid Lange and Peggy Mackenzie were generous with time and help.

I would like to thank Elinor Groom, librarian at Sandy Public Library, Bedfordshire, for information relevant to Carrie Davies's background, and Kathy Southee for sharing with me family details about her great-grandmother, the remarkable Mrs. Huestis.

In the course of writing this book, I talked to many members of the legal profession who provided me with crucial feedback and suggestions for future reading. Justice Robert Sharpe and Susan Binnie gave me legal references and advice. I am particularly grateful to Justice James MacPherson, who invited me to speak to the Ontario Court of Appeal study day, where I met Professor Jim Phillips, editor-in-chief at the Osgoode Society for Canadian Legal History. Professor Phillips's encouragement ("The law is *part* of social history; it reflects and incorporates contemporary social values"), his insights into the "unwritten law" defence, and his rigorous review system have helped make this a better book.

Frank Jones, author of *Master and Maid,* generously shared the information and insights he had gathered while writing his novel about the Carrie Davies case. I am truly in his debt. Vincent Tovell helped me understand the Massey side of the story. I am also grateful to Dr. Sandy Campbell, Dr. Duncan McDowall, Dr. Tim Cook, Dr. Norman Hillmer, and Rosemarie Tovell, who carefully read some or all of the manuscript, suggested further dimensions of the story, corrected my more egregious errors (those that remain are entirely mine), and offered encouragement. Dr. Naomi Griffiths and Monique Begin gave me a sense of the challenges facing twentieth-century feminists. Thanks are due to friends who cheer me on: Patricia Potts, Maureen Boyd, Cathy Beehan, Wendy Bryans, Judith Moses, and Julie Jacobson.

Special thanks go to editor and publisher Phyllis Bruce, who championed this book from the start, and as usual provided extraordinarily constructive counsel on how to amplify and strengthen my first draft. I am grateful to the team at HarperCollins Canada, who shepherded the book to publication, particularly my editor, Jennifer Lambert—a pleasure to work with—and Noelle Zitzer, Lloyd Davis, Tilman Lewis, Alan

Jones, Greg Tabor, Maylene Loveland, and Dawn Huck. My agent, Hilary McMahon at Westwood Creative Artists, was helpful at every stage of the process.

My husband, George Anderson, remains my most rigorous and supportive reader, with a gimlet eye for clichés.

Finally, I am grateful to the Office of Cultural Affairs in the City of Ottawa and to the Canada Council of the Arts for financial assistance. Without their continued support for writers, Canada would be diminished in ways that most of us would recognize only when it is too late.

Index

women (*cont.*)
    educated, 42, 143
    elite, 40–43
    employment opportunities, 94–95, 97,
        100–101
    in factories, 94–95, 100–101, 269, 271
    "fallen," 21, 22, 97, 191–92
    as journalists, 140–42
    law and, 21, 22, 47, 284–85
    as lawyers, 173, 174
    moral issues around, 95–97, 191, 232, 254–55
    as murderers, 185, 186, 188
    protection of, 232, 254–55
    rights of, 270–71, 284
    social activities, 42, 95, 97
    in Toronto, 40–44, 268–71
    unmarried, 191–92
    violence against, 255–56, 285
    votes for, 22, 43, 45–46, 270
    and the war, 22, 41, 43, 100–101, 268–71
    working-class, 94–96, 256, 269
Women's Christian Temperance Union, 41
Women's College Hospital, 45
Women's Conservative Club, 41
women's groups, 282. *See also specific organiz-*
    ations
    in Toronto, 40–41, 42–44
    and war effort, 41, 269

working class
    newspapers favoured by, 107, 113
    support for own, 178, 255
    women in, 94–96, 256, 267
World War I. *See* First World War
World War II. *See* Second World War
Worts, James, 44

xenophobia, 117–18, 127, 155

YMCA, 280
York Motors Ltd., 6–7
Ypres (battle site), 76, 158, 263–64

Zeppelin, Count Ferdinand von, 158–59
zeppelins, 158–59
Zimmerman, Kenneth, 57

"THOUGHT OF HIS DOING ME HARM MADE ME RUN FOR REVOLVER"

Carrie Davies Says She Feared What Would Happen Her When Massey Came Home

FIRED AS SHE RAN

Girl Says She Had Never Used the Revolver Before—Knew Massey Would Carry Out What He Planned—He Had Given Her a Ring—Crown Closed Case Against Girl Early This Afternoon.

The interest being taken in the trial of Carrie Davies, charged with the murder of her employer, Chas. A. Massey, was exemplified by the throng of people who struggled and fought and resisted the police in their efforts to get admission to the Assize Court at the City Hall yesterday afternoon. The court-room was kept locked until five minutes before the court resumed, and by that time the wide corridors outside were blocked with people. When the doors were opened, the rush to get seats almost overpowered the strong force of police on duty, and reinforcements had to be summoned to press back the throng.

Inspector of Detectives George Kennedy was the first witness called in the afternoon. He spoke of his first interview with the accused girl the same night the shooting took place. He produced the statement he took down from the girl on that occasion, and read the questions and answers to the jury.

TOOK ADVANTAGE OF ME.

The statement read in part.
Q.—What did you shoot for?
A.—"I really shot him in self-defence."
Q.—"What do you mean by saying you shot in self-defence?"
A.—"He took advantage of me yesterday, and I thought he was going to to the same to-day."
Q.—"What did he do yesterday?"
A.—He caught me on Sunday afternoon and kissed me twice. I ran upstairs; then he called me to make his bed, and I obeyed. As soon as I went into his room, he said, 'This is a nice bed.' He caught me. I pushed him aside and ran upstairs. I dressed and went out and told my sister on Morley ave.

Cross-examined — "Was anybody else present at the time this interview took place?"
"Yes. Detective Wickett."
"What time was it?" asked Mr. Dewart.
"About eight o'clock on the night of February 8," replied the detective.
"Did you take everything down correctly?"
"Yes."

DIDN'T TELL HER OWN STORY.

"You didn't ask the young lady to say in her own words or give her own account of the matter?"
"No. I just put the questions and she gave the answers."
"So that I took it that you didn't give her any opportunity or make any suggestion to her that she should give a continuous statement of matters?"
"No. I didn't ask her to tell her story."

HEARD SHOTS FIRED.

Joseph Pearson, of Dovercourt rd., said he was staying at his grand-

"The direction of the head; the doctor said it was pointing to the south. Did you move it?"
"No."
"How did he fall?"
"He looked as if he had fallen backwards; one arm was underneath him."

PHOTOGRAPHS OF SCENE.

Hugh Duncan, the police photographer, produced photographs of the scene on Walmer road, which were taken this morning. He also took some measurements. The distance from the bottom of the steps to the sidewalk was 38 feet 6 inches, and the distance in a straight line from the bottom of the steps to the door was 14 feet, making a total distance of 52 feet 6 inches.

This closed the case for the Crown.

IS A PURE GIRL.

Dr. A. J. Harrington, the first witness called for the defence, said that at the request of Mr. Dewart and Mr. Maw, he made a physical examination of the accused girl last night, in order to ascertain whether or not she was a virgin. He had no doubt that she was a virgin.
"Were you alone in the examination?"
"Dr. Duncan Anderson was associated with me."
"Are you agreed on that point?"
"Quite."

HOME ASSOCIATIONS.

Mr. Fairchild, brother-in-law of the prisoner, said he was a foreman bricklayer.
"How much older is your wife than Carrie?" asked Mr. Dewart, K.C.
"About six years older," was the reply.
"Did you know your wife and the little girl in the dock in their home in England?"
"Yes."
"Where did they live?"
"At Aldershot."
"That is the military headquarters?"
"Yes."
"That is where you courted your wife?"
"Yes."
"What was her father?" Mr. Dewart went on.
"He was an army pensioner," the brother-in-law replied.
"Do you know how long he had served?"
"My wife told me he had served the fall 21 years."
"Had he been in action?"
"Yes, in the South African war."
"And as a result of that service what was his condition?"
"He was a sergeant-major."
"I mean his physical condition. Was he wounded?"
"No; he fell off his horse, and had a leg broken."
"After that was he able to resume active service?"
"It was quite a long time since."
"Did you know the character of her father?"
"Yes."
Mr. DuVernet—"I am not objecting, but there is no suggestion against the respectability of this young girl or anyone connected with her."
"It is only to show what kind of displine obtained in the home," said Mr. Dewart.

FATHER VERY STRICT.

Witness said the girl's father was very strict. He died in September last as the result of a tumor.
"Did you know the little girl's mother?"
His Lordship—"Do you mean the

CARRIE DAVIES

would have to be careful. If he interfered with her she was to leave the house."
"Had anything passed between your wife and Carrie when she was endeavoring to make a statement?" counsel for the girl proceeded.
"After she commenced to tell about Mr. Massey kissing her, my wife kind of stared hard at her as much as to say, 'Don't speak before the little boy there.'"
Witness said the accused's family lived at Sandy Beds, Bedfordshire. The next youngest child to her was May, aged 15, and the youngest, Margey, was three or three and a half.

WOULD LOOK AFTER HER.

Cross-examined—"So far as you know, she was well and kindly treated?"
"Yes."
"On Sunday, what time did she come to your house?" asked Mr. Du Vernet.
"About four or five o'clock."
"She explained she had something to tell you?"
"She only told me that Mr. Massey tried to kiss her, nothing else."
"It didn't occur to you not to let her go back?"
"No, for this reason. When she was sick at the Island I had occasion to go and see her Mr. Massey told me then that he was interested in that girl. He said he would look after her and that his wife would look after her, that she would see that Carrie did not keep bad company. That alone threw me off. She told me herself that he had offered her the dollar for the way she had done her work."
"He offered her the dollar for the way she had done her work?"
"Yes."
"Afterwards he had given her a ring?"
"Yes."

GUESSED HE'D BE SORRY.

"Did you consider his kissing her was a serious matter from any indication she gave to you—from the way she said it?" queried the Crown Counsel.
"To take her own words for it, she said she thought he must be drunk,

for Mrs. Massey?" the accused was next asked.
"On the 28th of May, 1913," she answered.
"Did they live at Walmer road the year?"
"No. In the summer they went Centre Island."
"What were you paid?"
"Fourteen dollars for the first two months. After that I got $15, after eight months I received $16"
"Apart from paying the money back to your sister, did you g anything to anybody else?"

HELPED MOTHER.

"I used to send my mother w I could spare."
"How much?"
"When I received $14 I gave sister $10 and $2 or $3 to mother. Sometimes only one dollar, as I needed money myself. When father died I sent mother $30."
"Have you from time to time s her all you could?"
"Since father died I sent her $ and sometimes $5."
"What was the reason for sending that money?"
"Because mother had a family a she was not able to work."
"Where was your father?"
"In the hospital."
The witness was then question by Mr. Dewart as to her illness at Island in the summer of 1913, in gard to which she said she learn from the doctor that the trouble caused through not digesting her f properly.
Up till the time Mrs. Massey w on holidays, there was nothing Mr. Massey's conduct so far as was concerned, to which she co object, the girl said.

THE DINNER PARTY.

"Was there any special work did at the house during the she was away?" asked Mr. Dew on resuming.
"There was a dinner party."
"When?"
"On the Friday evening."
"Were there many there?"
"There were twelve."
"How did you know what to for dinner?"
"Mr. Massey gave me a slip paper with some things on. He me he would leave the rest to He brought home several things."
"Did you look after the liquors"
"No."
"You cooked and served the ner?"
"Yes."
"Did anything strange happen that dinner?" queried the girl's co sel.
"Ladies and gentlemen were dr ing rather heavily," said the witn in reply.
"Did it have any effect upon of them?"
"Yes, sir, except Mr. Massey didn't notice that it affected him"
"How do you know liquors served?"
"I knew there was glasses and by the bottl sent out afterwards to the cellar."
"Were there many liquor?"
"Several."
"What time did the up?"
"I think it was afte They gave Mr. Massey as they left the door came and thanked me had done."
"Anything unusual of"
"No."
"On Sunday what too Dewart went on.
"Nothing unusual un ner time. He came dov his bathrobe, and the h dressed for dinner."
"What became of the"
"He went out after d"
"What did you do?"

GAVE HER A RING

"I had been busy in the di room when Mr. Massey came d and thanked me for what I had on Friday night. He gave me a r